# Second Language Literacy Practices and Language Learning Outside the Classroom

SECOND LANGUAGE ACQUISITION

*Series Editors*: Professor David Singleton, *University of Pannonia, Hungary* and Fellow Emeritus, *Trinity College, Dublin, Ireland* and Associate Professor Simone E. Pfenninger, *University of Salzburg, Austria*

This series brings together titles dealing with a variety of aspects of language acquisition and processing in situations where a language or languages other than the native language is involved. Second language is thus interpreted in its broadest possible sense. The volumes included in the series all offer in their different ways, on the one hand, exposition and discussion of empirical findings and, on the other, some degree of theoretical reflection. In this latter connection, no particular theoretical stance is privileged in the series; nor is any relevant perspective – sociolinguistic, psycholinguistic, neurolinguistic, etc. – deemed out of place. The intended readership of the series includes final-year undergraduates working on second language acquisition projects, postgraduate students involved in second language acquisition research, and researchers, teachers and policy-makers in general whose interests include a second language acquisition component.

All books in this series are externally peer-reviewed.

Full details of all the books in this series and of all our other publications can be found on http://www.multilingual-matters.com, or by writing to Multilingual Matters, St Nicholas House, 31-34 High Street, Bristol BS1 2AW, UK.

SECOND LANGUAGE ACQUISITION: 127

# Second Language Literacy Practices and Language Learning Outside the Classroom

Miho Inaba

MULTILINGUAL MATTERS
Bristol • Blue Ridge Summit

DOI https://doi.org/10.21832/INABA2104
Library of Congress Cataloging in Publication Data
A catalog record for this book is available from the Library of Congress.
Names: Inaba, Miho - author.
Title: Second Language Literacy Practices and Language Learning Outside the Classroom/Miho Inaba.
Description: Bristol, UK; Blue Ridge Summit, PA: Multilingual Matters, [2019] | Series: Second Language Acquisition: 127 | Includes bibliographical references and index.
Identifiers: LCCN 2018029634| ISBN 9781788922104 (hbk : alk. paper) | ISBN 9781788922111 (pdf) | ISBN 9781788922128 (epub) | ISBN 9781788922135 (kindle)
Subjects: LCSH: Japanese language—Study and teaching—Foreign speakers. | Second language acquisition.
Classification: LCC PL519 .I53 2019 | DDC 495.68/0071—dc23 LC record available at https://lccn.loc.gov/2018029634

British Library Cataloguing in Publication Data
A catalogue entry for this book is available from the British Library.

ISBN-13: 978-1-78892-210-4 (hbk)
ISBN-13: 978-1-78892-634-8 (pbk)

**Multilingual Matters**
UK: St Nicholas House, 31-34 High Street, Bristol BS1 2AW, UK.
USA: NBN, Blue Ridge Summit, PA, USA.

Website: www.multilingual-matters.com
Twitter: Multi_Ling_Mat
Facebook: https://www.facebook.com/multilingualmatters
Blog: www.channelviewpublications.wordpress.com

Copyright © 2019 Miho Inaba.

All rights reserved. No part of this work may be reproduced in any form or by any means without permission in writing from the publisher.

The policy of Multilingual Matters/Channel View Publications is to use papers that are natural, renewable and recyclable products, made from wood grown in sustainable forests. In the manufacturing process of our books, and to further support our policy, preference is given to printers that have FSC and PEFC Chain of Custody certification. The FSC and/or PEFC logos will appear on those books where full certification has been granted to the printer concerned.

Typeset by Deanta Global Publishing Services Limited.
Printed and bound in the UK by CPI Books Group Ltd.
Printed and bound in the US by NBN.

# Contents

Tables and Figures     vii
Acknowledgements     ix

1   Introduction     1
    Out-of-Class Literacy Practices in L2: Why Sociocultural Perspectives?     2
    Literacy Activities and Literacy Practices     4
    Research Questions     6
    Research Context     6
    Outline of the Book     8

2   Out-of-Class Literacy and Language Learning from Sociocultural Perspectives     9
    Out-of-Class Language Learning     9
    Research into L2 Reading and Writing in Naturalistic Contexts     16
    Activity Theory     20
    Key Insights of Activity Theory     22
    Participant Backgrounds and Japanese Subjects     31
    Data Collection Methods     37
    Summary     44

3   Types of Literacy Activities Performed Outside of the Classroom     45
    Existing Classifications of Out-of-Classroom Learning     45
    Class-Related Literacy Practices     49
    Non-Class-Related Literacy Practices     56
    Features of the Participants' Literacy Practices     61
    Summary     64

| | | |
|---|---|---|
| 4 | Class-Related Literacy Practices Outside the Classroom | 65 |
| | Individual Differences in Class-Related Literacy Practices | 65 |
| | Learners' Activity Systems for Learning Japanese at University | 67 |
| | Factors Influencing Learner's Emphasis on Class-Related Literacy Practices | 70 |
| | Contradictions and Transformations of Class-Related Literacy Practices | 77 |
| | Summary and Discussion | 86 |
| 5 | Non-Class-Related Literacy Practices | 88 |
| | Overview of Non-Class-Related Literacy Practices | 88 |
| | Motives for Non-Class-Related Literacy Practices | 93 |
| | Multiple Motives | 101 |
| | Learners' Interests and Expansion of Literacy Activities | 103 |
| | Roles of the Internet in Expanding Opportunities for Non-Class-Related Literacy Practices | 108 |
| | Summary and Discussion | 113 |
| 6 | Language-Related Mediation in L2 Literacy Practices | 116 |
| | Mediation in Class-Related Literacy Practices | 117 |
| | Mediation in Non-Class-Related Literacy Practices | 131 |
| | Summary and Discussion | 143 |
| 7 | L2 Literacy Practices and Language Learning in Out-of-Class Contexts | 146 |
| | Out-of-Class L2 Literacy Practices and Language Learning: Major Findings | 146 |
| | Recommendations for Language Teaching in Formal Settings | 155 |
| | Directions for Future Research | 159 |

| | |
|---|---|
| Appendix 1: Background Interview | 162 |
| Appendix 2: Interaction Interview | 163 |
| Appendix 3: Final Interview | 165 |
| Appendix 4: Semi-Structured Interview with the Teachers | 167 |
| Appendix 5: Diary about Literacy Activities | 168 |
| References | 171 |
| Index | 185 |

# Tables and Figures

**Tables**

| | | |
|---|---|---|
| Table 2.1 | Background of the participants | 32 |
| Table 2.2 | Data for each participant | 38 |
| Table 2.3 | Interviews with teachers | 41 |
| Table 2.4 | Transcription symbols for the interview data | 42 |
| Table 3.1 | Materials and assessment tasks of the Japanese subjects | 50 |
| Table 5.1 | Non-class-related literacy activities undertaken by Chris, Patrick and Joshua | 89 |
| Table 5.2 | Non-class-related literacy activities of the second and the third groups | 91 |
| Table 6.1 | Students' dictionary use patterns for class-related reading practices | 118 |
| Table 6.2 | Available word search techniques and material types | 120 |

**Figures**

| | | |
|---|---|---|
| Figure 2.1 | The structure of a human activity system (Engeström, 1987, in Engeström, 2001: 135 - reprinted with the permission of Taylor & Francis and the author) | 22 |
| Figure 2.2 | L2 literacy practices | 29 |
| Figure 2.3 | Basic procedures of data collection | 41 |
| Figure 3.1 | Four dimensions for the participants' literacy practices in out-of-classroom contexts | 49 |
| Figure 4.1 | A model of the central activity system for class-related literacy practices | 68 |
| Figure 4.2 | Examples of linked activity systems | 69 |
| Figure 6.1 | Melissa's electronic dictionary with a stylus (used with permission from Sharp Cooperation) | 119 |
| Figure 6.2 | IME pad for Windows 10 (used with permission from Microsoft) and an online dictionary (Jim | |

|  |  |  |
|---|---|---|
|  | Breen's WWWJDIC http://nihongo.monash.edu/cgi-bin/wwwjdic?1C – used with permission from Mr Breen) | 119 |
| Figure 6.3 | An example of Japanese subtitles in a Japanese news programme (used with permission from NHK International, Inc.) | 139 |
| Figure 7.1 | Links between language classes/class-related tasks and non-class-related literacy practices | 154 |

# Acknowledgements

First and foremost, I would like to express my sincere appreciation to the 15 student volunteers and 6 teachers who generously participated in my research. I also owe a huge debt of gratitude to the many individuals who helped me develop the ideas and arguments in this book. I would particularly like to thank Adjunct Associate Professor Helen Marriott, Dr Robyn Spence-Brown, Professor Ikuo Kawakami and Professor Satoshi Miyazaki who provided constructive and insightful feedback allowing me to develop my research.

I am also grateful for the encouragement given by Dr Catherine Chabert to publish this book and for the generous support of Dr Matthew Piscioneri, Dr Thomas Baudinette, Mr Michael Slater and Mr Erik Beyersdorf in proofreading my manuscript. The assistance provided by Dr Ruselle Meade in proofreading several chapters of this book is especially appreciated.

I would like to extend my sincere gratitude to the series editors, Professor David Singleton and Associate Professor Simone E. Pfenninger, for their valuable advice on the revision, and an anonymous reviewer for his/her insightful and beneficial comments on this book. I am also grateful to my editor, Ms Laura Longworth, for her constant and professional support, and all at Multilingual Matters who have been involved in publishing this book.

I also wish to thank my friend, Ms Chieko Hartono, for her support throughout this long journey from conducting the research in Melbourne to writing up the book. Finally, I would like to sincerely thank my family in Japan, particularly my parents, Takae and Katsuji Inaba, who have always encouraged me to pursue my interests in language learning and move forward in my career.

# 1 Introduction

This book reports on research exploring out-of-class language learning and use activities undertaken by learners of Japanese at an Australian university, placing a particular focus on literacy activities in their target language, Japanese. This research was derived from my personal experiences as a teacher of Japanese when I taught the language at a Swedish university in the 2000s. Although Japanese culture was becoming popular in Sweden at that time, there were no other resources for my students to refine their knowledge of the language other than Japanese textbooks in the city where I taught the language. However, my students told me that they enjoyed various materials related to Japanese pop culture, such as *manga* (Japanese comic books) and *anime* (Japanese cartoons). Some students also told me that they used online resources to aid their Japanese study. Another striking discovery was that many first-year students knew at least a couple of words in the language, which they picked up from Japanese movies and *anime*, when they started learning Japanese at university. This anecdotal evidence made me realise that various resources in Japanese were easily accessible even outside of Japan, and I naturally developed my interest in out-of-class language learning.

This personal experience reflects the transformation of language learning environments triggered by the development in information and communication technology (ICT) around the turn of the 21st century. Traditionally, it was often said that learners in a foreign language (FL) environment, where learners learn a target language in their own country or in a country where the target language is not utilised as a common language of communication, needed to make a conscious effort to seek target language resources (Thomson, 1997). However, this situation has changed significantly due to the expansion of the internet, even for learners who study languages other than English (LOTE) (Benson, 2013). In the case of Japanese, for example, the prevalence of the internet in combination with the popularity of Japanese pop culture overseas (Japan Foundation, 2011; Sakuma, 2006) makes it possible for learners of Japanese to access Japanese language and cultural resources, even when they are situated outside of Japan (Akahori, 2002; Sasaki, 2006). In fact, research into the effects of Japanese pop culture on learning Japanese, including how to use Japanese pop culture materials in language classes overseas, has been conducted since the mid-2000s (Fukunaga, 2006; Kawashima & Kumano, 2011; Makino, 2008; Shibata, 2008; Williams, 2006). The advances in ICT also enable learners to access resources and tools for learning Japanese, such as online dictionaries and websites focusing on Japanese grammar (Sasaki, 2006). It is anticipated that such online tools may affect the ways in which learners approach assessment tasks, as well as self-directed use of Japanese in authentic contexts. Although I only illustrated the case of Japanese in this context, the advancements in ICT have significantly influenced not only the opportunities for language learning as well as authentic language use but also the manner in which students engage in assessment tasks and any activities involving their target languages. In particular, literacy skills in a second language (L2) or FL have become crucial in order to expand the possibility of out-of-class activities in a target language in this digital world (Benson, 2013), in addition to utilising paper-based materials. This is the reason why I primarily focused on literacy skills rather than speaking and listening skills.

L2 literacy practices undertaken outside of the classroom can be regarded as one form of autonomous language learning and authentic language use activities, which has been viewed as an important factor in mastering target languages (Benson, 2011). In particular, an effective combination of authentic language use outside of the classroom and classroom-based instructed language learning activities is thought to accelerate the language learning process (Ellis, 2008; Hall, 2009; Miyazaki, 2006). Drawing on these points of view, a comprehensive analysis of both class-related tasks and voluntary L2 use activities is beneficial to better understand the relationship between formal language learning and authentic language use outside of the classroom. However, the existing research explored either assignments for language classes or learners' voluntary L2 learning in out-of-class settings. In the latter type of research, the role of language classes in out-of-class language learning has been underexplored, although many learners still learn a target language in classroom settings (Inaba, 2013; Lai, 2015). I was thus motivated to investigate not only voluntary L2 learning and use activities but also class-related tasks undertaken outside of the classroom.

## Out-of-Class Literacy Practices in L2: Why Sociocultural Perspectives?

Research focusing on reading/writing in out-of-class settings first flourished in the field of literacy studies. In the 1990s, scholars in the field of literacy studies established the New Literacy Studies (Barton, 1994; Gee, 1992, 2008; Street, 1993, 1995), which views literacy as social practice situated within social and cultural discourses, and claimed the necessity of exploring literacy outside of the formal education parameters (Schultz & Hull, 2002). Consequently, a number of studies have been conducted to investigate the literacy practices undertaken by schoolchildren or adolescents outside of the classroom (e.g. Camitta, 1993; Finders, 1996; Mahiri & Sablo, 1996; Neilsen, 1998; Schultz, 2002). Although these studies produced a number of interesting results, such as the function of literacy practices in adolescents and the divergences between students' private writing activities in comparison to school activities, most of these studies addressed literacy practices in their first language (L1 – English), though the research into L2 literacy practices conducted by adolescents with an immigrant background has also been expanding recently (e.g. Black, 2005, 2008; Lam, 2000, 2004, 2006, 2009a, 2009b; Yamada, 2005; Yi, 2005, 2007). Moreover, although the New Literacy Studies has emphasised the social aspects of literacy practices, Haneda (2007) indicates that it does not provide a rigid framework for analysing literacy practices of language learners and their relation to social and contextual factors.

In the field of second language acquisition (SLA), L2 reading and writing research has been predominantly conducted from the perspectives of cognitive psychology, for example, L2 reading research driven from the bottom-up or top-down model as well as schema theory (Eskey, 2005) and L2 writing research based on a process approach (Leki, 2002). These studies view reading and writing as mental processes that occur in individual learners, and therefore, employ experimental settings. Although previous studies have revealed the complexities of reading and writing processes, contextual factors, such as personal, social and educational considerations, which have the potential to heavily influence L2 learning were not emphasised in these studies. That being said, in consonance with the social turn in SLA during the mid-1990s (Block, 2003) that is the growing attention to social and contextual aspects of language learning (e.g. Firth & Wagner, 1997; Lantolf & Johnson, 2007; van Lier, 1996), prominent researchers in the area of L2 writing and reading research have advocated the importance of integrating sociocultural perspectives (e.g. Atkinson, 2002; Eskey, 2005; Leki, 2002; Santos *et al.*, 2000). Indeed, particularly in the area of English for academic purposes (EPA), an increasing number of studies have begun to explore writing activities in naturalistic contexts from socio-cognitive (e.g. Leki, 1995; Manchón *et al.*, 2007; Riazi, 1997; Spack, 1997) or sociocultural perspectives, including Activity Theory (e.g. Cumming *et al.*, 2002; Haneda, 2005, 2007; Lei, 2008; Park & De Costa, 2015; Yang *et al.*, 2004).

Out-of-class language learning research has expanded due to interests in autonomous language learning and qualitative investigation in L2 learners' lives. Nevertheless, the number of studies on this topic is still scarce compared to studies in language teaching and learning in classroom settings (Benson, 2011). Moreover, Benson (2013) suggests that because of the development of ICT, the nature of autonomous language learning today has changed considerably from when learner autonomy was introduced into SLA in the 1970s. A shift in the focus of autonomous language learning research has already occurred, from discussing the way to facilitate out-of-class and independent learning by providing resources (e.g. self-access centre) towards revealing the complex and dynamic nature of contexts for autonomous language learning beyond the classroom (Benson, 2013). For example, a growing number of studies have examined out-of-class language learning in relation to the individual and societal factors of learners' learning contexts from sociocultural perspectives once more (e.g. Gao, 2010; Kalaja *et al.*, 2011; Menezes, 2011). This study, therefore, employs sociocultural perspectives and, in particular, Activity Theory, which enable us to observe reading and writing activities within individual and social contexts.

**Literacy Activities and Literacy Practices**

Before proceeding to a discussion, an explanation of the important terms used in this study will be provided, such as 'literacy', 'literacy activities' and 'literacy practices', relying on the discussions in the field of literacy studies. Literacy traditionally refers to reading and writing skills (Mayer, 2008). However, the contemporary view of literacy often includes visual and audio modes because textual information is inextricably linked to the visual and the audio in multimedia environments, such as the internet (Cope & Kalantzis, 2000; Mayer, 2008; Pailliotet & Monsenthal, 2000). This study employs this viewpoint of literacy to include textual information in visual resources (e.g. subtitles in Japanese TV serials).

In this book, I use 'literacy activity' to indicate an individual and concrete action involving written language, for example, writing the draft of an essay assignment, reading a Japanese novel. In the field of literacy studies, the term 'literacy event', which represents 'any occasion in which a piece of writing is integral to the nature of participants' interactions and their interpretive processes' (Heath, 1983: 93), has been preferred. However, I employ literacy activity rather than literacy event, because literacy event seems to include a nuance of focusing on the situations in which reading and writing activities happen. Literacy activities also include audio/visual (viewing) activities, which may involve reading activities (e.g. reading subtitles and textual information).

Another important term utilised in this study is 'literacy practice'. According to Schultz and Hull (2002), Scribner and Cole (1981) introduced the term 'practice' in order to conceptualise literacy within the

Sociocultural Theory framework. In their study, Scribner and Cole (1981: 236) expound the concept of practice as 'a recurrent, goal-directed sequence of activities using particular systems of knowledge'. They also state that 'literacy is not simply knowing how to read and write a particular script but applying this knowledge for specific purposes in specific contexts of use' (Scribner & Cole, 1981: 236). Scholars of the discipline of New Literacy Studies adopt the term 'literacy practice' in order to maintain social and cultural perspectives on reading and writing activities. In particular, Street (1984, 1993, 1995, 2000, 2003: 79) developed the concept of literacy practices in order to 'refer to the broader cultural conception of particular ways of thinking about and doing reading and writing in cultural contexts'. In other words, this term includes values, beliefs and cultural models (or patterns) that are illustrated through literacy activities (Rush, 2003).

In the current study, there are at least two types of literacy practices that participating students undertook outside of the classroom:

(1) *Class-related literacy practices* that students undertake for their language classes that are, however, physically located outside of the classroom (e.g. reading a textbook in preparation for a quiz).
(2) *Non-class-related literacy practices* which are not directly related to students' language classes (e.g. reading *manga*, writing emails) and are motivated by various factors.

I differentiated these two groups as literacy practices because it is anticipated that participants' values, beliefs, motivations and activity types differ depending on the relationship with their language classes. For instance, although the influence of assessment tasks is common for class-related literacy practices, such factors do not seem to directly influence non-class-related literacy practices. These differences are crucial in exploring students' values and their motivations for various literacy activities. I also employ the term 'literacy practice' in the forms of 'L2 literacy practices' and 'out-of-class literacy practices' in order to indicate students' literacy activities in the target language in an out-of-classroom context.

In SLA, the phrase 'beyond the classroom' has often been utilised because 'out-of-class' indicates a setting in contrast with classroom-based learning, and does not reflect the variety of settings in which language learning occurs (Benson, 2011). However, out-of-class is more appropriate to clarify the target of this study, which consists of literacy practices undertaken outside of the classroom compared to learning in the classroom. Hence, this study utilises expressions including out-of-class, such as out-of-class literacy practices and L2 literacy practices in out-of-class contexts.

## Research Questions

This book aims not only to provide a comprehensive and detailed picture of out-of-class literacy practices but also to discuss implications for teaching practices in order to facilitate out-of-class language learning. To achieve these aims, the present study endeavours to examine what and how language learners use a target language outside of the classroom by employing Activity Theory, a sociocultural approach, through addressing the following questions:

(1) What literacy activities in the target language and related to the language do participants undertake in out-of-class contexts?
(2) What factors encourage or constrain participation in such activities?
(3) How do the participants undertake their literacy activities outside of the classroom, and what tools do they use to support their literacy activities?

In environments outside of the classroom, it is expected that language learners may utilise either their first (or second, in the case of multilingual speakers) language alongside the target language, Japanese. For example, this may include watching Japanese movies with English subtitles. Although this is not a Japanese literacy activity, it could nevertheless still be connected with using the target language. For instance, viewing activities with English subtitles could be a source of vocabulary and expression necessary for written assignments or in-class reading or writing tasks. Consequently, these types of literacy activities were also considered to be a data source for analysis in this study.

## Research Context

This study focused on learners who study Japanese at a university in Melbourne, Australia, that is, Japanese as an FL. As previously mentioned, it is anticipated that ICT may increase the opportunities for using a target language even when learners are situated in FL contexts, by providing resources and online tools to support their language skills. As a number of previous studies have shown (e.g. Kurata, 2011; Pasfield-Neofitou, 2009, 2012), Australian university students learning Japanese engaged in a number of L2 activities outside of the classroom and utilised the internet in a variety of ways to assist with their language learning and use of Japanese. Moreover, as explained in more detail below, Australia is a significant context for learning Japanese as an FL. For this reason, Australian university students provide an interesting target group for a study of out-of-class literacy practices.

Australia is one of seven countries that have more than 100,000 Japanese language learners, and is ranked the top country among English-speaking countries with regard to the number of Japanese students (Japan Foundation, 2017b). The incentive for this growth in

Japanese language education in Australia mainly derives from its economic relationship with Japan since the 1960s, with the support of the government-level promotion of LOTE and related programmes (e.g. National Asian Languages and Studies in Schools Program started in 2009) (Japan Foundation, 2017a). In Australia, approximately 95% of the learners of Japanese study during primary and secondary education (Japan Foundation, 2017a). Although the number of learners at tertiary level is relatively small, Japanese is still the most widely taught language in Australia, not only at school level but also at universities (de Kretser & Spence-Brown, 2010). Japanese is thus one of the popular languages in Australia, which is supported by the Australian education system. Indeed, the majority of this study's participants commenced their study of Japanese as a compulsory subject in either primary or high school, and chose Japanese as one of the subjects for the Victorian Certificate Education (VCE), which proves the completion of secondary education in Victoria and also functions as an entrance examination for higher education (see http://www.vcaa.vic.edu.au/vce/). Such pre-tertiary study may in fact influence their decision to learn the target language while at university.

The university where this research project's participants studied Japanese was located in Melbourne, which is the state capital of Victoria in Australia. Approximately 17,800 Japanese residents were registered in 2016 at the Consulate-General of Japan, Melbourne, which ranked 11th in terms of numbers of Japanese citizens in overseas cities from 2013-2016 (Ministry of Foreign Affairs of Japan, 2017). There are Japanese communities in which both Japanese nationals (immigrants and expatriate families from Japan) and locals have taken part, and a number of shops selling Japanese food and goods, including materials on Japanese pop culture.

The university at which the participants studied Japanese has a *Manga* library that holds a large number of *manga* (Japanese comic books) in Japanese, and is run by student volunteers. Since the *Manga* library opened to the public, Japanese nationals living locally in addition to Australian students and Japanese international students have used this resource. Furthermore, student volunteers occasionally run *manga* translation lessons. Some of the participants reported that this library was a place not only for reading *manga*, but it also served as a venue for meeting friends who were studying Japanese or were interested in Japanese pop culture. In addition, the Japanese Club, which is a student association at the university, has also organised gatherings among the students and Japanese international students. Such events include BBQs and the screening of Japanese TV serials and movies. A number of participants in the present study also reported that they participated in these Japanese Club gatherings.

The university also has an Asian studies research collection. According to the university's website, the Japanese collection has over 25,000 volumes, including books on the history of modern Japan, contemporary Japanese society, economics, literature and language. The library also holds Japanese language resource materials for teaching Japanese, such as textbooks, workbooks and flash cards. A number of participants reported that they utilised this collection's books and teaching materials for their assignments and also borrowed books for voluntary reading. Although the use of these resources depends on individual students, there seems to be opportunities for learners to employ Japanese literacy skills utilising paper-based materials in addition to online resources, both at this university and those available in the city of Melbourne.

## Outline of the Book

As previously stated, this book attempts to provide a comprehensive and detailed analysis of out-of-class literacy practices undertaken by language learners, and will assume the following form. Chapter 2 will first review the relevant literature from SLA perspectives in order to illustrate the gaps that the present study fills and the importance of sociocultural perspectives for L2 literacy practices in out-of-class contexts. It will also introduce the theoretical framework of Activity Theory and the methodology employed in this study, including the background of the participants and their Japanese courses.

The next four chapters will focus on the research questions, and present an analysis of the data and discussions on the study's findings. Chapter 3 will address the first research question, providing detailed information about the types of literacy practices undertaken by the participants during the data collection period. This chapter also examines the differences and similarities between class-related and non-class-related literacy practices.

Chapters 4 and 5 will analyse class-related and non-class-related literacy practices, respectively. These two chapters will address the second research question. Focusing on the social and contextual factors that affect the range of opportunities for L2 literacy practices to take place outside of the classroom, the chapters will discuss which factors facilitate or impede the possibilities of language learning and authentic language use activities in out-of-class contexts.

Chapter 6 will analyse the manner in which learners engage in literacy activities in L2, placing a particular focus on the tools and resources that the participants utilised to support their Japanese language skills. This chapter will address the third research question, which aims to identify the challenges L2 learners face while learning and using their L2 outside of the classroom.

Finally, Chapter 7 will conclude with the major findings of the preceding chapters, and discuss their significance and implications for L2 teaching, learning and future research.

# 2 Out-of-Class Literacy and Language Learning from Sociocultural Perspectives

As stated in Chapter 1, the main purpose of this chapter is to demonstrate and justify the integration of sociocultural perspectives into out-of-class literacy and language learning research. In the following sections, I will first present a brief review of relevant studies on out-of-class language learning and second language (L2) writing as well as reading activities. By doing so, I will illustrate the gaps in the field, which should be further explored, and the importance of research from sociocultural perspectives. Then, the theoretical framework in the present study, namely Activity Theory, will be described in comparison to the related topics in second language acquisition (SLA), for example, language learning motivation and autonomous language learning. This chapter will also outline the methodological approach employed in the present study, including the background of the participants and a brief explanation of the Japanese subjects that the participants studied. The investigation of previous studies, theories and research methods provides the fundamental perspectives necessary for the analysis and discussion in the following chapters.

## Out-of-Class Language Learning

L2 literacy practices can be regarded as one form of out-of-class language learning because it is highly likely that students learn and use a target language in the form of literacy with the expectation of improving their language skills. Although studies on out-of-class language learning have been conducted from time to time along with the introduction of autonomous learning into SLA since the Council of Europe's Modern Language Project commenced in 1971 (Benson, 2007), the number of studies on out-of-class language learning is still scarce (Benson, 2007, 2011). However, this research area has been attracting more attention as a result of the theoretical pursuit of learner autonomy and naturalistic as well as qualitative research (Benson, 2011), in addition to the rapid change in out-of-class language learning environments following the implementation of computer technology (Benson, 2013; Nunan & Richards, 2015). Indeed, multiple studies have explored L2 learning and use activities outside of the classroom setting, and a wide range of topics have been addressed in more recent research, for example, exploring learning opportunities in L2 digital gaming (Chik, 2011, 2013, 2014; Rama et al., 2012; Thorne, 2008).

The research into out-of-class language learning is roughly divided into three categories depending on the data collection methods: research aiming to quantitatively identify what types of activities learners do outside of the classroom; research exploring the factors affecting out-of-class autonomous learning relying on students' retrospective data; or a combination of both. In the following sections, I will cover studies particularly related to the first and second research questions of the present study, the types of out-of-class activities and the factors influencing the opportunities for learning and using L2 in out-of-class contexts (for a comprehensive overview of this research area, see Sundqvist & Sylvén, 2016).

## Types of out-of-class L2 use activities

Research in this category often conducted large-scale questionnaires in order to determine the tendency or overall picture of what learners do in their L2 outside of the classroom. These studies in the 1990s and the early 2000s revealed the dominance of activities that rely on receptive skills, such as reading and listening (de Bot & Evers, 2007; Freeman, 1999; Pearson, 2004; Pickard, 1996; Yap, 1998). However, writing emails in English was the most common activity in some studies after the 2000s (Hyland, 2004; Inozu et al., 2010; Spratt et al., 2002), and the popularity of viewing and listening activities utilising streaming sites was identified in the studies conducted in the 2010s (Lin & Siyanova-Chanturia, 2015; Toffoli & Sockett, 2010). It is highly likely that this transition in common out-of-class activities reflects the prevalence of information and communication technology (ICT).

Moreover, a series of studies were conducted to statistically examine the relation between certain types of authentic language use activities and L2 proficiency development, for example, by young Swedish learners of English (Sundqvist, 2011; Sundqvist & Wikström, 2015; Sylvén & Sundqvist, 2012) and by Chinese middle school students who learn English as a school subject (Lai et al., 2015). With reference to the studies on young Swedish learners of English, it was found that there was a positive correlation between entertainment activities in English (e.g. playing online games and listening to pop songs) and their oral proficiency in English (Sundqvist, 2011; Sylvén & Sundqvist, 2012) and between gaming in English and vocabulary size (Sundqvist & Wikström, 2015). Lai et al. (2015) found that the variety of meaning-focused activities (i.e. L2 use activities) was positively correlated with their learning outcomes, including their grades in the English subject. These studies revealed the popular activities in L2 outside the classroom and verified the possibility of authentic use activities to improve L2 proficiency. However, the influential factors in developing opportunities for such L2 use activities, which are related to the second research question of the present study, were not explored in these studies. Consequently, a need for in-depth studies focusing on individual learners and their learning environments has been identified.

## Motivation and interests

A growing number of studies qualitatively examined out-of-class language learning, often in combination with quantitative data from questionnaires (Hyland, 2004; Lai, 2015; Lamb, 2004, 2007; Ma, 2017; Murray, 2004; Murray & Kojima, 2007; Palfreyman, 2006, 2011; Pearson, 2004; Pickard, 1995; Sockett & Toffoli, 2012; Yap, 1998). The focus of these studies was not only to identify what types of activities students engage with in their L2 outside of the classroom, but also to explore the factors facilitating or constraining such opportunities.

For example, motivation has been identified as one of the crucial factors in autonomous language learning (Benson, 2007). With the aim to investigate the relation between motivation and out-of-class language learning, Pickard (1995) interviewed three advanced-level German learners of English about their motivation for learning English and their out-of-class language learning experiences. A detailed analysis of the interview data revealed that the participants' authentic language use experiences in an English-speaking country and abroad had a great impact on their motivation and triggered their further efforts to study the language. Lamb (2007) also focused on the motivation of Indonesian L2 English learners at junior high school level. Analysing the interview data, it was found that students maintained a high level of motivation to improve their English proficiency for their future career, and the amount of L2 use and learning activities that the students undertook outside of the classroom was in fact increased. Although the students in Lamb's (2007) study emphasised the influence of societal factors (i.e. importance of English for a future career in the Indonesian context) on their motivation rather than the personal experiences found in Pickard's (1995) study, these findings clearly demonstrated that motivation supported learners' engagements in out-of-class language learning activities.

In relation to motivation, Yap (1998) explored 18 English as a foreign language (EFL) high school students' out-of-class language learning activities in Hong Kong, and revealed that enjoyment or interest played an important role in students' choice of activities. This finding is supported by Lam's (2000) case study on multilingual digital literacy practices of a Chinese-background immigrant adolescent, Almon. He was a fan of Japanese pop culture, and improved his English language skills and gained confidence as an English as a second language (ESL) student by actively utilising English related to Japanese pop culture, for example, creating an English homepage about his favourite Japanese pop singer and communicating with other fans of Japanese pop music. Although the focus of her study is young immigrant students' identity construction, this finding indicates the importance of individual interests in expanding authentic language use activities.

As more recent research, Ma (2017) and Sockett and Toffoli (2012) also found that learners' interests were one of the influential factors shaping out-of-class language learning on the internet or using mobile devices. The interest in American pop culture was also a key factor in the out-of-class language learning activities of Japanese adult learners of English in Murray's (2008) study. Yet, learners' interests have tended to be touched upon as one factor influencing their choices of out-of-class activities and have not been fully explored in the studies on out-of-class language learning. This might be because out-of-class language learning is often perceived as 'the efforts of learners taking classroom-based language courses to find opportunities for language learning and use outside class' (Benson, 2007: 26). In other words, the focus of research into out-of-class learning is likely to be placed on the learners' purpose to improve their L2 proficiency. However, the internet environment enables learners to easily gain materials and resources in a target language based on their interests (Sockett, 2014). Given this change of learning environment, the role of learners' interests in facilitating out-of-class language learning should be further explored.

## Factors in learning contexts

As mentioned in the previous chapter, the context of out-of-class learning is rather complex, and a number of factors affect students' engagement in voluntary L2 learning and use activities. Hyland (2004) conducted case studies on out-of-class English language learning involving eight trainee English teachers who studied a bachelor's degree or a post-graduate certificate in education at a university in Hong Kong and the quantitative data collected from large-scale questionnaires. The multiple case studies found that not only individual but also sociopolitical factors affected their opportunities to practise English in authentic contexts. Examples included learners' beliefs about effective L2 learning activities, ease of access to materials and learners' social identities with regard to speaking English as English teacher trainees in public settings, where Cantonese is usually utilised as a local language.

Placing a particular focus on the role of social networks in language learning opportunities, Palfreyman (2011) analysed interview data from five United Arab Emirates (UAE) female university students and their families. The most interesting finding in his study is that families, in addition to local communities and an online fan community based on the learners' interest, played an important role in the students' language learning as a learning community. Families provided a number of supports for learning L2, for example, teaching English or talking in English with each other among siblings, and encouragement from parents. Based on this finding, Palfreyman postulated that social networks contribute to language learning by providing opportunities for language use, information about language resources and encouragement to enhance learners' motivation.

A number of studies also examined how learners organise their learning environment from the viewpoint of learners' agency in sociocultural perspectives. For example, the study conducted by Kalaja *et al.* (2011) discussed how learners perceive their learning contexts, analysing the data from an open-ended questionnaire about Finnish university students' out-of-class language learning experiences of English or Swedish at their school age. In Finland, Swedish is one of the official languages, and both English and Swedish are taught as compulsory subjects at school. However, a striking difference was found: although the students actively searched for opportunities to use English, they missed the similar resources (e.g. TV and magazines) available in Swedish. Kalaja *et al.* claimed that learners' beliefs about Swedish as an obligatory language and English as an internationally important tool in the Finnish context might affect learners' agency to organise their learning contexts.

Similarly, in his extensive longitudinal study on language learning strategies by mainland Chinese undergraduate students at an English medium university in Hong Kong, Gao (2010) examined the role of agency in their strategy choices. Drawing on sociocultural perspectives, Gao revealed that learners' choices in how to improve their L2 skills were affected by a number of factors in multilayered social contexts: for example, macro-level factors (e.g. the great emphasis of the economic value of education in general as well as English), institutional factors (e.g. local students' community where Cantonese is used) and individual factors (e.g. motivation, beliefs and capacity for L2 learning). Moreover, it was found that their individual factors were often formulated through the influence of their social networks, such as parents, teachers and peers. Based on these findings, Gao concluded that strategic language learning was still the learners' choice, but should be recognised as interactions between learners' agency and various factors in their learning contexts.

The findings of the studies surveyed above contribute to understanding that out-of-class L2 learning and use opportunities are affected by various individual and contextual factors. In particular, the studies by Gao (2010) and Kalaja *et al.* (2011) demonstrated that sociocultural perspectives could shed light on the complex and dynamic nature of how learners exercise their agency to shape their language learning activities outside of the classroom. However, the role of language classes was not particularly discussed in these studies, though Gao's study found that language teachers at school influenced learners' beliefs and motivation.

It might be because the majority of the participants in these studies were not students taking classroom-based language courses. Only Lai's (2015) study examined how students develop their voluntary L2 learning and use activities outside of the classroom in relation to their in-class experiences. Lai conducted interviews with 11 Chinese students who were studying a foreign language as a major or minor degree at an English medium university in Hong Kong, and revealed a number of interrelations between in-class and out-of-class learning experiences. Examples include the influence of the content addressed in class on out-of-class activities (e.g. searching for French food because a teacher talked about it in class); the intentional use of the languages picked up from authentic materials in class; and out-of-class L2 use activities as compensation for in-class learning activities. These findings provide interesting implications to build an effective connection between in-class and out-of-class learning activities in order to facilitate the L2 learning process. However, Lai's (2015) study did not integrate class-related tasks undertaken outside of the classroom, which might also be connected to their voluntary L2 activities. In addition, the in-class and out-of-class connections were only discussed in terms of language learning opportunities outside of the classroom, and other aspects, for example, mutual influence at language level and strategy use, were not included. Thus, a more in-depth study to examine the connection between in-class and out-of-class language learning activities is necessary.

### ICT use

ICT can be understood as one factor influencing learning contexts. However, the role of ICT is significant in that the development of computer technology has altered the nature of autonomous language learning by enabling learners to easily attain materials and resources for learning and practising a target language (Benson, 2013). The quantitative research after the 2000s mentioned above (e.g. Hyland, 2004; Inozu *et al.*, 2010; Lin & Siyanova-Chanturia, 2015; Spratt *et al.*, 2002; Toffoli & Sockett, 2010) demonstrated that the activities frequently undertaken were mediated by computer technology, for example, emails and viewing activities on the internet.

Examining how ICT shapes L2 use activities, Sockett and Toffoli (2012) conducted eight-week diary studies and follow-up interviews with five French learners of English at tertiary level, whose proficiency levels were B1-B2 in the Common European Framework of Reference for Languages (CEFR). They found that the students engaged in a variety of activities that were characterised by the use of ICT, for example, watching movies in different languages with English subtitles, communicating with friends on Facebook and listening to the music of their favourite pop singers via on-demand music sites. It was also revealed that students did in fact learn the language, or at least built vocabulary through these L2 use activities, even if the students' language level was relatively limited. Based on this finding, Sockett and Toffoli claimed that technology enabled the students to create a personalised learning environment that allowed them to engage in L2 use activities in connection with their real lives.

As previously mentioned, Ma's (2017) study focused particularly on how mobile technology (e.g. mobile phones and tablets) mediates learning and using L2 in out-of-class contexts. Analysing multiple cases of 10 Chinese students who studied different majors at an English medium university in Hong Kong, Ma illustrated that students utilised various tools and resources (e.g. online dictionaries, dictionary apps, e-books) via mobile technology and that their use of such tools was affected by individual contextual factors, such as their motivation, learning strategies, interests and time as well as physical/space conditions (e.g. where learners study). Similar to Sockett and Toffoli (2012), Ma concluded that mobile technology functioned as a mediator to shape students' personalised learning experiences.

The key finding in these two studies is that ICT facilitates students to organise their own language learning environment based on their preferences as part of their private lives. However, Lai and Gu's (2011) study, analysing a large-scale questionnaire ($n = 279$) as well as semi-structured interviews on self-directed language learning by students in foreign language courses at the University of Hong Kong, revealed somewhat contradictory findings. Of the participants, 30% did not realise how to apply online communication tools, such as text messaging and online chatting, in order to learn their target languages even though they utilised them daily in their first language (L1). Students also claimed that authentic language resources on the internet were far beyond their language proficiency level, and therefore, not useful. These findings imply that not all the students recognised and gained benefit from the use of ICT to organise their out-of-class language learning (Levy, 2009).

To summarise, research on L2 out-of-class language learning as surveyed above not only contributed to our knowledge regarding the types of activities language learners undertake outside of the classroom, but also brought light to the individual, contextual and social factors that facilitated or constrained such L2 learning and usage opportunities. However, as identified above, a number of areas need to be further explored. Moreover, the majority of studies analysed the examples of learners of English, and more research is needed to examine cases of learners who study a foreign language other than English. In addition to this, learners' concrete actions while they were engaged in literacy activities, such as how to utilise online tools and peer assistance, were not explored in the studies discussed above. In order to investigate this aspect of L2 literacy practices, it is useful to turn to the studies of L2 reading and writing, which have investigated learners' strategy use in naturalistic contexts.

## Research into L2 Reading and Writing in Naturalistic Contexts

As briefly explained in Chapter 1, although research driven by cognitive psychology remains dominant in the area of L2 reading and writing, an increasing number of studies have examined how students read and write in out-of-class settings after the social turn in SLA (Block, 2003). This section will first review studies on L2 writing activities from sociocultural perspectives and subsequently focus on the L2 reading undertaken in contexts outside of the classroom. Finally, this section will discuss implications from experimental research into L2 reading in computer environments, which is relevant to research question three in the present study.

### L2 writing research

In the field of L2 writing, studies concerned with contextual factors influencing L2 writing activities were conducted from the late 1990s onwards, mainly in reference to the English for academic purposes paradigm. Scholars who have adopted a socio-cognitive perspective, in particular, argue that it is important to explore L2 writing strategies as actions that students actually employ in order to fulfil day-to-day requirements (Manchón *et al.*, 2007). Consequently, in conjunction with the increasing popularity of the sociocultural approach to language learning strategy research (e.g. Donato & McCormick, 1994; Gillette, 1994), a number of qualitative research studies into ESL students' writing strategies to complete assignments within their study disciplines were conducted from a socio-cognitive perspective (e.g. Leki, 1995; Riazi, 1997; Spack, 1997). Although these studies illustrated various individual contextual factors, such as students' goals, their beliefs and time limitations, affecting the manner in which students approached academic essays in their L2, a particular conceptual framework for exploring the sociocultural influences on L2 writing activities was not employed. In the 2000s, however, sociocultural perspectives, including Activity Theory, started to be employed in order to analyse the ways in which L2 learners engaged in essay assignments (e.g. Cumming *et al.*, 2002; Haneda, 2005, 2007; Lei, 2008; Yang *et al.*, 2004).

For instance, Lei's (2008) study examined the writing strategies utilised by two proficient Chinese students of English while engaging in written assignments for an English course at a Chinese university. The strategies found in Lei's study partially reinforced previous findings from L2 writing strategies in experimental settings, such as L1 use, seeking writing models (Leki, 1995) and the orchestration of strategies (Anderson, 2005). However, the crucial difference between those studies and Lei's (2008) study is its theoretical framework. In order to analyse strategy use in context, Lei employed Activity Theory, which is a sociocultural approach to learning. Drawing on Activity Theory, Lei's study illustrated how students utilised identical or similar resources differently throughout their writing process. It was also found that the two students were seriously concerned about teacher and peer feedback in order to draw on this resource to help improve their writing, yet they held different attitudes and goals when considering their writing assignments. Based on these findings, Lei concluded that her study data exemplified how learners' agency functions in context, and writing strategies should be analysed according to their social contexts.

Yang *et al.* (2004) also employed Activity Theory to investigate six ESL learners' engagement with written assignments from an ESL academic preparation programme at a Canadian university. Yang *et al.* revealed that the participants' objectives, resources and communities, in relation to their written assignments, transformed over the duration of the programme. In particular, the participants gradually sought useful resources, such as peers' written assignments, newspapers and books as writing models, for improving their essays. Similar to Lei's (2008) study, these findings indicate that writing in a target language is not a purely cognitive process, but it is an internal process influenced by learners' goals, motivation and beliefs. Yang *et al.* also claimed that external factors, such as students' learning environments, teacher and peer assistance and the utilisation of various material aids provided invaluable assistance to this learning process.

As studies focusing on language learners other than English, Haneda's (2005, 2007) studies explored learners' attitudes towards L2 writing from sociocultural perspectives, focusing on students of Japanese as a foreign language (JFL) at a Canadian university. Her first study (Haneda, 2005) explored the influence of two participants' learning trajectories as well as their perceptions about past and future communities on students' attitudes towards writing in Japanese. By drawing on the sociocultural perspectives of learning and related concepts, such as community of practice (Lave & Wenger, 1991), identity and investment (Norton, 2000; Wenger, 1998), Haneda (2005) claimed that the participants' attitudes towards and objectives for L2 writing were inextricably linked to their life histories. In her following paper, Haneda (2007) drew on a modified version of Wells' (2002) Activity Theory, and examined nine Canadian university JSL students' orientations towards their writing in the target language. The analysis revealed that the writing strategies employed by each participant were directly related to their Japanese proficiency, though they perceived the written tasks differently depending on their purposes and motivations for learning Japanese.

The findings of the above studies illustrate the relation between learners' approaches towards writing activities and learners' individual and contextual factors, such as objectives/goals for L2 learning, learning history and available language resources, including their social networks. However, Park and De Costa (2015) pointed out the underestimation of the role of motive in these previous studies driven by sociocultural and

Activity Theory perspectives. In their study on the L2 writing strategies undertaken by a student from a South East Asian country in a master's course in teaching English to speakers of other languages (TESOL) at a university in the United States, Park and De Costa (2015) revealed that the student's multiple motives, for example, the desire to be a role model as a female professional as well as an educated teacher in her home communities, drove her to employ certain strategies and development in her strategy use. The finding of their study indicates motive as one crucial factor in understanding how students read and write in authentic contexts. The concept of motive will be discussed in detail later in this chapter, addressing the importance of understanding reading and writing strategies as not only actions situated in sociocultural contexts but also as strategic activities driven by motives.

## L2 reading research

Compared to L2 writing research, studies on L2 reading in out-of-class contexts have been underdeveloped, though academic writing activities usually involve reading skills in the preparation process of writing essays (e.g. reading articles). However, a number of research studies on L2 reading in out-of-class contexts have been conducted predominantly in connection with extensive reading. For example, studies focusing on the effects of extensive reading on L2 reading proficiency development (e.g. Mason & Krashen, 1997; Nash & Yuan, 1992); the correlation between learners' attitudes towards L1 and L2 reading and extensive reading (Yamashita, 2004); individual and contextual factors influencing L2 extensive reading (Crawford Camiciottoli, 2001; de Morgado, 2009); and the relationship between learners' motivations and the amount of reading undertaken outside of the classroom (Mori, 2004). These studies quantitatively revealed that individual factors, such as the learners' past L2 reading experiences and their motivations for L2 reading, influenced their attitudes towards extensive reading as well as their overall performance.

Although there are few qualitative studies in this area, Leung (2002) conducted a case study to investigate the effects of extensive reading undertaken by a JSL learner. The subject was, in fact, Leung herself, and explored what the participant learned through extensive reading as a means of self-study and how she engaged with the reading activities, in particular, when problems arose. Although Leung focused on the effects of extensive reading, it was also revealed that the participant's individual factors, such as her social network with Japanese friends and her learning experience in the past, influenced the way in which she tried to resolve the problems.

A 2.5-year longitudinal case study conducted by Nishino (2007) into extensive reading in the FL context (EFL) examined two Japanese middle school students' reading strategies and motivations for reading in the target language. The interesting finding of Nishino's study is the influence of various contextual and individual factors, such as their reading experiences in their L1 and university entrance examinations, on the participants' motivation for extensive reading. Moreover, it is worth mentioning that the students became more interested in reading authentic texts and spontaneously sought authentic reading materials after their successful experience of reading an English novel. The aforementioned two studies did not apply sociocultural perspectives in their analyses, yet their findings clearly indicate that societal and contextual factors as well as learners' motives affect their reading activities outside of the classroom.

## L2 reading in computer environments

With particular regard to reading activities, the internet has the potential to provide various opportunities for voluntary reading, as well as information related to assessment task topics, such as essay and oral presentations. According to Chun's (2006) review, a large number of studies into the effects of computer-assisted language learning (CALL) technology on L2 reading, such as the effects of multimedia glosses and annotations addressing vocabulary acquisition and reading comprehension, have been conducted (e.g. Chun & Plass, 1996; Hulstijn *et al.*, 1996; Knight, 1994; Sakar & Erçetin, 2005; Taylor, 2006). In particular, since the 2000s, a number of studies have examined learners' strategy use and its relation to online dictionary/glossary resources and other features of online reading (e.g. Akyel & Erçetin, 2009; Ariew & Gulcan, 2004; Konishi, 2003; Laufer & Hill, 2000; Sankó, 2006; Tabata-Sandom, 2016; Yamane, 2007). In this section, I will only cover the studies on learners of Japanese because the support of online tools is crucial for learners of Japanese due to its complex writing system, including the difficulty of *kanji* (adapted and modified Chinese characters in the Japanese writing system).

Tabata-Sandom (2016) and Yamane (2007) examined L2 reading strategies and dictionary use by learners of Japanese. As reading hard copy materials in Japanese is often problematic for those who are not familiar with *kanji*, Yamane's (2007) study compared students' dictionary use in both computer and hard copy environments. In Yamane's study, 10 intermediate tertiary students studying Japanese at an Australian university were assigned to read two authentic Japanese texts on a computer and in hard copy form. In terms of dictionary use, Yamane's study identified several features of online and electronic dictionaries, for example, allowing students to write *kanji* characters on screen using the handwriting function enabled students to look up words in a dictionary. It was also revealed that students searched for more words in computer environments than they did in hard copy environments because of the easy access to online glosses. Based on these findings, Yamane concluded that expanding students' knowledge about dictionary choices and reading strategies would enhance learners' reading proficiency.

Tabata-Sandom (2016) particularly explored how intermediate to highly proficient learners of Japanese read authentic digital texts with online pop-up dictionaries. The data from think-aloud protocols and interviews revealed that less proficient students heavily relied on the pop-up dictionary, and those students positively evaluated the ease of searching for words that supported them to understand the gist of the reading texts. However, it was also identified that less proficient students faced problems in using the pop-up dictionary. For example, these students did not understand the sentences when incorrect segmentations of words occurred because of their lack of grammatical knowledge. Moreover, the pop-up dictionary provided multiple definitions for certain words, and the less proficient students struggled with identifying the appropriate definition.

Both Tabata-Sandom's (2016) and Yamane's (2007) studies provide interesting implications for the present study in terms of the usefulness of digital dictionaries, how these tools impact on the reading process on a computer and potential problems that students might face in using such tools. However, the influential factors on strategy use identified in the studies on L2 writing discussed above, such as learners' objectives and motivations for their activities and their preferences for strategy usage, were not explored. In other words, the findings only offer us fragmentary information about the actual processes of reading on computers, which might differ depending on individual learners and relevant contextual factors. That is to say, it is necessary to investigate how language learners utilise digital texts and online dictionary resources when reading in naturalistic contexts, employing a rigid framework for analysis. As the studies exploring L2 writing activities indicate, Activity Theory will also be beneficial for examining how learners approach reading activities. The next section will introduce Activity Theory, which serves as an analytical framework for the present study.

**Activity Theory**

Activity Theory incorporates L.S. Vygotsky and his colleagues' work on human mental development, which is often referred to as cultural-historical psychology. Vygotsky's fundamental claim is the notion of 'mediation' (see Lantolf, 2000; Lantolf & Thorne, 2006). Vygotsky (1978) argued that humans rarely interact with the world directly, but utilise various artefacts in order to achieve their objects in the social-material world. These artefacts include physical and symbolic tools (e.g. books, pictures and technology) and cultural concepts (e.g. numeracy and logic), which have been created and modified by human culture(s) over time.

Building upon Vygotsky's (1978, 1981) work concerning mediation, A.N. Leont'ev – one of Vygotsky's colleagues – constructed Activity Theory. The crucial difference between Vygotsky's work and Activity Theory is the fundamental unit of analysis. While Vygotsky (1978, 1981) focused on individual actions mediated by cultural tools and signs, Leont'ev (1978) employed the concept of activity as the fundamental unit of analysis for unifying and understanding individual actions and social contexts (Engeström & Miettinen, 1999). In Leont'ev's framework, the hierarchical distinction between activity, action and operation was added to the analysis of the complex nature of activity. The highest level includes activities that can be understood to be any interaction between subject (human) and object, and this interaction is mediated by tools (mediating artefacts). Activity is inextricably connected to the concept of motive, which is the biological or social need or desire to lead human activity towards a specific object. The second level of analysis is action, which is directed by a concrete goal. Goal-directed actions are realised by employing specific mediational means or strategies. The third level, operation, refers to the ongoing means through which an action is carried out under certain circumstances. This hierarchical distinction in Leont'ev's framework illustrates the multilayeredness of an activity and allows us to analyse a single event from different perspectives.

Engeström (1987, 1999, 2001) expands on Activity Theory in order to form a more comprehensive model of an activity system, including socially and culturally constructed contexts as part of an activity. The traditional conceptualisation of mediated activity consists of subject, object and mediating artefacts, and does not fully illustrate the societal and collaborative dimensions of each action (Engeström, 1999). In order to observe human activities in a broader context, Engeström (1987) added three elements to Activity Theory: the community or communities in which the subject is embedded; the rules that regulate the activity at various levels; and the division of labour between members of a community and the subject (Figure 2.1). In this model, the activity system itself is the unit of analysis, in other words, the relationships that resonate between all the components of an activity system constitute the analysis.

A central activity system (targeted activity system) is linked to multiple neighbouring activities, which influence the elements of the activity system, such as subject, rules, material and symbolic tools, and also future activity in which the outcomes of a central activity are embedded (Engeström, 1987, 1999). Lantolf and Thorne (2006) discuss such multiplicity of activity systems by exemplifying a particular educational context. For instance, in the current study, learners' literacy practices outside of the classroom may be situated in various different activity systems: language classes, other subjects at university as well as learners'

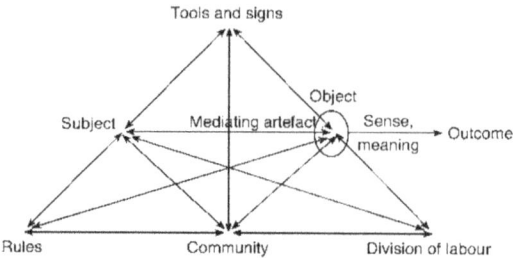

**Figure 2.1** The structure of a human activity system (Engeström, 1987, in Engeström, 2001: 135 - reprinted with the permission of Taylor & Francis and the author)

personal activity systems outside of formal education parameters, such as part-time jobs, networking with friends and communicating with people on social networking services, for example, Facebook and Twitter. Thus, activities of learning and using an L2 might be influenced by various activity systems, which include activities that are not directly connected to education. The multiplicity of activity systems also enables us to systematically understand the historical dimension of an activity, including the influence of the past (e.g. language courses at high school) as well as potential future activities (e.g. jobs in the future).

Engeström's (1987, 1999, 2001) approach focused on a collective activity system (how individuals act in a collective activity system) because he aimed to study organisational change. In contrast, L2 literacy practices are often undertaken individually. However, language learners belong to various communities, such as language classes, friendship groups and families. Their activities within their target languages are influenced by the rules and norms of these communities and community members. Therefore, Engeström's framework is also a useful analytical tool for examining the activities that learners undertake individually. The current study will particularly draw on Engeström's version of Activity Theory and its key concepts during the analysis, alongside relevant discussions in SLA, such as language learning motivations and language learning strategies.

## Key Insights of Activity Theory

### Motives

The notion of motive plays a key role in Activity Theory. In Activity Theory, a learner's needs (or purposes) behind a particular task are viewed as motives for an activity (Leont'ev, 1978). When a subject's need meets its object (i.e. the need is objectified), the need becomes a motive, and an activity emerges. In other words, a motive could be understood as a factor that drives the subject to undertake an activity. Additionally, as Engeström's (1987, 1999, 2001) theory of activity systems visualises, the subject's need is transformed into a motive under the influence of social and historical factors. With regard to the influence of such factors, Gao (2010) and Gillette (1994), for example, revealed that the attitudes of a student's family towards a target language or foreign languages generally affected the student's motives and goals, and eventually the performance of studying a target language.

Motives are a crucial factor in shaping each activity. The studies by Gillette (1994) and Spence-Brown (2004, 2007) illustrate the relation between learners' motives and their actual actions. For instance, Gillette's (1994) study reported two interesting findings: the influence of motives on students' approaches to studying the target language and the effectiveness of strategy use. Similarly, Spence-Brown (2004, 2007) revealed that students' motives affected their actual actions in an interview project. As these studies indicate, L2 learners' motives affect how they engage in similar activities differently outside of the classroom. In the case of the L2 literacy practices of Japanese language learners, one student may utilise an online dictionary in order to read passages in a textbook and thereby understand the content perfectly, whereas the same student may not utilise any dictionary when he/she reads *manga* in Japanese because he/she would like to enjoy the story without the distraction of using a dictionary.

Leont'ev (1978: 123) also postulates that an activity can be driven by multiple motives, suggesting two types of motives, namely 'sense-forming motives' and 'motive-stimuli'. While sense-forming motives refer to more important motives that provide the main meanings for activities, the motive-stimuli indicate less important motives that provide additional meanings but do not alter the primary meaning of the activity.

It is also necessary to explain the notion of motive in relation to the object of an activity. According to Leont'ev (1978: 62), 'the object of an activity is its true motive', that is, the object of an activity indicates the same thing as does the motive. In the case in which a subject has multiple motives, a sense-forming motive can become the object of an activity. However, the term 'object' has been utilised interchangeably to indicate 'the goal of an activity, the motives for participating in an activity, and material products that participants try to gain through an activity' (Yamagata-Lynch, 2010: 17). According to Yamagata-Lynch (2010), this issue has stemmed from problems related to translating from Russian into English because object in Russian has several meanings. In the case of class-related literacy practices, students have their own motives as well as learning objectives, which teachers expect the students to achieve through attending classes. Such objectives often differ from students' motives for learning the language. In order to avoid such confusion, the present study will articulate who sets up the object of activity if necessary. In addition, the aforementioned study by Spence-Brown (2004) indicates that a dominant motive may change over time. Rather, as Kaptelinin and

Nardi (2006) maintain, the multiple motives that students have as well as the learning objectives assigned by teachers collaboratively drive an activity while being influenced by various contextual factors. Accordingly, the current study will utilise two terms (motive and object) interchangeably, only when the dominant motive is obvious; motive will be employed to indicate students' needs and purposes for an activity, particularly when they have multiple motives for an activity.

Motive in Activity Theory thus differs from the traditional conceptions of motivation in SLA, which has often been understood as a relatively stable psychological trait or state of language learning in general (Spence-Brown, 2007). Because of this view of motivation, research on language learning motivation has historically employed quantitative data in order to reveal the correlation between the types of motivation and learning achievements (Ushioda, 2001). Although a reconstruction of the motivation theory has emerged, for example, the value-based and identity-oriented framework as represented by Dörnyei's (2005, 2009) L2 Motivational Self System, motivation is still predominantly depicted as a decontextualised static state as long as quantitative data is utilised. Yet, Ushioda (2009: 220) asserts that sociocultural and situated perspectives should be employed to explore the dynamic nature of motivation, as 'an organic process that emerges through the complex system of interrelations' between an individual learner as a real person and contexts.

The focus of the analysis in the present study is to depict how motives shape an activity in a context rather than on how motivation is formulated or developed. However, Activity Theory has the potential to explore the developmental and situated nature of motivation by looking into how learners' motives, in combination with a number of contextual factors, impact on their out-of-class literacy practice opportunities and their concrete actions in such opportunities.

## Mediation

As mentioned previously, mediation is another key concept in Activity Theory. In Engeström's (1987) model of an activity system (Figure 2.1), a subject's (learner's) actions towards the object of each activity are mediated by four interrelated factors: mediating artefacts (e.g. textbooks, dictionaries, computers, L1 and L2), rules (e.g. rules for assessment tasks, norms of online communities), community (e.g. language classes and peer groups) and division of labour (e.g. power relations between teachers and students, between classmates and native speaker friends). Mediation is also influenced by experiences in past activities (e.g. acquired language skills through in-class learning activities), including subjective factors, for example, beliefs formulated through experiences in the past.

In SLA, learners' concrete actions in reading and writing activities have been examined from the perspective of language learning strategies driven by cognitive psychology. However, the concept of mediation differs from the view of these strategies. On the one hand, language learning strategies are often understood as cognitive and meta-cognitive behaviours or techniques situated in individual learners, and therefore, those studies in cognitive framework employ experimental approaches that decontextualise learners' strategy use (Gao, 2010). On the other hand, mediation in sociocultural perspectives refers to goal-oriented actions, which are realised through available resources, tools and other factors in a specific context, for example, dictionaries, support in L1 as well as L2 and time constraints. From this concept of mediation, it can be claimed that learners' strategy choices are the result of an interaction between the subject of an activity (i.e. a learner) and the factors emerging from his/her activity system.

Among the aforementioned studies of L2 writing research employing Activity Theory, for example, Lei's (2008) study revealed that Chinese ESL learners utilised various strategies related to the four mediators presented in Engeström's (1987) activity system, in order to complete their writing tasks. In other words, a number of individual contextual factors mediated their writing activities. As Lei's study exemplified, the concept of mediation thus provides an analytical framework to explore how learners actually read and write in naturalistic contexts and how various contextual and individual factors influence their actions when it comes to reading and writing activities.

## Contradictions

Contradictions have been defined as 'a misfit within elements, between them, between different activities, or between different developmental phases of a single activity' (Kuutti, 1996: 34). They have also been expressed as 'historically accumulating structural tensions' (Engeström, 2001: 137), as 'problems, conflicts, clashes and breakdowns' (Dippe, 2006: 3) and as 'discoordinations' (Russell & Yañez, 2003: 341). Engeström (1987, 2001) proposes that four levels of contradictions can be identified within and between activity systems. Primary contradictions exist as inner conflicts within each component (e.g., within objects, subjects, rules) of a central activity system; secondary contradictions appear between the components of the central activity system (e.g. between tools and objects); tertiary contradictions occur when the object/motive of a culturally more advanced activity is introduced into the central activity system (e.g. teachers introduce a motive of learning into a student's activity in which he/she aims at playing with classmates); and quaternary contradictions are found between the components of the central activity system and those of neighbour activity systems (e.g. between the rules of the central activity system and the rules of another activity system).

Furthermore, Engeström (1987) draws on Marxist theory to explain that a primary contradiction could occur between the 'use value' and the 'exchange value' of a commodity. Products that are produced by individuals within a capitalist economy will have use value, but will also be assigned an exchange value when used as a commodity. This dual nature of products carries the potential for a basic contradiction in objects of an activity. In regard to schooling activities, Engeström (1987) emphasises the potential conflict between these two objects: reproducing texts for gaining grades that determine the future value of students in the labour market (i.e. exchange value), and mastering texts as tools that are useful outside of school (i.e. use value). These twofold objects for schooling activities may cause conflicts, such as between the desire to gain a good mark versus mastery of the subject content for its use value in their out-of-school lives. It is reasonably assumed that such conflicts may ultimately influence university students' engagement with learning language as well.

In Activity Theory, contradictions are considered an impetus for change and development in activity systems, and are essential in order to understand what prompts individual concrete actions within an activity system (Barab *et al*., 2002). With reference to L1 writing research at a tertiary level, Russell and Yañez (2003) examined the alienation that undergraduate students often identified in writing requirements in the US tertiary setting, focusing on an Irish history course. Russell and Yañez particularly discussed the case of Beth, who experienced contradictions between her motive of becoming a journalist and the course objects (mastering specialist writing in the history subject) determined by the teacher. Although Beth struggled to find meaning in the essay assignments at the beginning of the course, she gradually understood the potential of acquiring new writing skills for her future career. Based on her example, Russell and Yañez concluded that such contradictions might be overcome when students envisage the link between the objects of the course and their current or future activities.

Contradictions are more likely to occur in class-related literacy activities than in extra-curricular activities. This is because such activities can be interpreted as being part of a collective activity of classroom learning and can be influenced by the objects defined by teachers or institutions, the rules/norms of the classes and the power relations between teachers and students or between classmates. For instance, Nelson and Kim (2001) identified contradictions in an international students' ESL writing tasks: tensions existed between the students' notions, conceptual tools and motives for learning at university and those expected by the host university. In the present study, the concept of contradiction will be mainly utilised in relation to class-related tasks in order to identify which factors constrain learners' engagements in this type of literacy practice.

## Learner autonomy and agency in Activity Theory

As stated at the beginning of this chapter, L2 literacy practices can be viewed as one type of out-of-classroom language learning that is inextricably connected to autonomous language learning perspectives. The majority of the research studies into out-of-class language learning introduced above have discussed learners' efforts to identify opportunities for language learning outside of the classroom in relation to autonomy. However, the term 'autonomy' is often used in the literature in this field without mentioning any clear definition. This might be because the theoretical framework of learner autonomy in SLA is still under debate, including the most basic term, that is, 'autonomy' (Benson, 2001, 2007; Oxford, 2003). Furthermore, an increasing number of research studies on out-of-class language learning have often employed agency rather than autonomy (e.g. Gao, 2010; Kalaja *et al.*, 2011; Menezes, 2011; Toohey & Norton, 2003). However, agency and autonomy in SLA research are often used interchangeably without stating the distinction between these two concepts (Huang, 2011; Huang & Benson, 2013). Although the purpose of this section is not to elaborate on discussing the differentiation of the concepts of autonomy and agency, I shall present the most often cited definitions of autonomy and discuss the relation with agency from sociocultural perspectives (see studies by Huang and Benson [2013] and Lantolf [2013] for a detailed examination of the differences between autonomy and agency).

Discussions surrounding autonomy in language learning and teaching appeared in the Council of Europe's Modern Language Project in 1971 (Benson, 2007). This project led to the seminal report by Holec (1981: 3) in which he defined autonomy as the ability 'to take charge of one's own learning'. Holec (1981: 3) also described autonomous learning qualities as having 'responsibility for all the decisions concerning all aspects of this learning', such as determining the objects, contents of learning, selection method and techniques for learning, monitoring the learning process and evaluating what has been acquired.

Benson (2001) further developed the concept of autonomy in language learning in a more concrete fashion and discussed an individual's capacity to take control of his/her learning by outlining three facets of autonomous language learning: learning management, which refers to learners' behaviours in relation to how they manage the planning, coordination and evaluation of their learning; cognitive processes, which are the psychological elements of learning (e.g. attention, reflection and metacognitive knowledge); and learning content. Benson claims that learners have the capacity as well as the freedom to take control of these aspects in autonomous language learning.

Researchers studying the theory of autonomy have also proposed different types of learner autonomy. Littlewood (1999), for example, highlights the importance of reactive autonomy in formal educational settings. Reactive autonomy is a form of autonomy that 'does not create its own directions but, once a direction has been initiated, [it] enables learners to organize their resources autonomously in order to reach their goals' (Littlewood, 1999: 75). Littlewood's standpoint indicates that each learner may possess different capacities for autonomy and that the context of formal education only partially allows learners to exercise their autonomy. More recently, the concept of autonomy has started to be understood as 'a social capacity' (Benson & Cooker, 2013: 8), which indicates that learner autonomy is socially developed through interaction with others and shaped by contextual factors (Benson & Cooker, 2013; Murray, 2014). The definitions of autonomy, however, are united in that an individual learner's ability/capacity to control his/her learning constitutes its core (Huang & Benson, 2013).

Agency is one of the central concepts of Sociocultural Theory and its derivative theories, including Activity Theory. Similar to the concept of autonomy, many researchers have expounded agency from sociocultural perspectives (e.g. Ahearn, 2001; Lantolf & Pavlenko, 2001; Lantolf & Thorne, 2006; van Lier, 2008; Wertsch et al., 1993). Wertsch et al. (1993: 342), for example, pointed out the difficulty in distinguishing human actions from the utilisation of mediational means, and proposed 'mediated agency' to signify 'individual(s)-operating-with-mediational-means'. Similarly, Ahearn (2001: 112) remarked that 'all action is socioculturally mediated, both in its production and in its interpretation' and defined agency as 'the socioculturally mediated capacity to act'. Although scholars in the field of SLA (e.g. Lantolf & Pavlenko, 2001; Lantolf & Thorne, 2006; van Lier, 2008) have tried to explicate the concept of agency, the common ground in these discussions is the ability/capacity to 'act through mediation' (Lantolf, 2013: 19). As explained previously, from sociocultural perspectives, all human actions are mediated through tools and artefacts that have been socially and historically developed in societies. In other words, agency is realised in such mediated actions that are 'more concrete, specific and observable' (Huang, 2011: 242). Integrating the Activity theoretical point of view, it can be further argued that individual learners' agency is both simultaneously enabled and constrained by the elements of an activity system, not only by material and symbolic means but also by the rules/norms of a community and other linked activity systems (Lantolf & Pavlenko, 2001; Lantolf & Thorne, 2006).

Summing up, from sociocultural perspectives, it can be said that agency is always recognised in learners' specific actions of, for example, creating or disregarding out-of-class literacy opportunities and learning as well as using a target language in specific contexts. This might be a crucial difference from autonomy, which is concerned more about learners' control of their learning process (Huang & Benson, 2013). Agency from sociocultural perspectives is thus more suitable than autonomy for the present study because this concept enables researchers to depict the ways in which learners organise their out-of-class language learning taking into consideration various factors in their learning contexts, including from wider societal factors (e.g. online tools triggered by the advancement of ICT) to specific contextual factors (e.g. time constraints for exam preparation). In this regard, moreover, it is reasonable to say that agency is one of the crucial aspects to understand how students autonomously learn a target language (Gao & Zhang, 2011).

Before closing this section, it should be noted that the existing categorisations for out-of-class language learning have developed based on the concept of learner autonomy discussed above (e.g. Benson, 2001; Jones, 1998). Accordingly, such classifications do not cover all types of L2 literacy practices in the current study. The problems in such categorisations, and the primary but more comprehensive framework to explore features of different out-of-class activities proposed by Benson (2011), will be discussed further in Chapter 3.

## Applications of Activity Theory to the current study

How is Activity Theory applied to examine L2 out-of-class literacy practices? Figure 2.2 illustrates how L2 out-of-class literacy practices can be located within the contexts of both learning and using Japanese. The upper half of Figure 2.2 presents the literacy activities located in the classroom, which are tasks that have been assigned by teachers. The shaded parts in the lower half of the figure represent the target area of inquiry of the current study: namely, class-related and non-class-related literacy practices outside the classroom. As presented in Chapter 1, reading, writing and viewing activities, which are directly related to the requirements of a Japanese course, such as assignments and preparation for classes, are categorised as class-related literacy practices. Activities that are not directly connected to in-class activities, assignments or class preparation are viewed as non-class-related literacy practices. However, it is anticipated that this distinction might not always be clear-cut, and the overlapping parts in Figure 2.2 reflect such interrelations among or influences from each category.

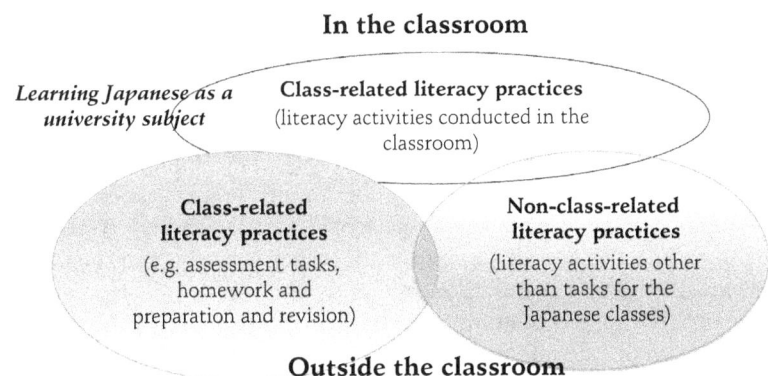

Figure 2.2 L2 literacy practices

For example, learners' motivation for conducting non-class-related literacy practices may be related to their Japanese classes: for instance, reading news websites with the purpose of improving their Japanese language skills in order to gain better grades in their Japanese classes. In this case, the distinction between class-related and non-class-related practices may become unclear. Moreover, it is highly likely that the in-class activities influence out-of-class literacy practices because the participants in the current study are students who study Japanese as a university subject. Therefore, this study will also try to depict the relationship between the Japanese classes and the two types of out-of-class literacy practices undertaken by the students.

From an Activity Theory perspective, although the previous studies discussed above depicted a single assignment task or a series of assignments for academic writing as an activity, this study will interpret that individual class-related literacy practices (i.e. reading, writing and viewing activities for class-related tasks) take place within the broader activity of studying Japanese as a university subject. Non-class-related literacy practices may be embedded in a number of additional activity contexts, such as social activities with peers, personal leisure activities and language learning activities. Activity Theory, as discussed above, provides the underlying conceptual framework for examining which contextual and societal factors afford or constrain opportunities for reading and writing in the target language. The notion of motive is crucial to understanding the reasons why participants in the current study prefer class-related or non-class-related literacy practices, or select particular types of activities. The concept of contradictions is particularly vital for understanding students' engagement with class-related tasks, which are embedded in the collective activity of language learning in a formal educational setting. The exploration of such factors, drawing on activity systems, will enable us to understand how opportunities for reading and writing outside of the classroom are created or not created.

As outlined above, learners' actions in undertaking each literacy activity are mediated by various tools, signs and social resources, such as dictionaries, learners' knowledge of the L2 and peer assistance. In addition, learners' choice of tools and other mediational means will be shaped by individual and contextual factors, such as the learners' motives/goals for literacy activities, the availability of tools, their ability to utilise the tools and the rules and norms of a community (e.g. Japanese classes). The concept of mediation and Engeström's (1987) activity system thus offers a comprehensive viewpoint for the in-depth analysis of the manner in which learners undertake literacy activities in naturalistic contexts. Before proceeding to the analytical chapters of the inquiry, the next section will present information about the participants and the data collection methods.

## Participant Backgrounds and Japanese Subjects

The participants were recruited in August 2008 and March 2009. I have focused on students who were enrolled in Japanese subjects from intermediate to advanced levels at an Australian university. The reason why students in these particular levels were chosen is that students participating in intermediate to advanced levels have the potential to engage in various types of literacy activities outside of the classroom. The total number of participants in this study is 15, comprising 8 male students and 7 female students. In Semester 2, 2008, 6 students completed every stage of the data collection, which I will explain in the following section. In Semester 1, 2009, 9 students, including 3 students who already took part in the 2008 study, volunteered to participate in the current study.

The 15 participants have been assigned pseudonyms. As Table 2.1 shows, their ages ranged from 18 to 24 years at the time of the data collection period. They are all English native speakers, except for one student who is an international student from a South East Asian country. However, she reported that English was her L1 for studying because the schools in her home country employed English as the primary language of communication. Although the majority of the participants started learning Japanese at primary or high school in Australia, a diverse range is evident in their learning histories. Moreover, the majority of the participants had learned other foreign languages in high school and at university or studied their family's cultural language at the Saturday Language School or at home. In particular, it is anticipated that the international student from a South East Asian country and the two Chinese background speakers might have advantages in Japanese literacy practices because Japanese *kanji* stems from Chinese characters.

## Students in Level 7

According to the unit outline of Japanese Level 7, this unit aims to develop students' Japanese skills from an intermediate to an advanced level. This subject utilised a textbook for intermediate level consisting of a one-hour lecture, a one-hour tutorial and a two-hour seminar every week. In the lectures, a teacher explained targeted grammar items and vocabulary, and students practised these items by writing short sentences in their tutorials. In seminars, students engaged in reading tasks in the textbook, answering comprehension questions and discussing the topic of each chapter in groups. The teacher also arranged listening practices. Since the textbook employs authentic Japanese passages from books and newspapers, the participants reported that there was a considerable difference between this unit and the classes that the participants took in the previous semester with regard to vocabulary, especially *kanji*.

Table 2.1 Background of the participants

| Name | Gender | Level of Japanese subjects (during data collection) | Nationality | Home language | Other languages | Pre-university length of Japanese study | Length of Japanese study at university | Experience in Japan |
|---|---|---|---|---|---|---|---|---|
| Brenda | Female | Level 7 | Australian | English | French, Italian (high school and university) | 7 years | 1 year | 2-week school trip |
| Grace | Female | Level 7 | Australian | English | French (high school and university) | 7 years | 1 year (enhancement course in Year 12) | 3-week school trip; 2-week cultural exchange programme |
| Kate | Female | Level 7 | Singaporean | Cantonese and English | Mandarin (primary and high school) | None | 2 years | 1-month cultural trip as a university subject; private trips (3 or 4 times) |
| Melissa | Female | Level 7 | Australian | English | Italian (high school) | None | 2 years | Approx. 10-week in-country summer programme at an exchange university |
| Nancy | Female | Level 7 | Australian | English | None | 4 years | 1 year | 1-year high school exchange programme |
| Joshua | Male | Level 8 | Australian | English | German, Chinese and Korean (high school or university) Estonian (his parent's language, self-study) | Approx. 2 years (self-study) | 1 year (from Semester 2, 2007) | None |
| Scott | Male | Levels 8 and 9 | Australian | English | French (high school) | 6 years | 1 and a half years | 4-week school trip |
| Frank | Male | Level 9 | Australian | English | Hebrew (prep and primary school) French (primary school) | 10 years | 2 years | Approx. 3-week school trip; 6-week homestay programme (to improve his Japanese for a university entrance exam) |

| Name | Gender | Level | Nationality | L1 | Other languages | Years studying Japanese | Additional study | Experience in Japan/abroad |
|---|---|---|---|---|---|---|---|---|
| Eric | Male | Level 10 | Australian | English | Polish (his parent's language) | 7 years | 2 and a half years | 2-week school trip; private trip with his family; approx. 10-week in-country programme undertaking a university subject |
| Alice | Female | Level 10 | Australian | English | None | 6 years | 2 and a half years | A few-weeks school trip; approx. 10-week in-country programme undertaking a university subject |
| Lisa | Female | Level 10 | Australian | English | Chinese (at Saturday School as her home language) German (high school and university) | 6 years | 2 and a half years (1 year interval – stop studying at university) | None |
| Patrick | Male | Level 11 | Australian | English | Chinese (university) | 7 years (including 2 years in Japan) | 2 years | 2-year stay (because of his father's job); 3-year study at a university in Japan (including 1-year Japanese course) |
| Thomas | Male | Level 11 | Australian | English | Chinese (university) | 3 years | 2 years | 10-day and 3-week trips |
| Daniel | Male | Level 11 | Bruneian (immigrated to Australia at 5 years of age) | English | Chinese (his home language, at Saturday School and university) | 3 years (including TAFE) | 3 years (including study at another university) | A half-year work experience; two short trips |
| Chris | Male | Level 12 | Australia | English | Chinese (3 years at high school and 2 years at university) | 4 years | 2 and a half years (including 1-year study abroad in Japan) | 1-year study abroad in Japan as an exchange student |

Five participants (Brenda, Grace, Nancy, Kate and Melissa) enrolled in this level. Their learning trajectories and their motivations for commencing Japanese studies differed considerably. Brenda and Grace started learning Japanese as a compulsory subject at school. Nancy first studied Japanese when she visited Japan as a one-year high school exchange student. In contrast, Kate and Melissa commenced their Japanese study at university. Melissa had a strong desire to study Japanese since high school, because of her interest in Japanese pop culture. Kate also started watching Japanese TV serials and movies in her home country, Singapore. Such differences in their learning trajectories seem to affect their preferences for learning styles and literacy activities (see Chapters 4 and 5). Furthermore, Grace participated in an in-country summer programme during the data collection period. Her experience in this programme constituted an interesting example as will be discussed in Chapter 4.

### Students in Level 8

Japanese Level 8 was the subsequent unit following Level 7, and the same textbook and class patterns (a one-hour lecture, a one-hour tutorial and a two-hour seminar) were employed. According to the subject outline, the aims of Japanese 8 were to enhance students' competence in both spoken and written Japanese, especially to develop their skills: (1) to gather information about a wide range of current issues in Japan from both spoken and written resources and (2) to report the findings and state their opinions about these issues in Japanese.

Joshua and Scott were enrolled in this course. Once more, there were significant differences in their Japanese learning experiences. On the one hand, Scott started learning Japanese as a compulsory subject at school. On the other hand, Joshua had independently studied Japanese for approximately two years before university, using textbooks and websites for learning Japanese and watching Japanese *anime*. Moreover, he had never been to Japan. As will be discussed in Chapter 5, Joshua read and wrote in Japanese almost every day, regardless of his Japanese language skills as an intermediate student. Both Joshua and Scott continuously participated in this study over two semesters in 2008–2009, although Joshua took temporary leave from studying at the university in Semester 1, 2009, because of his job.

### Students in Level 9

Japanese Level 9 and more advanced units were content-based subjects. The main theme of Level 9 was Japanese pop culture. According to the outline of this subject, students were expected to develop their competence in Japanese to advanced levels in both spoken and written Japanese by studying Japanese popular culture. In addition, the acquisition of digital literacy skills, for instance, to manage PowerPoint presentations in Japanese and to seek information in Japanese on the internet, was one of the aims of Level 9. This subject comprised a two-hour tutorial and a two-hour seminar per week, and since it is content based, there was no specific lecture to explain grammar items and vocabulary. In both tutorials and seminars, students engaged in reading Japanese passages from a wide range of materials such as books, online newspapers and magazines; watching Japanese drama, *anime* and TV shows; and listening to Japanese popular songs.

The two participants, Frank and Scott, studied this unit for the second semester of the data collection period. Similar to Scott, Frank also commenced his Japanese study as a compulsory subject in primary school, and had studied it as a school subject for 10 years before commencing university. Frank's vast experience in learning Japanese as a school subject seems to influence his attitudes towards class-related literacy practices (see Chapter 4).

## Students in Level 10

Japanese Level 10, which consisted of a two-hour interpreting class and a two-hour translating class per week, provided an introduction to interpreting and translation between Japanese and English. Students not only engaged in practical exercises such as basic interpreting and translating tasks but also studied theories related to such skills. Accordingly, students needed to read articles about interpreting and translation theories in Japanese.

Alice, Eric and Lisa enrolled in this unit. All these students had studied Japanese as a compulsory subject before university, although there were still differences in terms of their learning experiences while at university. For instance, while Alice and Eric took part in an in-country programme at a sister university in Japan, Lisa had never been to Japan and had taken a one-year interval in her studies at university. Also, Lisa was a Chinese background speaker, and had studied Chinese at Saturday School. Although Lisa struggled with *kanji* at an advanced level of Japanese, she also highlighted the advantage of her knowledge of basic *kanji*.

## Students in Level 11

Japanese Level 11 explored the theme of current issues in the Japanese media. The aim of this subject was to enhance students' academic skills in Japanese: for instance, gaining various resources in Japanese, forming their opinions through interpreting and analysing these resources, writing an essay and giving an oral presentation. This subject comprised two two-hour classes a week. In both classes, students engaged in reading Japanese articles from books, magazines and newspapers, and participated in debates about the topics. As an assessment, students were required to conduct an individual oral presentation about their own topics related to Japanese current affairs.

The three students (Daniel, Thomas and Patrick) who studied in Level 11 had considerably different learning experiences. Patrick lived in Japan for approximately five years in total, and attended junior high school, high school and university in Japan. Patrick often showed his high level of Japanese competence via private communication with me before or after the interview sessions. Daniel started learning Japanese after graduating from high school because of his interest in Japanese pop culture, and had attended several institutions for learning Japanese, including a private language school. Daniel also completed a half-year work experience in Japan, and gained confidence in his speaking skills through communicating with Japanese native speakers. Another student, Thomas, also started learning Japanese at a private language school when he was a high school student, because of his interests in Japanese culture, pop culture in particular. Unlike the other two students, Thomas had no long-term experience in Japan. However, Thomas won first prize in a Japanese speech contest in Australia, and had already acquired a high level of Japanese language skills.

The following chapters will reveal that these evident differences in their learning trajectories and Japanese competences affected their choices in their literacy activities. Furthermore, Daniel and Thomas were not only classmates from previous courses, but also good friends outside of the classroom. Such a relationship also affected Daniel's class-related literacy practices.

## Students in Level 12

Japanese Level 12 was the highest level at the university. The theme of this subject was history and current issues in Japan and the Asia-Pacific Region. This unit consisted of a one-hour lecture, a one-hour tutorial and a two-hour seminar. In the lectures, the teacher explained the overview of the topic in Japanese, while in the tutorials and seminars, students engaged in text reading and reading comprehension, writing practice and oral practice, such as informal discussion in groups and by conducting formal speeches about topics.

Only one participant, Chris, took part in the current research in this level. Chris had experienced a one-year exchange at a Japanese university. During the exchange study, Chris took classes specialised in reading skills, and he recounted that attending the classes improved his reading skills. Indeed, Chris reported on various types of reading activities. Moreover, Chris participated in the current study after he finished studying Japanese at university. Importantly, his reports reveal how he attempted to maintain his Japanese proficiency level after the course was completed (see Chapter 3).

## Data Collection Methods

This inquiry aimed to provide a detailed description and analysis of learners' literacy practices undertaken outside of the classroom. In order to achieve this aim, I employed a multiple case study approach. The case study approach has been widely implemented as an important tool to investigate the process and outcomes of language learning in the SLA field (Nunan, 1992). Compared to quantitative data (e.g. data from a large-scale questionnaire), the sample size of the case study approach is limited, and findings from such data cannot be generalised (Duff, 2006). However, conducting multiple cases enables researchers to make comparisons among cases, which can provide 'insight into an issue or to redraw a generalization' (Stake, 2005: 445). Indeed, the majority of the previous studies surveyed above employed a multiple case study approach and provided us with beneficial implications based on both an in-depth analysis in single cases and comparisons between the cases. Moreover, because of the nature of the case study approach where researchers hope to gather detailed information about a particular case, case studies in SLA often adopt a longitudinal and naturalistic approach, which does not include 'any attempts to manipulate the situation under study' (Dörnyei, 2007: 38). The data for this research was also collected over a semester or throughout an academic year, utilising several qualitative data collection methods: a semi-structured interview about students' background, a diary study which incorporates photos and a collection of written materials and a retrospective type of interview after the diary study. A combination of several qualitative data collection methods is also crucial in order to enhance the validity of a study by compensating the shortcomings of each data collection method (Dörnyei, 2007; Duff, 2008; Mackey & Gass, 2005; McDonough & McDonough, 1997; Silverman, 2005). Moreover, all the interviews were recorded for analysis purposes. The availability of this data for each participant is shown in Table 2.2.

In the following sections, I briefly explain the data collection methods, why I employed these methods and the data collection procedure.

### Background interview (semi-structured)

I initially conducted semi-structured interviews with the student participants in order to obtain information about their backgrounds, including their primary motivation for learning Japanese and the history of

**Table 2.2** Data for each participant

| Name | Background interview | 1st diary and interview | 2nd diary and interview | 3rd diary and interview |
|---|---|---|---|---|
| Brenda | √ | √ | √ | |
| Grace | √ | √ | √ | |
| Nancy | √ | √ | √ | |
| Kate | √ | Only diary entries | Only diary entries | √ |
| Melissa | √ | √ | √ | |
| Joshua (two semesters) | √ | √ | √ | |
| | | √ | √ | |
| Scott (two semesters) | √ | √ | √ | |
| | | √ | √ | √ |
| Frank | √ | √ | √ | √ |
| Eric | √ | √ | √ | |
| Alice | √ | √ | √ | |
| Lisa | √ | √ | √ | |
| Patrick | √ | √ | √ | |
| Thomas | √ | √ | √ | |
| Daniel | √ | √ | √ | √ |
| Chris (two semesters) | √ | √ | √ | |
| | | √ | √ | |

their Japanese learning. In order to avoid language proficiency influencing the quality and quantity of the interview data (Mackey & Gass, 2005; Nunan, 1992), I conducted all the interviews, including those that will be explained later, in the participants' L1, English. During the interviews, however, the participants and I occasionally utilised Japanese, which is my L1, when I did not immediately recall appropriate English words, or when the participants simply spoke in Japanese.

While the interview has been widely utilised as a research tool in the field of applied linguistics (Nunan, 1992), interviews or other subcategories of interviews such as stimulated recall interviews are characterised by a number of problems, such as the influence of the interviewer's status, the power relationship between interviewers and interviewees and the limitation of participants' memories (Block, 1995). As for the first two problems, the participants and I differed in terms of age, nationality and social status. I admit that such differences in the status of the participants and mine might affect conducting the interviews. In addition, I actually taught 4 of the 15 participants in the preceding year, though I did not teach any of the participants during the data collection period. However, having taught them in the past could be an advantage because I had already developed a rapport with them, which is crucial to collect in-depth data through interviews (Dörnyei, 2007; Richards, 2003). In order to reduce the problem of participants' memories in their reports about out-of-class literacy practices, I decided to employ a diary study.

## Diary study with photos and collection of written materials

After the first semi-structured interview about the participants' background, the participants were requested to report detailed information about their literacy activities for one week, using the diary format which I prepared. The diary format included the date, time, place, types of literacy activities and with whom they undertook these. The participants were also requested to take photos of the media that they used in Japanese, for example, Japanese *manga* and screenshots of websites, alternatively the website addresses.

I employed diaries because they are widely recognised in SLA as a useful as well as a non-intrusive method of collecting data about participants' experiences and the process of learning from an 'insider' (Dörnyei, 2007: 157) perspective, which might otherwise be overlooked by researchers and might not be revealed by such means as observations or interviews (Bailey, 1991; Dörnyei, 2007; Gibson, 1995; McDonough & McDonough, 1997; Mackey & Gass, 2005). The method of having participants take photos was originally sourced from Allen and Labbo (2001) and Allen *et al.* (2002) in their project PhOLKS (Photographs of Local Knowledge Sources). Using this method, Fukunaga (2006: 209) explains that the 'method provides a view of students' out-of-school lives'. Since the participants engaged with texts, including visual and audio modes, information from photos and websites was beneficial for gaining more concrete information about their literacy activities.

Along with the diary entries and the photos, the participants were also asked to submit written materials related to their literacy practices outside of the class setting, as well as in the classroom. The following kinds of materials in or related to Japanese were collected: copies of novels, magazines, local newspapers for Japanese residents in the city, *manga*, picture books, chat logs and emails with Japanese native speakers and fellow Japanese learner peers, assignment essays, classroom handouts, preparation memos for oral presentations in the classroom, classroom notebooks and textbooks. Some of the participants, moreover, submitted their past written assignments (essays), *manga* that they had read previously and textbooks which they utilised in high school. Although these materials were not directly related to their literacy activities during the data collection period, such information provided useful clues in order to understand their past experiences of learning Japanese.

As one of the shortcomings of diary studies, Bailey (1991) points out the quality and amount of description alongside the drawbacks commonly described in the case study approaches, such as generalisability and objectivity (see also Duff, 2006, 2008). Moreover, Bolger *et al.* (2003) presume that a formatted diary may result in less in-depth reports. In order to supplement the descriptions by participants, I employed the 'diary-interview method' (Zimmerman & Wieder, 1977: 479), which was first introduced in the field of sociology. In this method, the participants firstly maintain diaries, and then researchers prepare questions on the participants' diaries and conduct interviews.

Interaction interview

I employed an interaction interview for this purpose, and usually conducted the interview within a couple of days after the diary entries were submitted to me. The interaction interview, which was developed by Neustupný (2002) and others, is similar to introspection/retrospection or stimulated recall in terms of the interview techniques employed to elicit participants' actions and thoughts after they undertook specific actions. However, the interaction interview differs from the stimulated recall interview in that it focuses on concrete questions to examine what happened in a specific situation in cases where data collection methods such as observation or audio/video recording are unavailable (Muraoka, 2002; Neustupný, 2002).

Similar to audio- or video-tape recordings used in a stimulated recall interview (Gass & Mackey, 2000), in my interaction interviews I utilised the diary, the photos they took and any written materials which they submitted to me. By drawing on these materials, during the interviews, the participants often demonstrated how they undertook their literacy activities. Such use of stimuli should also reduce problems with memory in introspection interviews (Dörnyei, 2007; Gass & Mackey, 2000). Moreover, although interaction interviews aim to elicit descriptions about concrete behaviours (actions) during a specific event, it is necessary to explore participants' motives and past experiences because such factors may influence their current experiences. Hence, I flexibly changed questions during the interaction interviews in order to elicit their experiences and thoughts behind their literacy activities, as Muraoka (2002) suggested.

In order to collect rich data including a variety of examples at different points in time, I requested the participants to repeat this set of activities two or three times during one semester as well as during the university holiday. However, as it is similar to stimulated recall interviews, the interaction interview is usually conducted only once with each participant because the first interview will influence any subsequent interview (Gass & Mackey, 2000; Muraoka, 2002). In order to reduce this risk, the second focus week for the collection of diary entries and the

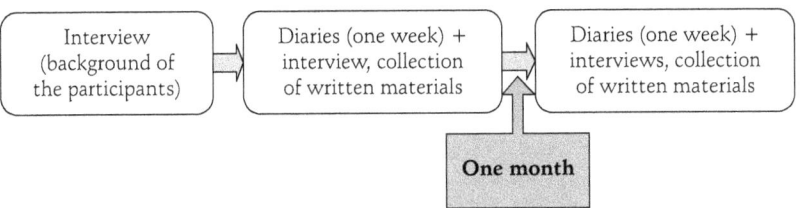

**Figure 2.3** Basic procedures of data collection

undertaking of interaction interviews was at least one month after the first focus week. Yet, there were exceptions when the participants started maintaining the second week of diary entries in the same month as their first focus week because of their study schedules. Figure 2.3 shows the basic procedures of the data collection.

## Data of Japanese classes

In order to understand the contexts of the students' literacy activities in a more comprehensive manner, interviews with teachers of the classes in which the participants enrolled were conducted at the end of each semester. Table 2.3 provides brief information about the teachers and their Japanese course. Japanese was employed in these interviews because all participants were Japanese native speakers.

Moreover, I conducted classroom observations of Japanese Level 7 in the second half of Semester 1, 2009, with teachers' permission. The main purpose of this classroom observation was to understand the contexts for the class-related literacy practices, which were inextricably related to the in-class activities. I basically employed non-participant observation because it is more objective than participant observation in which a researcher participates in activities as a full member of a group (Dörnyei, 2007). However, in order to be cooperative, I participated minimally in

**Table 2.3** Interviews with teachers

| Name (pseudonym) | Gender | Japanese subject | Interviews |
| --- | --- | --- | --- |
| Aoki | Female | Level 7<br>Level 8 | June 2009<br>November 2008 |
| Emoto | Female | Level 7 | June 2009 |
| Fukuda | Female | Level 8<br>Levels 9 and 11 | November 2008<br>June 2009 |
| Kimura | Male | Level 10 | October 2008 |
| Murata | Male | Level 10<br>Level 9 | November 2008<br>June 2009 |
| Suzuki | Male | Level 12 | November 2008 |

classroom activities when it was requested by the teachers or when students asked me questions.

While observing the classes, I took field notes on any activities related to reading and writing in chronological order based on the categories outlined by Mackey and Gass (2005), that is, the grouping format of participants (e.g. group work, pair work), the content and topic of each task/lesson (e.g. the topics of reading and writing exercises), the main characteristics of the interaction (e.g. writing short sentences on the spot) and the targeted language and linguistic skills of the students (e.g. grammar items students are required to use). After the classes, I documented these field notes in digital format.

I could not conduct classroom observations of the other Japanese courses due to ethical constraints. As for these courses, I collected data of the in-class activities by means of semi-structured interviews with teacher and student participants, as described above. Moreover, class-related materials such as copies of the subject outlines, textbooks, reading materials, handouts and worksheets were collected from the teacher as well as the student participants. Such data about in-class activities supported my understanding of the contexts relevant to class-related literacy practices.

## Transcription

All the interviews were recorded and transcribed drawing on the transcription conventions that Du Bois (1991) offers, with some modifications and simplifications. These transcription conventions are listed in Table 2.4.

As mentioned earlier, Japanese was occasionally utilised during the interviews with the student participants. These utterances in Japanese were transcribed in Japanese script, and were provided in Romanised spelling with italics and English translations. I employed the Hepburn system of Romanisation of Japanese and modified the Romanisation system according to Neustupný's (1991) guidelines. After each interview,

**Table 2.4** Transcription symbols for the interview data

|   |   |
|---|---|
| . | Final intonation |
| , | Continuing intonation |
| ? | Appeal, rising intonation |
| ... | Omission |
| <@@> | Laugh quality |
| (( )) | Researcher's comment |
| <X X> | Uncertain hearing |

I listened to the recorded interviews and marked unclear and incomprehensible parts. If these parts were important for analysis, I requested the participants to recall their utterances by email or in the next interview. However, in the cases in which they could not remember, I asked them to explain what they intended to say in the utterances. Also, the interviews with the Japanese teachers were transcribed in Japanese script and translated into English for citation.

## Data analysis procedures

The present study analysed the data inductively by utilising Nvivo, which is a qualitative data analysis software application. All the data, including transcribed interviews, diary entries and copies of the written materials, were imported into Nvivo and coded in order to identify significant themes and patterns.

The analysis of the types of literacy practices involved an examination of the diary entries, interviews and the collected written materials. The interview transcriptions of Japanese teachers and the field notes based on the class observations were also utilised in order to understand what types of literacy practices the participants undertook in detail. First of all, the data was categorised into either class-related or non-class-related literacy practices, and further categorised into subgroups, such as essays, oral presentations and voluntary reading activities. This data was also analysed in relation to categorisations in the area of autonomous language learning with the aim to reconstruct the categories best suited to the current study.

For the analysis of factors influencing opportunities for L2 out-of-class literacy practices, all the interview data and the students' comments in diary entries were utilised. The participants' cases were examined using a within-case analysis, where 'the data of a single qualitative case' (Merriam, 1998: 194) was analysed, in order to capture the full picture of an individual learner's learning context. Firstly, participant's data was categorised into either class-related or non-class-related literacy practices, and was coded based on factors found in activity systems (i.e. motives/objects, subjective factors, mediating artefacts, communities, rules/norms). This coding included a constant reconstruction of subcategories under higher categories, for instance, the types of motives under motive. Secondly, this coded data was compared across cases of individual students with the purpose of identifying important themes and testing out a tentative hypothesis (Silverman, 2005). This data was further analysed in relation to the key concepts of Activity Theory (i.e. multiple motives, contradictions).

A similar data analysis procedure was employed for an investigation into the ways in which the participants undertook each literacy activity. However, particular attention was paid to the participants' comments on how they relied on mediational means, that is, language-related resources, to support their literacy activities. Furthermore, the interview data was also coded based on the factors found in the activity systems in order to explore the contextual and individual factors which influenced participants' choice of resources.

**Summary**

This chapter commenced by reviewing studies related to L2 out-of-class literacy practices. The findings in these studies provide insight into the types of L2 activities that learners undertook outside of the classroom, and factors affecting these opportunities as well as their approaches towards reading and writing in a target language. Gaps still requiring further investigation were also identified. In addition, the chapter discussed the importance of integrating sociocultural perspectives in exploring L2 literacy practices in out-of-classroom contexts. Subsequently, this chapter outlined Activity Theory, which is the main framework in this present study. Key concepts, such as motive, mediation, contradiction and agency, were discussed in comparison to the relevant research topics in SLA, namely language learning motivation and learner autonomy. This discussion led to how this theory would be applied to the analysis of the current study.

This chapter also outlined the methodology utilised in this study. The description of participants' backgrounds combined with an outline of their Japanese courses was followed by the introduction of five types of data collection procedures: a diary study with photos, collection of written materials, semi-structured and interaction interviews and class observations. These multiple data collection procedures allowed me to triangulate the data and to provide a comprehensive description about the participants' L2 literacy practices. I also discussed problems evident in the methodology, and the attempts I took to minimise these problems. Finally, this chapter outlined the data analysis procedures while illustrating the processes of identifying theoretical categories and significant themes in the study in order to analyse what, why and how students undertook literacy activities in Japanese.

# 3 Types of Literacy Activities Performed Outside of the Classroom

This chapter presents a detailed description of the second language (L2) literacy practices that this study's participants undertook outside of the classroom. As mentioned in Chapter 1, there are two main types of literacy practices in out-of-classroom contexts: class-related and non-class-related literacy practices. In relation to this differentiation, I will first discuss important issues that influence the classification of out-of-class learning. Based on this discussion, this chapter will then present the types of literacy activities that students undertook and discuss the features of such activities in terms of the differences and similarities between the two types of literacy practices.

## Existing Classifications of Out-of-Classroom Learning

Literacy practices in out-of-classroom contexts can be viewed as opportunities for L2 learning outside of the classroom, and a number of studies have discussed such out-of-class language learning as being a form of autonomous learning (e.g. Freeman, 1999; Hyland, 2004; Inozu et al., 2010; Lamb, 2004; Murray, 2004; Murray & Kojima, 2007; Pearson, 2004; Spratt et al., 2002; Yap, 1998). In the field of autonomous language learning, several scholars propose theoretical classifications for out-of-class learning. Benson (2001) postulates three categories: self-instruction, naturalistic language learning and self-directed naturalistic learning. Self-instruction to a certain degree represents language learners organising their learning and studying a target language with little or no communication with teachers or target language speakers (Jones, 1998). In a broader sense, self-instruction indicates any situation where language learners study a target language without teachers' direct control, such as studying grammar by utilising a textbook (Dickinson, 1987). In the mode of naturalistic language learning, learners acquire the target language by means of direct interaction with target language speakers and authentic texts. According to Benson's categorisation, self-directed naturalistic learning implies that learners seek opportunities to utilise the target language, though the learners do not focus on learning the target language itself.

Benson's (2001) classifications are not suitable to discuss both class-related and non-class-related literacy practices. First, Benson's categorisations do not include any learning activities organised by teachers, such as assignments and homework. This might be because Benson postulates that control over content by individual learners is one of the main conditions of autonomous learning. Second, concerning the differences between self-instruction and naturalistic language learning, Benson (2001: 62) focuses on 'the degree of deliberate intention to acquire language content or skills at the time of the learning event itself'. However, it is often difficult to identify learners' intentions for a particular task because learners might have two different intentions for one practice, such as learning Japanese and enjoying private time by reading a *manga*. Finally, as a number of scholars have maintained (e.g. Firth & Wagner, 1997), it is also difficult to distinguish concepts such as learning or using in communicative activities. Indeed, participants in this current study also demonstrated that behaviour clearly related to learning a target language. They demonstrated this through their voluntary literacy activities, for instance, trying to memorise new words and constructing vocabulary lists. Such activities will be explained in more detail later in this chapter, as well as in Chapter 6.

Jones (1998: 378–379) proposed types of learning activities in relation to the degree of learners' independence. In his categorisations, learning activities allowing minimum learner independence include 'classwork' followed by 'homework' and 'self-access/teacher-led autonomy'. Jones (1998: 379) defined self-access and teacher-led autonomy in his categorisation as follows: self-access refers to learner-selected materials in order to support classroom learning, while teacher-led autonomy signifies 'the contracting out of elements of a taught language course to a solo work, but with teacher prompting and/or evaluation'. In other words, this category, along with homework, could be viewed as class-related literacy practices in the present study. Furthermore, Jones posited 'naturalistic immersion' as activities with maximum learner independence, followed by 'full autonomy' and 'teach-yourself'. These three categories are connected to non-class-related literacy practices in the present study. According to Jones (1998: 378), teach-yourself learning can be described as, for example, 'learning a target language with a language-learning package', and full autonomy indicates 'learning a target language with learners' own syllabus and materials'. Although Jones did not discuss concrete examples, full autonomy could also include activities through which students intend to learn a target language by utilising authentic materials.

Jones' (1998) classification includes tasks for language classes. However, participants in this study undertook several types of assignments other than just homework. Furthermore, Jones' classification does not cover self-study related to language classes, such as preparation and revision for classes. It is also important to note that the term 'learner independence', which was used to locate each category in Jones' categorisation, is ambiguous. For instance, on the one hand, preparation for classes may be spontaneously undertaken by students, but the materials used in the classroom are decided upon by the teachers. In other words, although students choose whether or not they prepare for classes, they cannot select the class content (what they prepare for the classes). On the other hand, in projects, such as oral presentations and essays, students may choose topics and materials even though the tasks are arranged and assessed by the teachers. This fact implies that each class-related task contains a different degree of learner independence. Furthermore, it is necessary to integrate other factors, such as the influence of language classes on the content level, so as to explore the relation between language classes and the activities that students undertake outside the classroom.

In Benson's (2011: 13–14) more recent study, however, a broader framework for analysing out-of-class L2 learning was proposed. This framework comprises two key concepts: 'settings' and 'modes of practices'. Setting does not simply refer to a physical place where the learning occurs, but also indicates a space or arrangement for learning, including relationships with others and resources that 'offer affordances and constraints on possibilities for language learning' (Benson, 2011: 13). The modes of practices are conceptualised as 'a set of routine pedagogical processes that deploy features of a particular setting and may be characteristic of it' (Benson, 2011: 14). The setting(s) and the modes of practices are analysed from four dimensions that are derived from the analysis of the terms often used to describe research on autonomous language learning: location, formality, pedagogy and locus of control. Benson describes these dimensions as follows: location refers to the place where a learning activity occurs (e.g. out-of-class and after school); formality is related to whether or not a learning activity is part of an educational programme and possibly leads to qualifications (e.g. informal vs. formal learning); pedagogy refers to whether a learning activity involves pedagogical factors, such as instructions, assessments and sequential materials (e.g. non-instructed and self-instructed learning); the locus of control indicates who makes the decisions related to a learning activity (e.g. independent and self-directed learning). Benson and Chik (2011) and Chik (2014) applied these four dimensions in order to examine the relationship between L2 gaming and autonomous language learning, and concluded that this framework could provide a starting point to understand how learners exercise their autonomy to learn an L2 through playing video games in the L2.

The terms proposed by Benson, however, are not very suitable for the aim of this chapter due to the following reasons. First, Benson's framework does not include a facet to examine the relatedness between language classes and out-of-class literacy practices, in particular, non-class-related literacy practices. Second, although assessment is an essential factor to discuss differences in class-related literacy practices, this element is integrated into pedagogy in Benson's framework. Third, it is often difficult to articulate who controls an activity. For example, the actual process to complete assessment tasks is arranged by individual students in consideration of a number of factors, such as the requirements set by teachers and the students' language skills. In this case, although students engage in the tasks in their own way, it is difficult to articulate who controls the tasks. Finally, location is not a crucial aspect when discussing the features of each type of literacy activity, though it might be an influential factor on how learners engage in literacy practices.

In order to illustrate the features of each literacy activity in the present study, I propose four facets: arrangement, assessment, content and pedagogy. Arrangement can explain the cases in which both teachers and students are involved in the decision processes of the task arrangements (e.g. teachers set up requirements for a task, but students can choose the topics and materials for undertaking it). Assessment, as mentioned above, should be a single element to examine features of class-related literacy practices. Content is also an important factor in order to identify what extent each literacy activity is incorporated into the language classes. Finally, I employ pedagogy from Benson's framework to discuss the language teaching aspects that exist in each literacy activity.

Figure 3.1 shows how I categorised participants' literacy practices based on the four dimensions of content, assessment, pedagogy and the person who arranges tasks (i.e. arrangement). As Figure 3.1 indicates, we can hypothesise that typical non-class-related literacy practices are arranged by students and are not assessed by teachers nor related to the content in the classroom. Moreover, such practices do not include any pedagogical aspect. The exact opposite applies to typical class-related literacy practices.

Although I differentiate between class-related and non-class-related literacy practices based on these dimensions, I acknowledge that the distinction between the two types of literacy practices may be ambiguous in particular cases. It is anticipated that some literacy activities for Japanese classes may share features of non-class-related activities and vice versa. In addition, the participants' purposes behind undertaking each literacy activity are also influential factors in differentiating between class-related and non-class-related literacy practices. However, in this chapter, I will focus on the four factors presented in Figure 3.1 to discuss the types of literacy practices rather than discussing the participants' objectives behind the literacy practices, as I will be discussing issues related to motive as the driving force behind their out-of-class literacy practices in the following chapters.

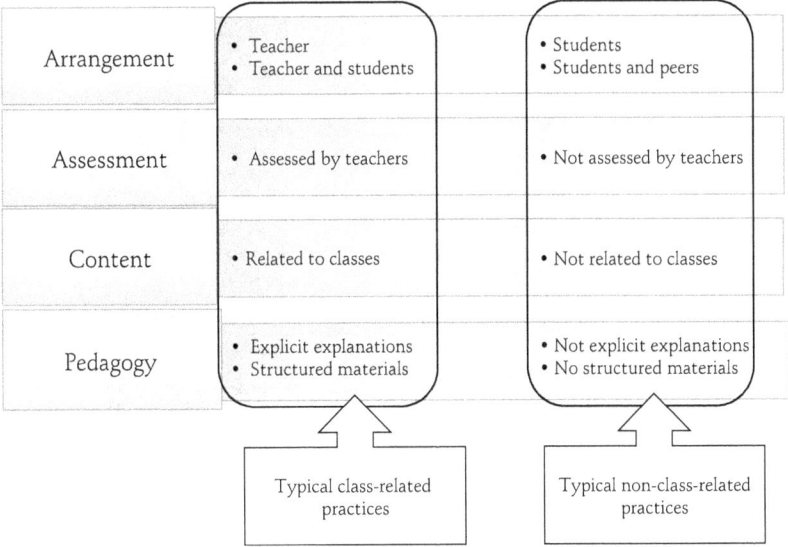

**Figure 3.1** Four dimensions for the participants' literacy practices in out-of-classroom contexts

## Class-Related Literacy Practices

The majority of the literacy activities that students undertook were clearly related to their Japanese classes. These activities included, for example, reading websites in preparation for an oral presentation, and reading textbook passages in order to prepare for classes. These literacy activities often occurred as a form or part of class-related tasks. In this vein, each literacy activity appears to be actions in Leont'ev's (1978) hierarchy of activity, and is significantly influenced by the task types. Hence, this section will discuss the task types, and explore what types of reading and writing activities were included in each task.

### Assessment tasks

Assessment tasks, such as quizzes, examinations, oral presentations, oral tests and essays, are essential in order for participants to pass their Japanese subjects. Table 3.1 presents the assessment tasks that the participants were required to undertake for their Japanese subjects. The assessment tasks that the participants reported on in interviews and in their diary entries are italicised.

All of the tasks were assessed by teachers; however, the degree of teacher intervention differed for each task. Moreover, although all the assessment tasks were part of the courses, which were structured based on progression, different types of tasks involved different degrees and types of pedagogical factors. In the following sections, I will focus on

Table 3.1 Materials and assessment tasks of the Japanese subjects

| Japanese subjects | Content (textbook) | Assessment tasks |
|---|---|---|
| Level 7 | Authentic Japanese: Progressing from Intermediate to Advanced (Kamada et al., 1998) | Vocabulary quizzes, mid-semester examination, oral test, final examination, a written assignment, a project report based on an interview with a Japanese native speaker |
| Level 8 | Authentic Japanese: Progressing from Intermediate to Advanced (Kamada et al., 1998) | Vocabulary quizzes, unit quizzes, oral test, final examination, two written assignments, an oral presentation in pairs |
| Level 9 | Japanese popular culture (No textbook. Reading materials were distributed in the class) | Quizzes, oral test, final examination, homework tasks (one translation task), a group presentation, an essay |
| Level 10 | Interpreting and Translation (a course book) | Mid-semester test and final test for interpreting, final test for translation, tasks for interpreting (dialogue presentation, live interpreting), translation assignments and oral presentation (about translation theories) |
| Level 11 | Current Issues in Japanese Media (a course book comprising reading materials) | Vocabulary and reading comprehension tests, final examination, an essay, an individual oral presentation |
| Level 12 | History and Current Issues in Japan and the Asia-Pacific Region | Vocabulary quizzes, mid-semester examination, oral test, final examination, an essay |

these two points, namely the degree of teachers' regulations and the pedagogical aspects, in order to discuss the various assessment task types.

*Preparation for quizzes and examinations*

Most of the participants reported that they used preparation for quizzes and examinations as opportunities for reading and writing in Japanese outside of the classroom. The questions in the quizzes and examinations were decided upon by teachers.

Although the ways in which and how much participants prepared for these tasks varied depending on each participant, it is thought that these types of tasks might allow for a small amount of learners' regulation in terms of selecting resources and learning contents. The questions in the quizzes and examinations were arranged by teachers to check students' understanding and progressions in the course content, which included the vocabulary, grammar items and reading materials that the students learned in the classroom. In this vein, it can be claimed that preparations for quizzes and examinations were closely related to the pedagogical aspects of the participants' Japanese classes.

The reading and writing activities undertaken in preparation for quizzes and examinations differed depending on the types of questions. In relation to vocabulary quizzes, the students read the vocabulary lists and wrote *kanji* a number of times in order to memorise pronunciations, meanings and how to write *kanji*. Several quizzes and final examinations also included grammar and reading comprehension questions. Accordingly, Melissa, Brenda and Scott reported that they wrote example sentences based on classroom materials (lecture slides and handouts) because 'If I write it out, I remember it more' (Melissa, Interview 3). Reading and writing activities for this type of task were thus used as a means of rote learning.

Preparations for quizzes also involved different types of reading activities. For instance, Scott needed to re-read the material in order to fully understand the content because Japanese 9 quizzes included comprehension questions on the reading material:

> Prepared for a Japanese quiz. Re-read the article on which the quiz was to be based on (ヒット ドラマは台湾発 ((*hitto dorama wa Taiwan hatsu* – popular Japanese TV serials came from Taiwan)). Made a list of all the 漢字 ((*kanji*))/words I didn't know. I found some parts of the reading to be quite difficult, since several Chinese names (of people and TV shows) were included (and not necessarily with ふりがな ((*furigana* – pronunciations of *kanji*))). I also had to look up a lot of Japanese words (for example: 瞬く ((*mataku* – instantly)), 塗り替える ((*nurikaeru* – rewrite)), 財閥 ((*zaibatsu* – company syndicates)), 御曹司 ((*onzōshi* – scion)), 憧れ ((*akogare* – yearning)), など((*nado* – etc.))). I used my normal sources (Jim Breen's WWWJDIC, Canon Wordtank G55, etc.), but also Google and Wikipedia (English and Japanese), to help with the Chinese names/words. (Scott's diary entry on 12 May 2009)

Here, Scott not only reads the article itself, but also consults websites and Wikipedia articles in order to understand unknown Chinese words. These examples indicate that different types of questions, which were set by teachers, seem to trigger different types of reading and writing activities among the students.

### Preparations for oral presentations/oral tests

Oral presentations in class and oral tests also incorporated a number of reading and writing activities. While oral tests were necessitated in all Japanese courses, and assumed a discussion format, oral presentations were required in Japanese Levels 8, 9, 10 and 11 in the form of group/pair or individual presentations. As opposed to the quizzes and examinations, the oral presentations and oral tests provided students with more choices in terms of topics, resources and arguments. Although the topics were related to the textbook content or reading materials, students were allowed to select alternatives that were arranged by teachers, or choose any topic related to the content of their Japanese classes. Where students were allowed to choose topics, they selected the topics that they thought were 'interesting' (Nancy, Interview 3) or 'easier than other topics' (Frank, Interview 2).

Preparation for oral presentations and oral tests involved a number of reading activities that differed from reading activities for quizzes and exam preparation in terms of student initiatives because students could choose what they read. The participants relied heavily on the internet, Google and Wikipedia in particular, and read websites for information. For instance, Patrick, who studied in Level 11, read several articles on the Japanese Wikipedia site and on Japanese news websites. Several students mainly relied on English internet resources for a number of reasons that will be explored in the subsequent chapters. However, it is noteworthy that all the references that the participants reported were online reading materials.

Oral presentations/oral tests also included writing activities that were presented in the form of writing scripts/cue cards, handouts and PowerPoint slides for their oral presentations. For these writing activities, most of the participants utilised computers (Microsoft Word and Microsoft PowerPoint) because they could type Japanese text without knowing how to write *kanji*. Thus, the participants relied heavily on computers and on the internet for these assignments.

Both the reading and writing activities described above did not clearly include pedagogical factors, such as utilising structured learning materials and explanations from teachers, though they did involve learners paying attention to the language, such as looking up new words in a dictionary. Rather, the way in which the students engaged in these reading and writing activities was comparable to how people read and write authentic materials in an L2. Combined with the fact that the students had more options to choose topics and materials, it can be reasonably stated that these literacy activities were closer to authentic language use outside the classroom.

*Essays and project reports*

Essays and project reports were also part of Japanese Levels 7, 9, 11 and 12 assessments. However, the other requirements for these tasks differed slightly depending on each individual Japanese subject. As for the project report in Level 7, the report's topic was set by the teacher. For the report, students also had to undertake an interview with a Japanese native speaker instead of relying on reading resources. In other words, this report did not involve reading activities in order to gather relevant information. Although the essay topic for Japanese Level 11 was set by the teacher, students were obliged to read resources in order to develop their own arguments. Students in Levels 9 and 12 could choose one topic based on the content that they studied in class and were required to search for and draw upon other resources. It can be claimed that the research project in Level 7 thus limited student initiative as opposed to other Japanese subjects, perhaps because of the students' lower level of Japanese proficiency.

Similar to the preparation undertaken for oral presentations and oral tests, students heavily utilised computers and the internet for their essays. Participants were required to type their essays, and therefore all the participants utilised computers for writing. Students also searched for resources on the internet and read material online. Chris, Frank, Patrick, Scott and Thomas also reported that they read parts or chapters of books or whole books in Japanese for their essay assignments. Reading such a broad range of material, including hard copy materials, was necessary for students because the incorporation of a variety of references was included in the essay's assessment criteria. In the interview, Ms Fukuda (a teacher of Level 11) explained the evident differences between the purposes of the oral presentation and the essay task. In regard to the essay task, Ms Fukuda stated that she encouraged students to search and read academic books in order to acquire basic academic skills, including Japanese academic language skills. Ms Fukuda also hoped that students would improve their presentation skills by means of the oral presentations, thus the types of resources were not important. Such differences in teachers' intentions were evident in the assessment criteria/requirements, and shaped learning experiences in terms of what types of materials students read and how to engage in the assessment tasks to some extent. However, these teachers' intentions did not appear in the form of teaching the language (e.g. explaining the meaning of expressions) and support by prepared materials, for example, vocabulary lists. Similar to the case of oral examinations and preparations, the reading and writing activities for essays and project reports did not explicitly include pedagogical aspects.

One of the participants, Daniel, also read the essays of students who had undertaken the same course the previous year as a model, and utilised these essays to construct his argument, structure his essay and gain information about useful references (Daniel's diary entry on 25 May 2009). However, Daniel's case seems to differ from the examples in the previous study whereby peers' written assignments were utilised (e.g. Yang *et al.*, 2004) in that Daniel directly utilised the contents of his peers' essays for drafting his own assignments rather than just as a model for his essay.

As illustrated above, most of the essays, oral presentations and oral tests of the participants' Japanese classes thus involved both reading and writing activities. This finding is the same as those in previous studies on English as a second language (ESL) academic writing (e.g. Riazi, 1997; Spack, 1997), that is, literacy skills included not only writing tasks, but also assessment for evaluating oral skills. Given that these tasks often formed a relatively large part of the assessment, literacy skills seem to be crucial for students who study Japanese, at least for the intermediate and advanced courses at the university. This finding also supports what Sakuma (2006) claims: reading and writing for academic purposes have been emphasised in the curriculum of Japanese language education, regardless of the necessity thereof.

*Translation tasks*

In Japanese Levels 9 and 10, translation tasks were part of the assessment, and translation materials were selected by teachers. In other words, it is likely that teacher intervention in translation tasks would be relatively high, despite the fact that students could choose what tools and which resources they utilised when undertaking the translation.

Translation tasks do not represent the typical reading and writing practices undertaken in Japanese classes, and therefore the literacy activities undertaken by the participants were different from the other assessment tasks presented above. For instance, formulating and expressing opinions in Japanese were necessary when composing written essays. In translation tasks, students needed to focus on how to convey the content of original texts into the target language. Alice and Lisa, who were enrolled in Level 10, reported that they deliberately examined words and phrases by comparing example sentences presented in an online dictionary. Moreover, as the task concerned translating an English advertisement into Japanese, both students researched Japanese advertisements on the internet in order to check their language styles (polite register or casual register). This usage of authentic materials differed from the other reading activities for the class-related tasks in that the students focused on the language rather than on the content.

Translation tasks thus incorporate language-focused actions. However, teachers' linguistic support was not available while students were engaging in the tasks out of the classroom, though there were opportunities to share translation strategies and feedback in the classes after the tasks were completed. In this sense, it is reasonable to claim that these translation tasks embraced pedagogical factors more explicitly than the other assessment tasks, where feedback primarily took the form of marking.

Similar to the other class-related tasks, the participants highlighted their reliance on internet-based resources once more, such as online dictionaries, Wikipedia and Google for finding relevant information. Chapter 6 will fully explore the manner in which the students utilised the internet for preparing the assessment tasks.

## Non-assessment tasks

*Homework*

Several students reported that homework activities, which were not assessed, were also an opportunity for reading and writing activities.

Since homework tasks included reading comprehension questions based on class reading materials, the students needed to read and understand the passages. Frank reported that, in order to answer the reading comprehension questions, he re-read the material by checking the meaning of unknown words and expressions using an online dictionary and Google.

The homework tasks involved structured instructions, in other words, factors of pedagogy, in that students answered the questions set by the teachers. However, in the participants' Japanese subjects, homework was basically the work that students could not finish during class time. Although teachers encouraged students to do their homework, students ultimately decided whether or not they undertook the task. In this respect, this type of homework was different from the aforementioned assessment tasks, which were the compulsory components that the students needed to fulfil in order to pass the subjects.

*Preparation/revision for classes*

The majority of students (10 out of 15) reported that they read the textbook/the reading materials in preparation for their classes. In order to understand the textbook passages or the materials, the participants searched for unknown words and expressions by utilising their electronic dictionaries, paper dictionaries and online dictionaries. As Frank did for his homework, Scott also reported that he often utilised Wikipedia and Google in order to search for unknown words and expressions that he could not find in dictionaries.

Grace also undertook extra study, which involved written exercises. In order to master the grammar items that she learned in class, she firstly constructed English sentences and then translated them by drawing on the grammatical rules. Ms Aoki, who was a teacher in Japanese Level 7, also commented in the interview that Grace sometimes asked her to correct the Japanese sentences that she composed during this extra study. Although Grace herself did not describe this practice as revision, we can observe that this practice was revision for the class because she tried to master the grammar items that she had learnt in the classes. In addition, after each Japanese class, Grace compiled extra vocabulary lists that included the words and expressions utilised by teachers during classes.

Class preparation and revision shared similarities with homework in that both types of tasks were directly related to participants' Japanese classes and were also undertaken on a voluntary basis. However, the difference between these two types of practices is whether or not they had been directly arranged by the teachers, which indicates the difference in the dimension of pedagogy. Different from homework, class preparation and revision did not directly include teachers' instructions and feedback, though these tasks prompted actions focusing on the language, such as looking up unknown words and creating sentences using new grammar items. Moreover, class preparation and revision were arranged by the students based on their own reasons, such as 'to follow the classes' (Frank, Interview 2), 'answer to the teacher's questions in the classes' (Daniel, Interview 2) and 'to get my Japanese back up to a comfortable level' (Grace, Interview 1). It can be assumed that class preparation and revision levels require a higher level of student initiative, which is ultimately motivated by students' personal goals. It is also important to note that only Grace reported extra revision activities after the classes. These issues will be further discussed in Chapter 4.

## Non-Class-Related Literacy Practices

Typical non-class-related literacy practices are arranged by either individual students or students and their peers in the case of written communication. In addition, it is assumed that these literacy practices are not directly linked to the content as well as the assessment of their Japanese classes, and do not include pedagogical aspects, for example, instructions from teachers about the language. Moreover, since these types of activities are not limited in terms of content, media types or the amount of activities, the range of activities can be broad and differs for each participant. In the current study, communication with Japanese speakers, personal reading, as well as writing activities, could be observed. Multimedia practices, such as watching Japanese TV shows and playing Japanese video games, also included reading activities in Japanese.

### Communication with Japanese speakers

All students except Frank, Lisa and Patrick reported that they communicated with Japanese native speakers or Japanese learners via the internet. Such online communication involved both reading and writing activities. For instance, Joshua exchanged messages on Facebook with his Japanese friend. He read the messages in Japanese and replied in Japanese. On Twitter, Joshua also read followers' tweets and posted his tweets in Japanese. In contrast, Scott only utilised English when participating in online chat with his classmate, although his classmate mostly utilised Japanese. For Scott, this online chat became an opportunity for reading, but not writing activities. These activity types are different from other literacy activities for the reason that participants needed communication partners. These practices were arranged by both students and their friends/acquaintances who were competent in Japanese.

Despite the fact that the majority of participants communicated with Japanese speakers via the internet, only Joshua, Nancy and Scott reported concrete examples of their online communication in their diary entries. The reason that other participants did not report these activities is that most of the students utilised English as the language of communication. Moreover, communication with Japanese speakers was not a frequent occurrence for most of the participants. These two reasons could be influenced by a feature common to these activities, namely, the necessity of having communication partners. It is also important to note that none of the participants reported factors of pedagogy in these activities, such as corrections or negotiation for meanings by native speakers or peers. This result might be influenced once more by the feature of communication in that both the learners' and the interlocutors' intention or purpose for the communication shapes how they engage in these types of activities (see Kurata, 2011).

## Reading activities

More than half of the participants undertook at least one reading activity during the data collection period, but the activity amount varied depending on the participant. Unlike communication with Japanese speakers, reading activities were completely arranged by the participants. In other words, participants could choose the topics and materials, depending on their interests and purposes. An analysis of diary entries shows that the students read various genres (content) using either paper-based or online reading materials.

Participants utilised a wide range of paper-based materials, including Japanese novels (Chris, Patrick and Joshua), a bilingual bible (Chris), a Japanese children's picture book (Nancy), an information magazine aimed at Japanese residents in Australia (Patrick), specialised magazines (Eric and Patrick), fashion magazines (Kate), Japanese *manga* (Chris, Eric and Thomas), a bilingual Japanese culture book (Brenda) and a bilingual short story book (Grace). Yi (2005) found that Korean adolescents at high schools in the United States undertook more online reading activities in their first language compared to paper-based readings. This was due to a lack of Korean paper-based materials. However, participants in the present study accessed the above paper-based materials through various means: purchased in Japan (Chris, Eric, Patrick and Grace), borrowed from the university library (Patrick and Nancy), read at the *Manga* library of the university (Chris and Eric), received as souvenirs from friends (Joshua and Brenda) and borrowed from a friend (Kate). Patrick and Kate also reported that they visited shops that sell Japanese books in the city of Melbourne. These comments indicate that it is possible to access Japanese paper-based materials in the city, at least around the time of the data collection period.

It is worth mentioning that the participants commented on the linguistic aspects/features of the materials they read. For instance, Chris reported that the Japanese novel he had read was rich in onomatopoeia, which he did not learn in the classroom. Eric claimed that casual conversation styles were utilised in Japanese *manga*. Patrick, who majored in law at a Japanese university, read a specialised magazine about judicial precedents and noted that the magazine included a large amount of terminology. Kate read a Japanese fashion magazine and remarked that this magazine utilised many loanwords related to fashion.

Participants also undertook reading activities on the internet: reading a Japanese host sister's blog (Kate), a classmate's blog which was written in Japanese and Chinese (Scott), browsing online discussion boards (Chris and Joshua), searching and reading articles on the Japanese version of Wikipedia or other useful websites (Joshua, Patrick, Scott and Thomas) and checking Japanese pop or *anime* songs' lyrics (Alice, Chris, Grace, Joshua, Melissa and Scott). Joshua also read the emails in Japanese that he received from a computer programming discussion group's email list. Again, it is assumed that participants were exposed to various Japanese language types (vocabulary items, grammar and registers) through these online reading activities, as Scott reported that he checked unknown words, which were used in his friend's blog posts.

These comments about both paper-based and online reading materials imply that the students were aware of these new vocabulary terms and expressions, which they might not have experienced in the classroom or gained from class-related tasks. However, it is apparent that authentic materials are not intentionally structured for learning the language. Moreover, online reading activities provide a broader variety of materials, which include different levels of language formality and styles. For instance, people use different writing styles with different levels of politeness in blogs and online discussion boards. The articles on Wikipedia resemble an academic writing style, which is completely different from song lyrics. In other words, participants could access numerous opportunities in order to learn new vocabulary and expressions, in particular on the internet.

Surprisingly, not a single participant reported utilising online learning websites, despite the fact that various Japanese learning websites are available on the internet. One possible reason for this is that the participants in this study were classroom-based learners and did not feel the necessity of utilising websites designed for learning Japanese. However, Joshua registered for an English–Japanese online dictionary project mailing list, and often received and read emails about Japanese grammar issues that were explained in English by the members of the mailing list. This reading activity is different, in terms of pedagogy, from the other reading activities presented above. Although this is not an example of a reading activity in Japanese, Joshua gained access to Japanese linguistic topics by reading these emails, which is comparable to teachers' explanation about the language in the class. Chik (2014) found that learning and teaching activities occurred in online communities on L2 gaming (e.g. gamers' blogs and forums), for example, discussing translations about gaming words and giving advice about using games for L2 learning. Such possibilities for learning L2 through participating in online communities based on learners' interests is one of the distinct features that the internet provides to L2 and foreign language (FL) learners.

### Viewing activities

In the current study, viewing activities were most commonly reported by the participants. These included watching Japanese variety shows, *anime*, TV series and movies. It is necessary to recognise that watching these videos is not a reading activity. However, since Japanese variety shows and *anime* often include written information, such as Japanese captions and the use of onomatopoeia as visual effects, several participants reported that they read this written information in order to understand the content.

For instance, Lisa watched a Japanese comedy show on YouTube and read short Japanese captions in order to understand content, stopping and repeating the video as necessary. Frank and Brenda also commented that this type of written information was useful in understanding the Japanese TV programmes' content. Although Lisa and Frank commented that they preferred to watch the TV shows with English subtitles when available, they would read the written information in Japanese if English subtitles were not available.

Melissa also reported a similar type of reading practice. She watched *anime* and tried to read *kanji* that were utilised by one of the characters:

> One of the, the panda character, because he can't talk and this panda, he has signs. So, yeah, I tried to look at them too. (Melissa, Interview 3)

Although Melissa could check the meanings of words written in *kanji* from the English subtitles, she also tried to recognise the *kanji* presented on the screen. Lisa, Frank and Melissa's examples thus indicate that viewing activities could involve opportunities to read Japanese texts. As previous studies on the effectiveness of captions for vocabulary learning and listening comprehension indicate (e.g. Fatemeh *et al.*, 2013; Lwo & Lin, 2014; Winke *et al.*, 2010), these viewing activities with captions in a target language have the potential of exerting a positive influence on L2 learning. Chapters 5 and 6 will further discuss what kinds of learning opportunities exist and how such written information will support learners who engage in viewing activities.

Japanese video games also provided Joshua with an opportunity to read Japanese texts and learn new vocabulary, as Chik (2014) found in her study on L2 gaming. In his diary entry, Joshua reported that he wrote down the words and phrases that he learnt from a Japanese video game. He then proceeded to search for these words using an online dictionary. Joshua also researched the game's special terms on the Japanese version of Wikipedia. Accordingly, we can assume that multimedia, such as TV shows, *anime* and video games, could include various reading activities in Japanese as well as students' language-focused actions, such as Melissa's attention to *kanji* and Joshua's action of looking up unknown words.

### Writing activities

Writing activities were scarce, apart from writing emails and communication via online chat with Japanese speakers. Otherwise, only Joshua and Chris regularly undertook Japanese writing practices. Chris wrote to-do lists, and Joshua wrote a personal diary and blog posts in Japanese. Joshua commented that he often utilised what he learned in his Japanese classes in his personal diary, as will be discussed in Chapter 6. Although this comment implies that Joshua's writing activities served as opportunities for practising the linguistic knowledge learned in class, these activities did not include structured materials and direct instructions by others.

These were the only apparent examples of writing activities in all of the participants' diary entries and information gained from the interview data. Considering the fact that the participants in the present research were studying Japanese in FL contexts, it is reasonable to assume that there were no situations where the students were required to write in Japanese in their everyday lives.

### The boundary between class-related and non-class-related literacy practices

Several practices were difficult to categorise into either class-related or non-class-related literacy practices. One of the participants, Scott, undertook a voluntary reading activity based on what he learned in the classroom:

> The textbook passage we looked at today in my Japanese seminar mentioned Gregory Clark, and our teacher said he was formerly an Australian diplomat and now an academic in Japan, which sounded interesting. English Wikipedia does not have an entry for him, so I tried to read the Japanese entry. (Scott's diary entry on 4 September 2008)

This reading activity bordered on being synonymous with that of a voluntary studies perspective. This is because the content was based on what Scott studied in class and was, thus, arranged by the student, ultimately not assessed by teachers and not given any instructions about the language. However, this example differs from other voluntary studies, such as homework and preparation for classes, that directly affected class activities, because the purpose of Scott's reading activity was to pursue his personal interest.

Chris also undertook an activity comparable to class practices; the only difference was that he arranged it himself. Chris completed his

Japanese study at the university in Semester 2, 2008. In order to maintain his Japanese proficiency, Chris set himself the goal to pass Level 1 (the highest level) of the Japanese Language Proficiency Test (JLPT). Although he said that he could hardly study Japanese due to his other study commitments during the semester, he started preparing for the JLPT by drawing on the material specialised for the test which he had purchased in Japan. Chris explained the reason why he chose this typical 'teach-yourself' (Jones, 1998: 378) style as follows:

> Firstly, obviously, I have to direct my own study. I have to choose like what I'm going to do. I think, if I get 1 級 ((*ikkyū* – first grade)), I feel good, and it's also formal recognition. So, that's like an obvious way, that's a sort of the first step I can take, and the way of studying, this is still quite structured. (Chris, Interview 5)

This statement illustrates that Chris tried to independently arrange alternative formal study because at the time he no longer studied Japanese in the classroom. Moreover, the process of studying for the JLPT holds several similarities to class-related literacy practices in terms of arrangement, assessment and pedagogy. Regarding arrangement, the questions in the preparation book were created by experts, just as quizzes and homework are arranged by teachers. In terms of assessment, the learning outcomes are assessed in the form of a proficiency test. As for the dimension of pedagogy, the materials are structured to gain enough language skills to pass the JLPT Level 1. It should also be noted that Chris reported this type of activities only after he completed his Japanese courses. Students might search for structured materials and opportunities for assessment as a substitute for classroom-based learning upon completion of their language course.

## Features of the Participants' Literacy Practices

### Variety of the literacy activities

The above analysis found that the participants undertook numerous literacy activities that were different from each other in terms of content, assessment, arrangement and pedagogy. Firstly, one feature evident in the participants' L2 literacy practices is the diversity of topics, materials and language adopted within the various materials. As predicted, many of the literacy activities reported by the participants were undertaken using a computer, which enabled students to easily search for information. In this vein, information and communication technology (ICT) contributed to this diversity of literacy activities, in particular reading and viewing activities.

With regard to the reading activities related to the Japanese classes, participants not only read the prescribed texts or course materials, but also authentic texts, such as websites and books. Moreover, participants were required to read resources written in more academic Japanese for their assessment tasks, such as newspaper articles, reports by scholars or authorities and articles on Wikipedia. Such a variety of reading activities was encouraged by the teachers, whose intentions were reflected in the assessment criteria and task arrangement. The content and text type of these materials, however, were limited to topics relevant to the class content and formal as well as academic text types.

Similarly, the topics of the class-related writing activity were limited to the content that the Japanese classes covered. However, it was also observed that participants undertook various writing activities through class-related tasks. Writing *kanji* and example sentences for memorisation purposes demonstrates writing at the word and sentence levels. The participants were also required to write longer texts, such as scripts for their oral presentations and essays. In addition, writing activities might involve different language styles, such as formal speech styles expected for oral presentations and academic writing styles for essays. This variation of writing from word level to text level was again produced by different types of tasks related to the language classes, in particular, by teacher intervention in the form of the requirements for the assessment tasks.

Non-class-related literacy practices provided students with different opportunities to use Japanese. The most distinctive feature of this type of literacy practice is the wide variety of materials that students draw on for their reading activities, from articles on the Japanese version of Wikipedia to fashion magazines, which were usually triggered by their interests in these topics. The popularity of the viewing activities was also inextricably related to the participants' pursuit of Japanese pop culture, such as Japanese *anime*, TV serials, variety shows and video games. Students' incentives, a salient feature of non-class-related literacy practices, thus resulted in literacy practices of using various types of materials that could provide them with new vocabulary and expressions that they might not have encountered in the classroom. Yet, this essential feature of this type of literacy practice also led to situations whereby students might not undertake any activities. The scarcity of writing activities might be indicative of this characteristic along with contextual factors, such as it being an FL context. The factors that influence learners' motives for undertaking non-class-related literacy practices will be explored in Chapter 5.

## Pedagogical factors involved in out-of-class literacy practices

The above analysis revealed that only limited types of literacy activities, including those for class-related tasks, clearly involved pedagogical factors. Regarding non-class-related literacy practices, Chris' use of the material specifically arranged for the proficiency test was the only example that included a pedagogical aspect, that is, using the textbook-type material including detailed explanations about the language (e.g. explanation about grammar). In regard to class-related literacy practices, it is assumed that both assessed and non-assessed tasks are embedded in formal education, which is carefully structured in consideration of students' progression. In this vein, all the reading and writing activities of this type of literacy practice subsumed pedagogical factors, for example, utilising the class materials chosen by the teachers and giving feedback on the students' performance in the assessments. However, the preparation for quizzes/examinations and of the assigned homework evidently involved factors of teaching in the form of questions about the class content. The other assessment tasks and non-assessed activities did not incorporate the teacher's explanation about the language, though all the literacy activities possibly triggered students' attention to linguistic aspects, for instance, looking up a new word in a dictionary and memorising it.

One possible reason for this is the level of the courses in which the participants studied. The participants in this study belonged to intermediate and advanced levels, and the assessment tasks required using the language rather than learning it explicitly, for example, engaging in grammar exercises. In particular, the advanced classes employed a content-based approach using authentic materials even in the classroom. The setting of out-of-class literacy practices might be another reason why there is little involvement of pedagogical factors. This is because students learn the language with teachers' support in the class and practice it through reading and writing outside of the classroom.

## Ambiguity in the distinction between class-related and non-class-related literacy practices

It is also important to note that the same or similar types of reading activities were undertaken for both class-related and non-class-related literacy practices. From the perspective of Activity Theory, as predicted in Chapter 2, similar actions could serve different activities. For example, Japanese Wikipedia articles were utilised by students both for reading activities for assessment tasks (e.g. oral presentations and essays) as well as for their voluntary reading to pursue their own interests. The other reading and writing activities for the assessment tasks also shared similarities with those for non-class-related literacy practices in that the students did not gain direct support in terms of language from the teachers. With regard to non-class-related literacy practices, an interesting example is Scott's case of reading a Japanese Wikipedia entry, which exemplified the connection between his extra out-of-class reading activities and his Japanese classes at the content level. This example also indicates the importance of adding content level to the analysis in order to examine the relationship between class-related and non-class-related literacy practices.

These shared similarities between class-related and non-class-related literacy practices indicate that the differences in the two types of literacy practices are not always clear-cut and cannot be viewed in a linear manner, with the classroom and full autonomy as polar opposites, as suggested in Jones' (1988) classification. The analysis based on the four dimensions of content, assessment, arrangement and pedagogy, thus revealed the complexity of students' literacy practices, which were previously not examined and accounted for by the existing categorisations centred on spontaneous out-of-class language learning.

## Summary

In this chapter, I have provided an overview of the out-of-class literacy practices that students undertook, while also examining the features of these practices based on four dimensions – assessment, arrangement, content and pedagogy. On the one hand, the analysis found similarities and connections between class-related and non-class-related literacy activities, which imply the possibility of encouraging students to undertake both types of practices. On the other hand, the differences in literacy activities for Japanese classes and those for students' own purposes were also salient in terms of material types and content. There seems to be a significant disparity between the Japanese language course curricula that emphasise academic language and the activities that learners actually undertake or want to undertake outside the classroom for other purposes. Paradoxically, it can also be claimed that non-class-related literacy practices can provide students with opportunities to learn what their Japanese classes did not provide. However, such discrepancy might affect students' motivation for engaging class-related tasks, which will be discussed further in the next chapter.

I would also acknowledge that these findings only draw on the examples provided by intermediate and advanced language students. In-class learning activities and assessment tasks at beginner level are often more language focused (e.g. grammar exercises), which requires more explicit instructions by teachers than those at the intermediate and advanced levels discussed above. Beginner students might utilise different types of resources for their voluntary activities because of limited language skills. It can be reasonably anticipated that class-related and non-class-related literacy practices by beginner level students share different types of commonalities or dissimilarities from those found in this chapter.

# 4 Class-Related Literacy Practices Outside the Classroom

Chapter 3 examined the various types of literacy activities undertaken by participants outside of the classroom. One of the notable findings was that students' mandatory Japanese class tasks provided opportunities for various reading and writing activities to emerge. In this chapter, the analysis will be narrowed to focus on class-related tasks that involved a number of reading and writing activities. As discussed in Chapter 3, even though, to a certain extent, most of these tasks were initiated by teachers, participants nevertheless individually engaged with tasks outside of the classroom. In other words, the degree of attention paid and the effort made in relation to such tasks differed among participants depending on their Japanese learning purposes and other second language (L2) learning-related contexts.

This chapter will firstly present patterns of students' out-of-class literacy practices and explore why several participants placed more priority on class tasks and what factors influenced their decisions. I will also focus on the contradictions evident in participants' activity systems for class-related tasks. This is important in order to examine the problems students identified and their strategic efforts to overcome them in relation to social and contextual factors. Contradictions are crucial to understanding what prompts concrete actions and the transformations of an activity system (Barab *et al.*, 2002). By focusing on contradictions, I am able to examine which factors influenced students to change their attitudes and approaches towards class-related tasks that involved reading and writing activities.

## Individual Differences in Class-Related Literacy Practices

Undertaking class-related tasks is clearly an essential factor for students to successfully complete their courses. All of the participants, therefore, reported on their preparations for assessment tasks and/or for their in-class work when they described their out-of-class literacy practices. However, three different patterns were identified.

The first group includes participants who placed emphasis on assessment tasks and other practices relevant to their Japanese subjects. These students reported less non-class-related literacy practices than did the other students. Brenda (Level 7) was a student of this group. She reported on her detailed preparation for class assessment tasks, such as project reports, vocabulary quizzes, speaking tests and examinations. She also consistently prepared for class reading activities. However, she scarcely had any extra opportunity to utilise Japanese other than for such class tasks. Likewise, Daniel (Level 11), Frank (Level 9) and Scott (Levels 8 and 9) directed all their efforts towards undertaking class tasks during the semesters, and only reported one or two voluntary literacy activities in their learning diaries. Grace (Level 7) also enthusiastically undertook extra study for class work other than that required for assessment tasks, for instance, studying grammar items by composing her own example sentences, as presented in Chapter 3. Interestingly, 3 students of this group reported modifications to their out-of-class literacy activities. In the interviews, Daniel and Frank commented that they increased the amount of time spent on class-related tasks in comparison to previous semesters to the data collection period. In contrast, Grace started to practise Japanese by utilising authentic materials, especially listening materials, in the second round of her diary study. The reasons behind such changes will be discussed in the following sections.

The second group includes students who prioritised assessment and class task preparation while also undertaking non-class-related literacy activities for extra study or for enjoyment on a more irregular basis when circumstances allowed them to do so, such as on weekends, semester breaks and occasions when there were no urgent assignments. The majority of the participants fall into this group. Kate, Melissa and Nancy (Level 7) enthusiastically prepared for the quizzes, project work and reading activities in the classroom, and also occasionally engaged with voluntary reading or viewing activities. The students who were enrolled in more advanced levels, such as Alice, Eric, Lisa (all Level 10) and Thomas (Level 11) also indicated a similar pattern to the above students.

The final group includes Chris (Level 12), Joshua (Level 8) and Patrick (Level 11), who frequently utilised Japanese other than for class tasks. In this study, they were atypical students. A crucial difference between these students and the other students described above is the amount of time that they spent undertaking voluntary literacy activities. Here, it must be acknowledged that these 3 students rarely prepared for their class reading activities. For instance, Chris claimed that he did not usually read the reading materials for the classes of Level 12 beforehand though he 'really really read in the class' (Interview 1). Although Patrick prepared for in-class reading activities by checking unknown words in his dictionary and writing down the meanings, he also stated the following: 'obviously, I don't have to write as many notes as do some of the other students' (Interview 2). Given that both these students had had long stays in Japan, Chris and Patrick seemed to have already acquired advanced levels of Japanese. Joshua's Japanese language skills were not as advanced as those of Chris and Patrick. However, he was studying a lower level course, and it might be reasonable to say that the level of his reading and writing skills in Japanese was sufficient for his Japanese classes. When considering these factors and their comments in the interviews, Chris, Joshua and Patrick did not have to devote time to prepare for Japanese classes, and in turn, could spend more time undertaking literacy activities other than the class-related tasks. Yet, one must be cautious about implying a causal relationship here. Alternatively, it could be argued that their regular participation in such voluntary activities in Japanese might have enhanced their competence, and therefore reduced their need for class preparation.

To summarise, the majority of the participants in the current study mainly undertook reading and writing activities for their Japanese classes during semesters. This tendency was, to some extent, predictable because the participants were university students who needed to pass their courses to gain degrees. However, as shown above, there was some evidence of an inverse relationship between time spent on assessment tasks and class preparation, and time spent on other literacy activities. The following sections will explore significant factors that influenced such individual differences with reference to students' motives and beliefs, as well as any contradictions, concerning class-related tasks. Prior to this discussion, I will describe the activity systems related to students' class-related literacy practices in order to illustrate the contexts in which the practices were situated.

## Learners' Activity Systems for Learning Japanese at University

As explained in Chapter 2, this study views learning Japanese at a university as an activity system. The assessment tasks, homework, preparations and revisions, which include various literacy activities undertaken outside of the classroom, are components of the activity of the language course. The participants' activity systems for learning Japanese at university varied depending on the students as well as the tasks. However, there were common factors that influenced students when they undertook these tasks for their Japanese classes. Drawing on the activity system(s) model of Engeström (1999, 2001), I will discuss the common factors observable in the students' activity systems.

Figure 4.1 illustrates the fundamental dimensions of central activity systems. In this activity system, each participant was the subject who undertook tasks for his/her Japanese courses. As subject-related factors, participants' learning histories and beliefs affected their current activity

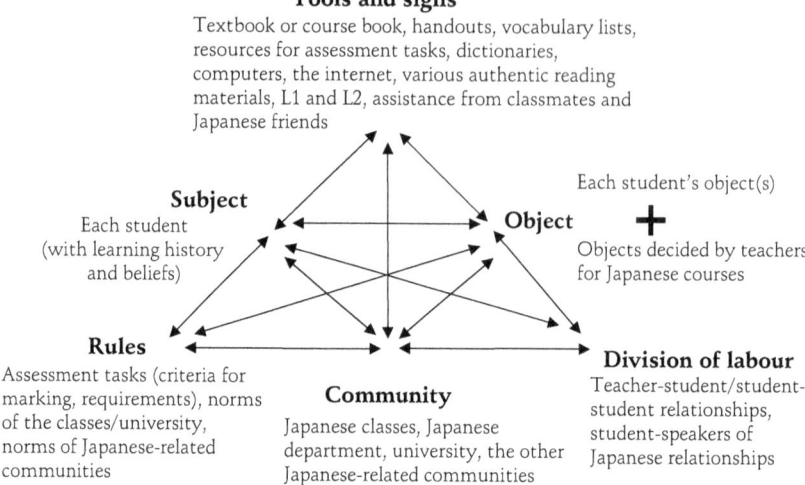

**Figure 4.1** A model of the central activity system for class-related literacy practices

systems. The objects of activities, which were the objects of each task and of learning Japanese at university, regulated the participants' literacy practices. While the students had their own motives for learning Japanese, the linguistic elements and topics (i.e. what the students should learn) as the objects of each Japanese course were decided by the teachers.

In order to achieve the objects, participants utilised various tools, such as textbooks, course material books, handouts, vocabulary lists, task sheets, websites and books as resources for their oral presentations and essays, dictionaries (e.g. paper, electronic and online dictionaries), computers and the internet. Their first language (i.e. English) and the target language (i.e. Japanese) were also tools used for undertaking the tasks. In particular, Japanese was a limited tool for learners to undertake class-related tasks, and often triggered problems. A number of students also relied on their classmates and Japanese friends' assistance.

For the majority of participants, their Japanese class was the only community that influenced their class-related literacy practices. However, Eric, Daniel and Melissa participated in other Japanese-related communities at university, such as the *Manga* library and Japanese Club communities. These communities were a part of linked-activity systems that influenced students' attitudes and concrete approaches towards Japanese class tasks, as will be discussed later in this section. Daniel also had Japanese-speaking friends in another subject. The relation between students and members of these communities (e.g. teachers, classmates, Japanese speaker friends) can be understood as a division of labour. Moreover, various rules related to the assessment and norms of studying at university also impacted on the ways in which participants approached assessment tasks and ultimately their preparation for in-class work.

Lantolf and Thorne (2006: 224–225) point out that language learning in an educational context is influenced by various factors that resonate in multiple activity systems and which are relevant to participating individuals. Russell and Yañez (2003: 340–341) name these activity systems 'linked activity systems'. Figure 4.2 presents a typical relationship between a student's central activity system and his/her linked activity systems.

One example of linked activity systems is participants' past activity systems for learning Japanese. These past activity systems included their Japanese classes at primary or high school, private language schools and their previous Japanese courses at university. Joshua's self-study also constituted his past activity of learning Japanese. The participants' beliefs and preferences for their method of learning the target language, their perceptions about assessment tasks and their Japanese language skills were formulated and evolved through their experiences in these activity systems.

As mentioned previously, Japanese-related communities, such as peer groups at the *Manga* library and the Japanese Club, were linked activity systems at the university. In particular, a peer group at the *Manga* library affected several students' class-related literacy practices in different ways. For instance, Daniel used to be an enthusiastic *anime* fan and volunteered at the *Manga* library in his first and second year at university. In the interview, however, Daniel reported that his friends at the *Manga* library negatively influenced his Japanese study in his first two years of university:

> Because every time at 漫画図書館 ((*Manga toshokan* – the *Manga* library)), my friends come, and when they come, you can't do any work, work is stopped because your friends come and play poker games, and watch movies... (Daniel, Interview 3)

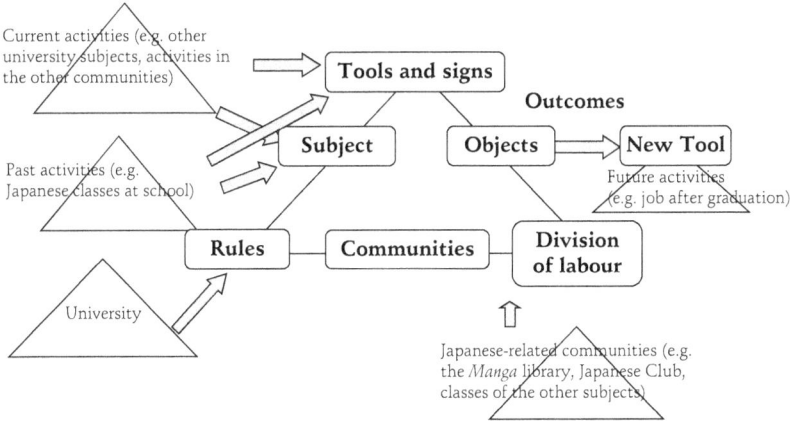

**Figure 4.2** Examples of linked activity systems

This excerpt illustrates that members of the *Manga* library community distracted Daniel from engaging in assessment tasks and appeared to turn his learning activity into a leisure activity. Since he did not want to be a 'part of that culture' (Interview 3) any more, he quit being a volunteer at the *Manga* library in his third year, when the data collection commenced. In contrast, Melissa, who also volunteered at the *Manga* library, had peers who were helpful. She claimed that the students who visited the *Manga* library helped each other with assessment tasks and preparation for vocabulary quizzes because some of the students studied at an advanced level or had already completed the highest level of Japanese classes at the university. Unlike Daniel's case, the *Manga* library in Melissa's case provided capable peers in assisting her in her studies.

Other subjects that the participants studied at university also affected their approaches to the tasks. Daniel had Japanese speaker friends in another subject who assisted him with his essay assignment. This is an example of the positive effect that other subjects had on Daniel's class-related activities. However, the majority of students commented on the difficulties encountered in managing Japanese assessment tasks simultaneously with assessments in other subjects. For instance, Nancy, who majored in Zoology as well as Arts, claimed that 'I only do what I have to do' (Interview 2) because of the effects of workloads in other subjects. In terms of time pressure from other subjects, participants' Japanese class study was affected, with voluntary literacy activities potentially being influenced as well. Participants' engagement in class-related tasks was thus connected with a number of activity systems in the past as well as in the present.

## Factors Influencing Learner's Emphasis on Class-Related Literacy Practices

In the following sections, I will explore the factors that affected the differences between individual students with regard to their attitudes towards and effort undertaken in preparing for assessment tasks and Japanese class activities. Furthermore, I will focus on contradictions related to Japanese class tasks in order to identify problems or conflicts that students experienced and tried to overcome. In doing so, I will discuss how students modified their routine of out-of-class literacy activities and placed more or less priority on class-related tasks.

### Subjective factors: Learning history and beliefs

According to Activity Theory, a learner's history is a critical element in understanding human behaviour (Lantolf & Thorne, 2006). Subjective factors, such as learners' beliefs about language learning, have been developed through learners' experiences in their past activity systems, with Engeström (1987: para 4 – 'The structure of learning activity') referring to this concept as 'subject-producing activity', such as education and schooling. According to Kalaja and Barcelos (2003: 1), while there are a number of definitions for beliefs in second language acquisition (SLA) and similar terms (e.g. metacognitive knowledge and learners' representations), beliefs can be defined as 'opinions and ideas that learners (and teachers) have about the task of learning a second/foreign language'. As reviewed in Chapter 2, drawing on sociocultural or socio-cognitive perspectives, a number of studies on L2 writing as well as learning strategies revealed that learners' history, including learning trajectories and family history, affected their beliefs about and orientations towards tasks and strategy choices (e.g. Gao, 2010; Haneda, 2005, 2007; Spack, 1997). The present study also identified the influence that students' learning history had on their preference for class-related literacy practices.

Brenda explained that doing homework and reviewing what she learned in class were her main study methods outside of the classroom; this was the same throughout her high school and university studies. As to the reason why she continued utilising the same method throughout the data collection period, Brenda stated the following: 'I think that's because that's the only way I've learned ((Japanese))' (Interview 1). Similarly, Frank explained that his high school Japanese study method consisted of following teachers' directions and studying for required assessed tasks. For Brenda and Frank, their focus on class-related tasks had thus been their Japanese learning method spanning their entire learning histories. In addition, both these students claimed that Japanese was their strongest subject at high school. It is reasonable to assume that these two students were satisfied with their Japanese learning methods, both of which produced excellent outcomes.

Frank also asserted that he enjoyed learning a language at school as well as at university:

> Other subjects just reading an article after an article, so this ((learning Japanese)) is always practical learning, practice speaking, watching TV... and also the assessments vary, like we have quizzes and speaking and listening and exams, whereas other subjects ((have)) just essay or exam, just boring <@@>. (Frank, Interview 1)

Frank's comment implies that he genuinely enjoyed class activities as well as the assessment tasks. Scott also claimed that he preferred to study grammar and vocabulary for tasks related to the Japanese classes (i.e. preparation for vocabulary quizzes and examinations) rather than listening or viewing activities using authentic materials, such as watching Japanese *anime*. Both students' comments indicated that their focus on class-related literacy practices derived not only from their habitual Japanese learning pattern but also their preferred learning style, which appeared to be formulated through their learning experiences.

Conversely, it can be said that these students did not acquire strategies to learn the target language by interacting with authentic materials. In the third interview, for example, Frank asserted that he did not know what to do without teachers' instructions. This comment indicates that such methods were not internalised as an effective learning strategy for Frank. However, beliefs can vary during a relatively short period of time, and in turn, learners' preferences can change to focus more on non-class-related literacy practices.

Grace's example clearly illustrates such short-term transformation in her beliefs through her learning experiences. Similar to the above 3 students, her main literacy activities in Level 7 were related to Japanese classes, including extra learning activities, such as compiling her own vocabulary lists and composing example sentences, as previously described. However, Grace's out-of-class literacy activities were transformed after participating in an intensive in-country programme during the semester holidays. The programme was based on a tailored curriculum emphasising productive practices, including discussions and presentations. In addition, several opportunities to use Japanese with local people, such as visiting a primary school and a Japanese university, were included in the programme. In the interview, after she came back from Japan, Grace claimed that she was impressed by the fact that the curriculum did not include any lessons on *kanji* or grammar items:

> Before I went there, I had all the information saying it would be no, there would be no grammar or 漢字 ((*kanji*)) classes, so I was like how I might get progress without ((explicitly learning *kanji* and vocabulary in the classroom)). But, it was about using it … so we didn't have to be actually taught vocab or be taught to memorise or tested on it, but when you were listening to that ((Japanese)) the whole time, I took on much more vocab than probably even in normal class. (Grace, Interview 3)

This comment illustrates her beliefs that explicitly learning vocabulary and grammar items was important in acquiring Japanese skills, and her extra studies in Level 7 reflected these beliefs. However, this excerpt also indicates that Grace's beliefs concerning her approach to acquiring linguistic elements of Japanese changed because of her experience during the programme in Japan. Grace described how she learned *kanji* during the programme:

> Like teachers write ((vocabulary in *kanji*)) on the board, and I see it like around the city, and in the centre, and even on the computer like 設定 ((*settē* – configuration)) and the stuff <@@>, settings and 表示 ((*hyōji* – display))… And I always, I was always writing down ((the *kanji* which Grace saw)). (Grace, Interview 3)

Although Grace adopted the same method (i.e. writing down unknown words) to learn *kanji* as the approach she took in Level 7, she encountered new *kanji* by actually using Japanese in and outside of the classroom. She also explained that she learned new expressions from what other students utilised as well as conversations outside of the classroom. In other words, Grace could learn new vocabulary and expressions without textbooks or other materials, such as word lists arranged by teachers. As a result, even though Grace still viewed learning grammar and vocabulary as important aspects of Japanese learning, she formulated her beliefs that using the target language was a 'constructive, effective' (Interview 3) way of learning it. Moreover, after she returned to university, she noticed that she did not have to search for so many words in the textbook and could 'read and understand the passages in the textbook more quickly than last semester' (Grace's diary entry on 4 August 2009). It is assumed that by recognising these positive results brought about by actual language use in and outside of the classroom, her newly developed beliefs were reinforced. As a result, Grace sought opportunities for authentic language use, such as reading a bilingual book and listening to Japanese pop songs, in the subsequent course.

From a sociocultural perspective, the cases of Brenda, Frank and Scott highlight the influence of ontogenesis, which is the 'life history of individuals in society' (Lantolf & Genung, 2002: 177); in other words, their relatively long history of learning Japanese at school. Alternatively, Grace's case demonstrated the influence of microgenesis on her beliefs, which is 'cognitive development that occurs moment by moment' (Ohta, 2000: 54). The longitudinal study by Spack (1997) of an English as a second language (ESL) learner's academic literacy skills revealed that the learner's beliefs and her ways of approaching assessments were developed over a few years of university study. As discussed above, however, learners' beliefs might evolve in an even shorter period of time, thereby affecting their approaches to learning the target language. This implies that other students might change their patterns of out-of-class literacy activities if their beliefs change. Grace's case also demonstrates that language classes play an important role in formulating learners' beliefs about effective language learning techniques. Allen (1996) studied the impact of teachers' beliefs about effective language learning on ESL learners' beliefs, describing how the latter gradually changed during the language course. In Grace's case too, it is reasonable to assume that teachers' beliefs were reflected in their teaching methods and this eventually affected Grace's beliefs. A learner's beliefs are thus not only historically but also socially constructed (Gao, 2010).

In addition to their beliefs, the nature of the assessment may also affect their foci on class-related tasks if it is the kind of assessment that rewards intensive study of class-related materials. This issue will be discussed in the following sections in terms of motives and contradictions.

## Motives related to exchange value and use value of learning Japanese

Motives/objects are important factors in determining the direction of an activity (Leont'ev, 1978). With regard to the objects of traditional schoolwork, Engeström (1987) points out that text is a tool for learning as well as an object of learning and postulates that its dual nature generates two types of objects in students. These are the exchange value and use value of learning at school: the former is an object related to gaining marks that eventually influences students' future value in the labour market, and the latter is another object to master living tools for society outside of school. It is assumed that participants' class-related literacy practices were influenced by these two types of objects because they were university students who studied the target language as a subject. Indeed, many of the participants referred to both types of motives/objects in relation to each assessment task or their Japanese studies at university.

Apart from motives related to exchange value and use value, participants in the current study also highlighted a variety of other reasons for learning Japanese: for instance, linguistic interest in Japanese as a foreign language (e.g. Scott and Frank), personal interests or enjoyment of learning and using Japanese (e.g. Alice, Chris, Frank, Joshua, Kate and Nancy) and the desire for intercultural communication with Japanese native speakers (e.g. Eric). Although these motives also might affect students' orientations towards class-related literacy practices, I primarily focused on exchange value and use value as significant motives which influenced their attitudes towards class-related tasks.

### *Exchange value: Gaining a good mark and a positive evaluation from teachers*

Many of the participants claimed that the exchange value of learning Japanese, such as 'gaining a good mark' or 'receiving positive evaluation from teachers', was important in conjunction with performing assessment tasks. Two students who centred their efforts on undertaking class-related tasks, Scott and Frank, repeatedly stated their concerns about receiving a good grade in each assessment task. In the interview, Frank explained in the following way why he invested his efforts in class-related tasks:

> Firstly, like any other subject, I still wanna do well, so that I get a good average, good grades. If I wasn't interested ((in the Japanese subject)), I still had to do it <@@>. (Frank, Interview 3)

This statement illustrates that Frank's aim to gain good academic results motivated him to study intensively for his Japanese course. Frank's motive related to exchange value significantly influenced his decision to prioritise reading and writing skills over speaking or listening skills because most of the assessment tasks involved literacy skills.

Nancy and Daniel explained their concerns about teacher evaluations. In the interview based on her vocabulary quiz preparations, Nancy claimed that she dedicated herself to the preparation because she wanted to impress her teachers. In the first interview of the semester, Daniel also highlighted his goal of being a good student in relation to teacher admiration and reported that he had maintained this type of objective since he started learning Japanese in formal education settings. These students might simply want to be praised by their teachers as a reward for maintaining their self-image as good students or for their own self-satisfaction. However, positive evaluation by teachers can also be interpreted as a form of exchange value in that teachers' evaluations are closely linked to the students' marks. More importantly, both Nancy and Daniel enthusiastically prepared for the assessment tasks and class reading activities which were being evaluated by their teachers. As will be discussed later, Daniel, in particular, changed his orientation towards Japanese classes and his routine of studying the target language outside of the classroom. This implies that his aspiration to receive positive teacher evaluations seems to have significantly influenced his efforts when undertaking class-related tasks.

Interestingly, Chris, Joshua and Patrick, who undertook various literacy activities other than class-related tasks, did not clearly state their concerns about academic results. As a possible reason why they did not focus on exchange value types of motives, their high level of Japanese language skills might have enabled them not to be overly concerned about gaining a good mark. As previously stated, Chris and Patrick already seemed to have acquired high level Japanese language skills through their learning experience in host country settings. Joshua also seemed to have acquired sufficient Japanese language skills from his intermediate Japanese studies in Level 8. However, for the other students, it seemed that their concerns with gaining a good mark motivated them to dedicate their efforts to class-related literacy practices.

*Use value: Acquiring Japanese for activities outside of the classroom*

In the case of the current study's participants, the use value of learning Japanese could be understood as gaining sufficient Japanese proficiency to utilise it outside of the classroom or in the future. Many participants highlighted this type of motive in association with their reasons for learning Japanese as a university subject rather than specific assessment tasks. They expressed the motive in regard to their career, communication with native speakers and living in Japan. For example, Brenda described why she studied Japanese at university as follows:

I was tossing up between doing Science and Arts or just Arts, and I decided to do Arts, and I sort of wanted to do this course, always with the intention of later doing interpreting or translating. So, I sort of always knew what I wanna do… now I'm actually at uni and I'm doing just languages, it's sort of encouraging, it's sort of confirming my goal. (Brenda, Interview 1)

In the second interview, Brenda consistently claimed this ambition to become an interpreter or translator, and it is highly likely that this use value motive had a longitudinal impact on her Japanese study at university. The following excerpt shows that Eric's motive for learning Japanese developed purely from an interest in learning Japanese in order to acquire useful skills from a careers perspective:

To be honest, when I first started ((learning Japanese)) in first year ((at university)), I think just because I loved Japanese, I really wanna to keep learning… But then, as I talked to career counsellors, it so became pretty clear to me that it would be very important, it will be good for my future, for the job prospects. So, my reason changed from loving, like doing it purely because I love Japanese, I am more into, you know, I actually wanna do this for my job. And the time when I got bit bored with Japanese, I thought like, 'Oh why', like 'Why am I doing this?', but I was going like, 'Oh, I would, I keep doing this because hopefully it will be really good in future'. So, that's more my reason now. (Eric, Interview 1)

This statement demonstrates how Eric's motive to master Japanese as a useful tool for his career encouraged him to study Japanese. Although Eric occasionally undertook non-class-related literacy activities, the relation of this motive to use value clearly affected his enthusiasm for undertaking assessment tasks and homework outside of the classroom. This will be examined later.

The other students (Alice, Daniel, Nancy and Thomas), who also diligently prepared for Japanese class tasks, maintained that their motives were related not only to their job prospects, but also to gaining good academic results. This might be because the prospect of gaining good academic results is simultaneously related to future career possibilities which require them to use Japanese. For this group of students, both exchange and use value types of motives seem to be internalised and become an impetus to enthusiastically study in their Japanese courses.

Chris, Grace, Joshua and Patrick only emphasised use value type motives in their interviews, as was also the case with Brenda and Eric. However, they differed in that these students constantly undertook extra literacy activities or study other than those required by the assessment tasks. As previously mentioned, Chris, Joshua and Patrick regularly undertook free reading or writing activities during the data collection period. Grace was the only student who employed a number of extra types of studies. As Gillette (1994) showed, the use value motive is one element that can trigger learners' extra study and authentic language use outside of the classroom, though the other factors (e.g. beliefs and Japanese language skills) influenced their patterns of out-of-class literacy practices as discussed previously.

It is also important to note that a few students, who focused more on class-related tasks, did not state a definite use value for learning Japanese. For instance, whereas Frank clearly stated his concerns about gaining good academic results, he remarked that he did not intend to use Japanese in his career because he hoped to work for law firms which were related to his major at university. Similarly, Scott also indicated the low probability of utilising the target language in the future; however, in the interviews, he described his attempts to gain good marks. As briefly mentioned above, both Frank and Scott stated their interest in the language or enjoyment of learning Japanese as their reasons for continuing their Japanese studies. These motives might possibly be responsible for their enthusiastic approach to class-related tasks. However, analysis of the interview data indicates that participants' concerns about receiving a good mark often dominated other motives and affected decisions to alter their attitudes and approaches towards class-related tasks. This will be illustrated in the following sections.

## Contradictions and Transformations of Class-Related Literacy Practices

This discussion will focus on the contradictions evident in participants' activity systems in relation to class-related literacy practices. By analysing the interview data, although I was able to identify various difficulties experienced by students that triggered a transformation of their activity systems and actions, I also found that other contradictions were not overcome by students.

## Contradictions between learners' Japanese proficiency level and task demands

### Influence of exchange value on learning Japanese

Participants who spent more time on class-related literacy practices identified a gap between their Japanese proficiency level and tasks related to their Japanese classes. Such tasks included assessment tasks and in-class reading activities. According to Activity Theory, this tension could be understood as a contradiction between a tool and an object dimension, in other words, a contradiction between learners' Japanese language skills and Japanese as learning objectives defined by teachers.

This difference in Japanese language skills and task demands often caused learning difficulties and prompted students to apply further effort to their Japanese classes. For example, Frank identified the critical tensions between his Japanese proficiency level and the tasks of Level 9, and adjusted his Japanese learning routine outside of the classroom in order to overcome these tensions. In the follow-up email to the interview, Frank stated that before studying Level 9, Japanese had not been too difficult for him, and he could gain satisfactory academic results. However, he recognised that there was a gap between his competence and the level of Japanese required to complete tasks in Level 9. The following excerpt describes his analysis of the reason why he experienced difficulties in this subject:

> Before level 9, we were based on the textbook, everything was based on the Japanese textbook, so it wasn't so bad. So, now I'm starting to use other sources, like journals, I think text like journals or newspapers and television stuff, so it's a very different language from what I'm used to. So, it's difficult <@@>. (Frank, Interview 1)

Since the textbook in Levels 7 and 8 utilised authentic texts from Japanese newspapers, journals and books, it is reasonable to say that they were relatively limited to formal and academic Japanese. In contrast, the range of authentic materials utilised in Level 9 was broader and included journal articles, newspapers, books, websites, lyrics of Japanese songs, *manga*, Japanese movies and TV programmes. It is assumed that this range of authentic materials provided the 'very different language' stated by Frank in the previous excerpt. Frank also highlighted that he constantly needed to look up unfamiliar grammar items, expressions and vocabulary found in the material used in Level 9.

This gap between Frank's Japanese proficiency and new class material types appeared to trigger another critical tension in his activity system, namely that between subject and object dimensions. Since one of Frank's motives as well as objects of learning Japanese at university was to gain good marks, a dilemma between his current condition in which he had difficulties in understanding the materials and his motive/object occurred. In order to overcome this dilemma, Frank planned to alter his Japanese study routine outside of the classroom. In the previous semester, Frank only prepared for assessment tasks. However, at the start of the data collection period, he intended to undertake extra study by utilising authentic materials, in particular, visual activities for improving his listening and speaking skills.

Frank, however, eventually focused more on preparations for class reading activities as well as preparing for assessment tasks:

> Because I usually base on, like focus first on the assessment, so because mostly the assessment is written. So, I usually focus first on like reading

and writing, and then I don't really have much time to worry about the rest. As for my listening, I'm probably not doing it very much, just because the other stuff is more important, I think. (Frank, Interview 2)

Here, Frank's concerns about gaining good academic results directed his actions in order to overcome the tensions he experienced. In addition, as a student who studied a double major, Frank could not devote himself entirely to studying Japanese. Although his initial intention to increase the time studied by utilising authentic materials was not achieved, Frank altered his learning habits outside of the classroom by, for instance, reading materials beforehand in order to follow his classes. The contradictions in Frank's activity systems thus triggered his move to transform his learning activities outside of the classroom.

This contradiction between students' Japanese language skills and required Japanese proficiency does not appear to necessarily generate transformations. Unlike Frank, Daniel had serious learning difficulties in his first and second years at university. He identified the crucial gap between his reading skills, especially his knowledge of *kanji*, and the language used in the textbook of Level 7, which Daniel was first enrolled in when he transferred to the university from his previous institution. As this textbook comprised of authentic Japanese texts, Daniel could not follow the classes and lost enthusiasm. This occurred even though he held the objective of enhancing his status by studying at a good Australian university as an exchange value and the improvement of his Japanese language skills as a use value. This learning difficulty also caused a negative influence on his orientation towards learning Japanese as well as his attitude towards teachers, as shown in the following excerpt:

…after two years of being at the top, and then, coming into XXXXXX ((his current university)), and then completely, you know, losing all ambition and becoming lazy, and you know, rude even to my teachers <@@>. (Daniel, Interview 4)

As mentioned previously, positive evaluation from teachers was one of Daniel's activity objects for learning Japanese throughout his Japanese learning history. However, this object disappeared, or was abandoned, alongside losing his confidence as a top student which he had developed during the course of his learning history.

However, Daniel aimed to be at 'the top of the class again' (Interview 1) and altered his class-related practices at the start of the data collection process. Here, I suggest that Daniel's motive was closely linked to the exchange value of learning Japanese at university. In a follow-up email after the first interview, Daniel claimed the following: 'I'm hoping to change my current Japanese record to something a lot more positive'. This was because he was in his final year of university and wanted to improve his résumé. In other words, his motive related to the exchange value of learning Japanese in fact became an object of his activity (learning Japanese at university) and motivated Daniel to change his attitudes towards class-related tasks. In the third interview, Daniel explained the differences between his third and second year at university:

> Whereas last year, if I hadn't had an assignment's due, I probably won't start it until the day before. I just completely forgot about it, you know, not do any work. And then, just handed it in last minutes. But this semester, I look at it, I get done, I get preparation ready and I finish it, with time to spare. (Daniel, Interview 3)

Aside from the fact that he seriously struggled with the level of the texts in Level 11, this statement indicates that Daniel altered his actions in order to achieve his object of learning Japanese and becoming a top student again. In addition, Daniel intentionally selected the peers he associated with for achieving his object. As mentioned earlier, Daniel's friends at the *Manga* library negatively influenced his attitudes towards assessment tasks. Instead of these friends, Daniel began to closely associate with another participant in this study, Thomas, who excelled in Daniel's Japanese class. As Chapter 6 will discuss in detail, Daniel asked Thomas for help with his assessment tasks. Moreover, Daniel's fellow students who had studied Level 11 helped him with his essay assignment. They were also classmates of Daniel in other subjects at the university.

In the interview, Daniel explained how having good friends positively influenced his Japanese study:

> …this year I made a lot more friends, so I was able to ask them for help because they needed help as well, so we were able to swap, which meant that this semester wasn't so stressful as it would be if I didn't have any friends at all. Like in 7 ((Japanese 7)), doing 7 and 8 ((Japanese 7 and 8)), I didn't have any 先輩 ((*senpai* – senior student who studied the same course before)) to ask for their help from. I did my work all by myself … But, this semester, I have been able to do the work by myself, but this time I have friends, like Thomas by my side to keep, for us to keep pushing each other to study, to make sure we get the work done. (Daniel, Interview 4)

This excerpt illustrates that Daniel's relationship with his classmates and friends contributed to the manner in which he prepared for assessment tasks. This is observable in terms of the concrete help he received as well as his positive mental attitude towards learning Japanese. In the same interview, Daniel maintained that choosing friends was a crucial factor for him to learn Japanese. These comments imply that Daniel consciously surrounded himself with people in order to achieve his object and evaluated the success of this attempt. In this way, Daniel's activity system for class-related literacy practices transformed with regard to its object and relationships with classmates and peers as community members. As Engeström (2001) claimed, contradictions within and between activity systems thus triggered the development of activity system(s).

Both Frank and Daniel's examples suggest that their exchange value motives seem to be key factors in the development (or change) of their class-related literacy practice patterns. This finding supports what Nelson and Kim (2001) revealed in their study based on the utilisation of online learning records in ESL writing classes. In their study, Nelson and Kim found that interaction with grades was a crucial factor for ESL students being able to master how to use online learning records as a tool in the writing course. In addition, it is important to recall that Frank and Daniel also highlighted other purposes for learning Japanese and these differed from motives related to exchange value. For instance, Frank studied Japanese for his current enjoyment rather than for his future career prospects. Daniel wanted to improve his Japanese in order to better communicate with his Japanese friends and have the potential to work in Japan. Nevertheless, both students explained the change in their study patterns only in relation to their concerns about grades and marks. Their emphasis on motives related to exchange value may be because their concerns about their assessment became the object for their Japanese study at university and affected their concrete actions to overcome the tensions between their Japanese language skills and task demands. Alternatively, while gaining a good mark seemed to be a task-specific motive, 'enjoying language learning' and 'improving Japanese language skills' may be motives for a larger activity, that is, learning Japanese at university.

### Influence of use value of learning Japanese

Similar to the cases of Frank and Daniel, Grace also highlighted the gap between her Japanese language skills and the level of her Japanese course (Level 7). In the year preceding the data collection period, she commenced her study of Japanese at university during her Victorian Certificate of Education (VCE) enhancement course, which was a special course offered to high school students in order to improve their university entry scores. While Grace was undertaking this course, she did not concentrate on studying Japanese because of the necessity of studying other subjects for the VCE examination. The following excerpt describes how she was frustrated with her Japanese level at the beginning of the data collection period:

> I didn't study as hard as I always had in Japanese, and I started to feel like I was getting behind, and I didn't always feel very pleasant for my

study because I didn't really understand, because I wasn't putting in enough hours of work. I talked to *Aoki sensei* ((Ms. Aoki – the coordinator of Japanese 7)) this year <@@>, because I have to work very hard now, to catch up again. (Grace, Interview 1)

Similar to both Frank and Daniel, this tension can be understood as a contradiction between tool and object dimensions. However, a crucial difference existed between Grace and the other students with regard to motives. As discussed above, Frank and Daniel highlighted their concerns about academic results. In contrast, Grace emphasised her motives in association with the use value of learning Japanese. For instance, Grace explained her experiences at the TalkBack Classroom programme, which is a forum for high school students in Australia providing opportunities for them to investigate national and international relations. Grace explained how her experience in the programme encouraged her to continue studying Japanese:

A lot of the interviews we did in Japanese, and I could sort of understand, especially level 5 and 6 Japanese, we studied about some whaling vocabulary. So, in the interviews we did with the Japanese Whaling Association, I could sort of understand what he was saying and maybe realized that I was nearly at the level of my Japanese that could be very useful to me, and so, I sort of decided to, going further. (Grace, Interview 1)

In addition to these comments, Grace also stated that her experiences in the programme presented her with the potential to use Japanese in the future, particularly from a career perspective. These comments imply that Grace's strong motive related to the use value of learning Japanese was in fact a contributor to her attempts to fill the gap between her Japanese language skills and the standard of her Japanese classes. Although studying a target language at university undoubtedly has an exchange value for the reason that it enables her to obtain a degree, it seems that such a motive was less important for Grace compared to her motive to improve her Japanese language skills for her prospective career. It is also useful to recall that Grace was the only student who undertook extra studies outside of the classroom, such as composing example sentences in order to master grammatical items. The concrete actions that Grace undertook to overcome the gap between her Japanese language skills and her class level also indicated that she did not only focus on receiving good marks in the assessment tasks.

Based on the analysis of Grace's experience, it appears that learners' motives related to the use value of learning Japanese may trigger efforts to improve their proficiency beyond undertaking the required Japanese class tasks. This is a crucial difference between Grace's case and those of Frank and Daniel, who only focused on assessment tasks and preparation for in-class reading activities. In other words, it can be said that their different motives prompted different approaches towards improving their Japanese language skills. It is also important to note that, among this current study's participants, Grace was an exceptional case. Although many of the participants proclaimed their aspirations to use Japanese in the future based on their career ambitions, only in Grace's case did her motive, which was related to the use value of learning Japanese, result in an increase in extra study activities outside of the classroom. Instead, as the following section will discuss, motives related to use value might negatively affect learners' attitudes towards class-related tasks.

## Contradictions between use value type of motives and topics/tasks of Japanese classes

Analysis of the interview data also identified conflicts between students' use value motive types and Japanese course topics or tasks. As mentioned previously, students' motives related to the use value of learning Japanese included their expectation of using the language in their lives outside of the classroom, for example, social activities with Japanese speakers or in their future careers. In a study that explored how a university student overcame difficulties associated with composing essay tasks, Russell and Yañez (2003) revealed that students in a history course could not identify the use value of writing such tasks. The detachment evident between students' motives and the task purposes (and the course) often negatively affected their attitudes towards the tasks themselves. In the current study, a number of students highlighted this type of conflict. For instance, students who studied in Level 7 commented negatively about the usefulness of vocabulary and expressions for their language use activities outside of the classroom. This was because the topics presented in the textbook were too specific. Nevertheless, these students spent a great amount of time preparing for quizzes and examinations because these were part of the required assessment.

Eric's experiences in Levels 9 and 10 illustrated contrasting examples of the connections and disconnections between his motive and the Japanese topics and tasks that he had to undertake. As presented in Chapter 2, Japanese Level 9 was a content-based course on Japanese popular culture. However, Eric was not particularly interested in Japanese popular culture apart from Japanese *anime* movies, and neither could he recognise the usefulness of studying Japanese popular culture from a career perspective. Although Eric needed to undertake the assessment tasks, he maintained in the interview that he unwillingly prepared for these. In contrast, Eric was motivated to undertake class-related tasks in Level 10, which focused on translation and interpreting exercises, because he regarded such skills as useful for working in Japan. Eric also highlighted his experiences of an in-country summer programme at a university in Japan. During this summer programme, students were required to read a great number of authentic articles from newspapers and journals, and also to write a number of essays. Eric enthusiastically engaged in these tasks both in and outside of the classroom because he became aware of the connection between these tasks and the Japanese skills which would be required for his future career. As Russell and Yañez (2003) argued, recognising connections between students' use value motives and their class content appears to encourage them to undertake class tasks.

However, as Eric's experience in Level 9 as well as the Japanese Level 7 students' comments indicate, a dilemma often exists between students' motives and what they actually need to study in order to pass the course. This dilemma may be difficult for learners to resolve because the content of the Japanese course (e.g. topics and tasks) is determined by teachers who are in a more powerful position to the students in the university environment.

*Contradictions between assessment activity and learning activity*

Focusing on Daniel's case, this section will discuss how the exchange and use values of learning Japanese compete as dual motives for studying Japanese in formal education settings, thereby influencing learners' approaches towards class-related tasks. Daniel provided a detailed account of his experience with an essay task in Level 11. His report illustrated apparent dilemmas within his motives as well as between his motives and the objects that the teacher defined, with which other students might also be faced. As previously discussed, Daniel struggled with the reading and writing tasks of his Japanese class, in particular, the essay assignment in Level 11 which required students to read several resources in Japanese and to write their opinions in an academic style of Japanese. This gap between Daniel's literacy skills and those required of tasks triggered a violation of the rules for the essay task:

> Being unable to read a high majority of resources has put me in a very difficult position in regards to finding good information to build my argument from. Which is why I once again called on the help of my *sempai* ((*senpai* – fellow students who studied the same course before)) to lend me their previous year's assignments and sit down and help me craft a good skeleton for my own essay building off from quotes and thoughts that they used last year. This is definitely cheating and I'm not proud of this at all, however what choice do I have if I want to pass. (Daniel's diary entry on 25 May 2009)

In the interview related to this essay assignment, Daniel maintained that he could not formulate his own ideas and mostly borrowed references, arguments and even expressions from his fellow students' essays. As the above excerpt illustrates, Daniel tried to overcome the tension between his Japanese language skills and the demands of the essay task with the help of his fellow students, although he recognised that this was not appropriate behaviour. As mentioned previously, Daniel highlighted his great concern about his academic results as a final-year student. Behind his decision to violate the assessment rules, his motive for gaining a good mark was evident. Although this coping strategy yielded a successful outcome, it can be said that Daniel also lost valuable opportunities necessary to improve his reading and writing skills.

With regard to conflict between assessment and language learning, Daniel noted the negative influence which the assessment's pressure had on his Japanese study:

> Because we're students, doing courses and you know, it's just not enough time to really learn something, you know… it's just always so much pressure. You might learn one thing or two, but it's more you're learning, you're forced to learn. (Daniel, Interview 2)

This comment implies that a contradiction occurred within Daniel's objects, which were learning Japanese versus passing the course, that is, the contradiction between the use value and the exchange value of formal education. As Spence-Brown (2004, 2007) argues, it can be claimed that students' concerns about assessment often dominate other motives and direct their engagement when undertaking assessment tasks. In addition, it is also necessary to take Daniel's Japanese proficiency level into account. Spence-Brown found that students with a high Japanese proficiency level did not experience a conflict between the motive to do well in assessment and their other motives, whereas students with lower proficiency levels tended to focus more on assessment. In Daniel's case too, he needed to concentrate on passing the course because of his low Japanese proficiency level. As discussed above, on the one hand, it is highly likely that Daniel's concern about gaining good academic results increased his efforts when performing class-related literacy practices. On the other hand, this concern might reduce his Japanese learning opportunities.

Furthermore, Daniel articulated his dissatisfaction with the structure of the assessment. As the following excerpt demonstrates, Daniel negatively evaluated the essay assignment in comparison with the ongoing assessment that he experienced at his previous university:

> It ((the essay task as assessment)) is also one of the reasons why I hate studying university level Japanese. I cannot understand or see the relevance of a 2,000 character essay being important in acknowledging a student's understanding of the topic. It would have served a better purpose to have ongoing assessments throughout the semester instead of one large written piece with high percentage scaling. All this is reading

and copy what the author wrote. However, it's not my decision to make so there is no excuse for not doing the work. (Daniel's diary entry on 21 May 2009)

This statement indicates a conflict between Daniel's understanding of meaningful assessment and the actual assessment method employed by the teacher. It is reasonable to say that this conflict might trigger Daniel's demotivation to prepare for the essay task. As Daniel pointed out, this conflict is unalterable because, as a university student, his agency is constrained by societal factors, that is, the power of the teacher and the university (see Lantolf & Genung, 2002). Engeström *et al.* (2002) claim that contradictions might repeatedly occur, and if they appear in a more aggravated guise, whereby contradictions are ignored or cannot be fixed, it is necessary for students to be supported in seeking possibilities to overcome these problems or for teachers to attempt to resolve the contradictions.

## Summary and Discussion

This chapter has particularly focused on participants' class-related literacy practices and explored the reasons why several participants placed more emphasis on Japanese class tasks than others. The major factors which influenced students' preferences for class-related tasks were related to their histories as learners and their beliefs about effective learning methods. The students who mostly undertook class-related literacy practices seemed to have been satisfied with their learning styles (i.e. focusing on the assessment tasks and the preparations for the classes) and the outcomes of their learning activities in light of their learning histories. However, Grace's experience illustrates that such beliefs concerning effective learning methods may be changed through learner experiences within a relatively short period of time. Additionally, Grace's case also provides valuable insights into the role that Japanese classes could play for developing learners' beliefs, and, in turn, lead to an expansion of a variety of literacy activities outside of the classroom.

This chapter has also discussed students' efforts towards class-related literacy practices, drawing on the concepts of motives and contradictions in the context of Activity Theory. I primarily focused on two types of motives, related to the exchange value and use value of learning Japanese, because these motives were inextricably linked to formal education (Engeström, 1987). The majority of the participants in this current study outlined both the exchange value and use value of learning Japanese as their motives for class-related tasks or learning Japanese at university: gaining a good mark and acquiring Japanese language skills for their lives outside of the classroom.

In examining the contradictions that students experienced in class-related tasks, the exchange value and use value motives appeared to influence their orientations towards tasks in a different manner. Students' motives for gaining good marks triggered an increase in class-related literacy practices and helped overcome the gap between their Japanese language skills and task demands. In contrast, learners' motives related to use value seem to trigger extra studies outside the classroom. However, if students could not identify any relation between their use values and their tasks or the contents of their Japanese classes, they were often demotivated when preparing for the tasks. My findings thus differ from the claim by Gillette (1994) that learners who recognise the use value of language learning are not demotivated by transient negative experiences. Rather, as Spence-Brown (2004, 2007) maintains, it appears that students' concerns about academic results were more influential on their attitudes and approaches towards class-related tasks. Moreover, as Daniel's case indicates, dominance of exchange value may lead students to cope with the assessment tasks rather than improve their target language skills through the tasks themselves.

It was also revealed that students found it difficult to overcome a number of conflicts within the learners' activity systems because of power relations between them and teachers or the university as a related community. Perhaps, these conflicts should be identified by both teachers and students in order to facilitate learners' class-related literacy practices. However, from the perspective of agency in Activity Theory, it can be interpreted that students manage their language learning in order to achieve their objectives while taking such constraints into consideration. Participants' efforts in class-related literacy practices were thus the consequences of interaction between learners' agency and factors that emerged in their activity systems. These social and contextual factors also affected learners' concrete approaches towards each literacy activity. This will be discussed in Chapter 6.

# 5 Non-Class-Related Literacy Practices

The previous chapter examined participants' class-related literacy practices in terms of their attitudes towards their required Japanese class tasks, and the factors that affected their decisions to mainly focus on assessment tasks. Although the majority of students' Japanese reading and writing tasks undertaken during the semester were class related, as shown in Chapter 3, participants also undertook various types of literacy activities which were not directly related to their Japanese classes. In terms of motives in the context of Activity Theory, this chapter will explore the reasons why students undertook literacy activities other than those that were required for their Japanese classes. I will also examine the contextual factors that influence the motives and develop opportunities for such second language (L2) literacy practices.

## Overview of Non-Class-Related Literacy Practices

Before exploring the factors that influence students' participation in non-class-related literacy practices, this section will briefly present an overall picture of the various literacy activities that students undertook during the data collection period. Although Chapter 3 presented the types of literacy activities that the participants undertook outside the classroom, this section focuses more on the differences and similarities in the non-class-related literacy practices among the participants.

### Individual differences in non-class-related literacy practices

As mentioned in Chapter 4, participants in the current study can be classified into three groups: those who undertook reading or writing activities more extensively; those who read and wrote irregularly; and those who mostly focused on class-related practices. In this section, I differentiate the first group from the second and third group because of the significant differences in terms of the amount of time spent undertaking literacy activities and the variety of activities involved.

The first group comprised Chris, Joshua and Patrick, who frequently engaged in spontaneous Japanese reading and writing at least several

Table 5.1 Non-class-related literacy activities undertaken by Chris, Patrick and Joshua

| | Paper based | | Electronic | | | | |
|---|---|---|---|---|---|---|---|
| | Reading | Writing | Reading | Writing | Online communication | Viewing | Listening |
| Chris (2008) | Novel | To-do lists | Arbitrary reading | | Mixi[a] | | Listening to radio |
| Chris (2009) | Bilingual bible, *manga*, studying for JLPT | Studying for JLPT | Pop song lyrics | | Mixi | *Anime* episodes, TV serials | Listening to J-pop songs |
| Patrick | Novel, book, legal magazine, legal textbooks, newspaper | | Websites of Japanese court cases | | | TV serials | |
| Joshua (2008) | | | Articles on Wikipedia, pop song lyrics, voluntary reading | Personal diary | Facebook, Twitter, online chat, emails related to his part-time job | Video games | |
| Joshua (2009) | Novel | | Emails from mailing lists | Weblogs | Facebook, Twitter, online chat, emails related to his part-time job | *Anime* episodes, video games | |

[a] Mixi is a Japanese social networking service.

times a week alongside their assessment task preparation. Table 5.1 shows that these 3 students undertook a variety of activities, including reading and writing.

It is important to note that there was a crucial difference between Chris, Patrick and Joshua. On the one hand, Chris and Patrick mainly engaged in reading both paper-based and online materials. On the other hand, Joshua mostly undertook online literacy activities, such as browsing websites and communicating with his Japanese friends and Japanese learners on social networking sites. Joshua only read one paper-based resource, a novel written by a famous Japanese contemporary writer. This might be because he had never visited Japan and might not have been presented with many opportunities to obtain paper-based resources. In contrast, Chris and Patrick had long-term stays in Japan and purchased books and *manga* while there.

The students from the second group reported only undertaking a limited number of literacy activities in their diary entries and interviews. The students from the third group basically focused on class-related tasks during semesters and reported only one or two instances of their voluntary literacy activities in the interviews but not in their diary entries. As Table 5.2 illustrates, although 9 out of the 12 students read either paper-based or online materials, none of the students in these groups had the opportunity to write, except for instances when they participated in online communication via the internet.

Moreover, it is notable that the majority of the participants undertook viewing activities, such as watching Japanese *anime*, TV serials and variety shows. The popularity of viewing activities highlights the influence of Japanese pop culture on participants' Japanese literacy activities. Although Fukunaga (2006) and Williams (2006) discussed the impact of Japanese pop culture on learning Japanese, these studies particularly focused on *anime* fan students. The finding in this study indicates that not only *anime* but also other aspects of Japanese pop culture (e.g. Japanese TV serials) and related materials seem to have influenced Japanese learners' lives.

As discussed in Chapter 3, viewing activities often involved reading skills because Japanese variety shows and *anime* include written information in Japanese, such as examples of onomatopoeia and brief Japanese captions. The mixture of audio, visual and linguistic modes, that is, multimodality, is a feature of modern literacy practices which Cope and Kalantzis (2000) pointed out in their discussion on Multiliteracies. However, the amount of written information in these visual resources is apparently limited in comparison with other materials that the participants read, such as Japanese books and websites. The students from this group thus had fewer opportunities to utilise written Japanese in comparison with Chris, Patrick and Joshua, who undertook various reading and writing activities.

Non-Class-Related Literacy Practices 91

Table 5.2 Non-class-related literacy activities of the second and the third groups

| | Paper based | | Electronic | | | | | |
|---|---|---|---|---|---|---|---|---|
| | Reading | Writing | Reading | Writing | Online communication | Viewing | Listening |
| Alice | | | Lyrics of *anime* songs | | Facebook | *Anime* episodes | |
| Brenda | Bilingual book | | | | Facebook | | |
| Daniel | | | | | Mixi, Facebook | *Anime*, TV serials | |
| Eric | *Manga*, specialised magazine | | | | Facebook | *Anime* | |
| Frank | | | | | Facebook | Variety shows | |
| Grace | Bilingual book, *manga* | | | | Facebook, emails to Japanese teachers | | Listening to pop songs, online radio |
| Kate | Fashion magazines | | Host sister's blogs | | | TV serials, movies | |
| Lisa | | | | | | Variety shows | |
| Melissa | | | Lyrics of pop songs | | Facebook | *Anime*, TV serials | Listening to pop songs |
| Nancy | A picture book | | | | Email to host family | Movies | |
| Scott (2008) | | | Article from Wikipedia, website | | Facebook | | |
| Scott (2009) | | | Lyric of pop song, classmate's blog | | Online chat, Facebook | Movies | |
| Thomas | | | Japanese online newspaper | | Online chat | *Anime* | |

## Common features among the participants

The most notable feature is that all participants, except for Brenda, undertook at least one viewing activity during the data collection period. This result is consistent with the findings in the studies on informal out-of-class learning activities by English as a foreign language (EFL) students in the 2010s, which demonstrated the popularity of online viewing activities (e.g. Lin & Siyanova-Chanturia, 2015; Sockett, 2014; Toffoli & Sockett, 2010). A possible reason for this result is that video-sharing sites became common during the first decade of the 21st century. For instance, YouTube, a well-known video-sharing site that participants in this study utilised for their viewing activities, was established in 2005 (see Graham, 2005). Netflix started its streaming service in the United States in 2007 (see Helft, 2007). Interestingly, Daniel's report reflects this change. He was a fan of Japanese *anime* and borrowed DVDs from a video rental store when he started watching it at high school. However, he mainly utilised the internet during the data collection period. Not only Australian students but also Swedish learners of Japanese regularly undertook viewing activities using such video streaming services (Inaba & Kurata, 2017). The diversity of these service types on the internet enables learners to obtain resources even in languages other than English and has become a significant factor for naturalistic language learning and use activities outside the classroom (Toffoli & Sockett, 2010). In addition, numerous video materials related to Japanese *anime*, TV serials and variety shows with subtitles in multiple languages have been provided by the fandom of Japanese pop culture. This may be another reason for the popularity of viewing activities in the present study.

Another salient feature commonly found among students from both groups is the infrequency of writing activities, including online written communication with Japanese speakers. Previous studies on out-of-class learning in foreign language (FL) contexts (e.g. Freeman, 1999; Pearson, 2004; Pickard, 1996; Yap, 1998) also identified tendencies similar to this current study's results. This is despite the fact that writing emails in a target language was the most common activity noted in some of the studies after the internet started to be commonly used (Hyland, 2004; Inozu *et al.*, 2010; Spratt *et al.*, 2002). A possible reason for the infrequency of online written communication in the current study might stem from an important feature of interactive activities, namely, the need for conversation partners. It can be argued that opportunities to participate in online written communication interactions are influenced by interlocutors' motives and circumstances. For instance, Nancy reported that she wrote an email to her host family in her first diary study. However, approximately two months later, she claimed that she had 'emailed them, but they haven't replied' (Interview 3). Moreover, the participants in this study often utilised English rather than Japanese when undertaking online written communication with their Japanese acquaintances. Consequently, the following sections will mainly focus on reading and viewing activities in order to explore students' motives and the influential factors which have had an impact on their motives.

## Motives for Non-Class-Related Literacy Practices

Participants reported various reasons for their choice and employment of each literacy activity. However, their motives can be roughly divided into four main groups: learning Japanese; entertainment, including pursuing their interests and relaxing; maintaining friendships or other social relationships with Japanese speakers; and other purposes, including part-time jobs. The first two motives were predominant in the current study and were similar to the findings by Yap (1998), who investigated EFL high school students' motivations for their out-of-class learning. Accordingly, I will focus on students' motives for learning Japanese and entertainment as an impetus for non-class-related literacy practices and the significant factors influencing these motives.

## Japanese learning motives

Analysis of the interview data suggested that the majority of participants viewed non-class-related literacy activities as learning activities which could be used to improve their Japanese language skills. In addition, Chris, Eric and Nancy described their reading and viewing activities as challenges which provided them with a sense of achievement, although this could be understood as a result (outcome) of the activity rather than its primary motive. These learning motives can mainly be derived from the following factors: learners' beliefs about the value and positive experiences of non-class-related literacy practices, and concerns about enhancing their Japanese competence in order to receive a good mark.

### *Learners' beliefs and positive experiences of voluntary literacy activities*

According to Barcelos (2003), it has been claimed that learners' beliefs about effective ways of language learning influence their learning strategies or approach to language learning. For instance, the quantitative research by Yang (1999) on EFL learners revealed a significant correlation between their beliefs of self-efficacy and functional practice strategies, thus indicating their actions to seek or create opportunities to practise a target language. Although participants in this study did not report beliefs of self-efficacy, several students commented on the usefulness of authentic language use for improving their Japanese. This is a similar finding to that of a study by Yap (1998) involving Hong Kong EFL high school students' out-of-class language learning. Yap established that EFL learners recognised the benefits that out-of-class activities had on improving their

English and held strong beliefs about the value of practising the target language outside of the classroom.

As already mentioned in Chapter 4, from an Activity Theory viewpoint, learners' beliefs can be viewed as a subject-related factor that is formulated and developed based on past activities, for example, education and schooling (Engeström, 1987). For instance, Grace's example in Chapter 4 illustrated that her belief about the effectiveness of learning the target language by utilising authentic materials was developed through the positive experiences she gained from her intensive in-country programme. This belief directly influenced her primary motive for learning Japanese and encouraged her to read a bilingual book of short stories written by Japanese contemporary writers as well as *manga* that she had purchased in Japan.

A number of students also claimed that their experiences of voluntary activities in Japanese appeared to have shaped their beliefs. For instance, Melissa reported several experiences of mutual influences between class-related learning and her voluntary activities using authentic resources. The following excerpt shows how she recognised a particular word that she had previously heard in a Japanese pop song when she was studying for a vocabulary test:

> …for instance, on today's test, there is 破る ((*yaburu*)), 'to tear'. I didn't know what it was, I wouldn't know if I just looked at it at the test. But I learnt 破る ((*yaburu*)) by listening to a song, because I understood all of the sentences except for 破る ((*yaburu*)), so I looked it in a 辞書 ((*jisho* – dictionary)) and it said 破る ((*yaburu*))… (Melissa, Interview 1)

She also explained that she noticed a phrase '間に合う (*ma ni au* – make it in time)', which she had recently used in her Japanese class (diary entry on 13 June 2009), in a Japanese *anime*:

> …I didn't realise what that ((the word *ma ni au*)) meant, but I learned it when I was studying for my exam. And when I was watching ((the Japanese *anime*)), I heard they said, you know, 間に合った ((*ma ni atta* – the past tense of *ma ni au*)) or something like that, and 'Ah=, that is the word'. (Melissa, Interview 3)

Although her spontaneous practices mainly involved listening and viewing activities, these examples indicate that Melissa recognised the value of her actual use of Japanese in relation to her studies. Likewise, Thomas reported his experiences related to watching Japanese *anime*:

> …what particularly useful I think is sometimes some *anime* have some person who speaks some dialects in Japanese, like 関西弁 ((*Kansaiben* – dialect of *Kansai* region around Osaka and Kyoto)) or something. I think

because I watch *anime*, I can understand almost all of those, I constantly understand most of the main dialects pretty much perfectly, which I think it gives me advantage over the other students in class because, of course, we don't usually do anything in some dialects ((in class)), but sometimes in reading or something, it would be like some 関西弁 ((*Kansaiben*)) or something, like I understand that because of the *anime*. (Thomas, Interview 1)

In the comment above, Thomas indicates that watching Japanese *anime* enabled him to learn something that Japanese classes did not usually deal with in detail. Thomas also claimed that his viewing activities gave him an advantage in acquiring new vocabulary necessary for the Japanese classes:

Because, you know, sometimes you would learn new vocabulary in the class and from the vocab list, but it's like, I sometimes have already heard that from *anime* or something, and I would already know, and I think that helps me to just study ((vocabulary)) quicker. (Thomas, Interview 1)

Watching *anime* was also an opportunity for Thomas to reinforce previously learned vocabulary because he heard these words several times in such contexts (Interview 1). Melissa's and Thomas's comments indicate not only that they learned extra vocabulary through viewing and listening activities but also that they noticed the bidirectional connections between what they learned in their Japanese classes and their authentic language use activities related to Japanese popular culture. It can be reasonably assumed that these experiences influenced their beliefs about the usefulness of such entertaining activities for learning Japanese. Moreover, Melissa's and Thomas's experiences imply that language classes and assessment tasks might become viable opportunities to encourage learners to realise the outcomes of their leisure activities in a target language.

Chris, Joshua and Patrick, who regularly read or wrote in the target language outside of the classroom, also stated their beliefs as follows: 'if you don't use the language in everyday life, you won't really learn it at all' (Chris, Interview 3); 'reading anything is helpful to improve Japanese' (Patrick, Interview 3); and '(...) 言語の練習も、え、なる、できます ((*Gengo no renshū mo, e, naru, dekimasu* – I can practice the language, too))' (Joshua, Interview 2). Due to data limitations, it was difficult to identify how their beliefs were formulated. However, Chris and Patrick had experienced long-term stays in Japan and reported undertaking voluntary reading and writing in Japanese. Although Joshua had never been to Japan, he had commenced learning Japanese by himself. Based on their past experiences, it is safe to assume that all of these students thus recognised the benefits of authentic language use on improving their Japanese proficiency levels.

### Influence of Japanese classes: Exchange value type of motive

Eric highlighted the influence that Japanese classes had on his motives to read *manga* and watch *anime* in terms of gaining good marks in his Japanese classes. As mentioned in Chapter 4, this is what Engeström (1987) called the exchange value of studying in formal education settings. It can be reasonably assumed that this exchange value influenced participants' motives to undertake extra literacy activities outside the classroom because they were students who studied the target language at university level. In the interview following the completion of his Japanese studies at university, Eric described how his main motive for extra reading and viewing activities outside the classroom was to enhance his performance in the Japanese classes:

> When I was studying Japanese, I really tried a lot to read *manga*, I tried to watch a lot of *anime* more than I normally would. I did definitely use more Japanese outside the classroom. That was because I was studying Japanese. So, it was sort of relevant at that time. But now I finished Japanese, the same reason to pick up *manga* isn't there anymore. Because I don't really like *manga*, so like I just ignore it, I just leave it alone. Of course, I still wanna learn Japanese, but when I studied Japanese, I really wanted to get good marks. If I can read *manga*, I can say to myself, 'even though this is really tiring, at least maybe I'll get a distinction', because this is going directly into my marks, like this is directly useful. (Eric, Interview 3)

Interestingly, Eric was the only informant who stated the direct influence that Japanese classes had on his motives for undertaking literacy activities other than assessment tasks. The study by Yap (1998) on motivations for out-of-class language learning also did not report this type of motivation except for an example where oral skills were practiced for an English proficiency test.

Leont'ev (1981) states that motives are not always recognised by the subject of an activity. Some of the students in this current study might simply be unaware of this type of motive. Alternatively, students might not intentionally mention their desire to gain a good mark as a motive because they did not want to be identified as being only focused on academic results. Another interpretation of this result is that students might expect a positive result for their performance in Japanese but did not regard it as their motive for non-class-related literacy practices. It is reasonable to assume that one of the students' motives for studying Japanese was to improve their language skills. In this vein, good performance in Japanese classes is a by-product of efforts to improve their Japanese language skills rather than their motive for informal language learning and use activities outside of the classroom. Students' concerns about good performance in Japanese classes thus only had a minimal impact on their motives to pursue the opportunities for authentic language use in the out-of-class contexts.

To summarise, participants' positive beliefs concerning the effectiveness of authentic language use prompted their spontaneous literacy activities in order to develop their Japanese language skills. It is also worth noting that Japanese classes possibly shaped students' positive beliefs and facilitated their non-class-related activities, though the language classes appeared not to have a direct impact on their motives.

## Motives of enjoyment and learners' interests

Another dominant motive for non-class-related literacy practices was entertainment, fulfilling interests and relaxing. Previous studies on language learning motivations have dealt with learners' interests as intrinsic motivations (Deci & Ryan, 1995; Ryan & Deci, 2000) for language learning and claimed a strong relation with their efforts in learning target languages (e.g. Noels *et al.*, 1999, 2000). In relation to non-class-related literacy practices, the participants in this study reported long-term as well as temporary interests in certain topics. This will be discussed in the following sections.

### Long-term interests in Japanese pop culture

A feature of participants' interests that appeared in the interviews was the strong influence of Japanese popular culture over a long-term period, which chimes with claims by Sakuma (2006) that interest in Japanese subculture is a salient reason to study Japanese. In this study, as Tables 5.1 and 5.2 show, the majority of students undertook at least one activity related to this. In the interviews, the students also described their involvement with Japanese popular culture from an early age, for instance, watching dubbed Japanese *anime* on TV or playing Japanese video games.

Participants' comments indicate that their interests in Japanese popular culture were socially constructed in their past activity systems and continued to prompt their voluntary activities over their learning histories. In his second interview, Daniel described how he was involved in watching *anime*:

> It was funny because my high school had never taught Japanese, never taught Japanese. And it was because my friends really liked *anime*, I started watching *anime* as well, and then I became addicted, I became オタク ((*otaku* – geek))… and my brother loved *anime* as well, so we used to borrow *anime* from *Hobby Japan* ((a video rental shop of Japanese *anime* in Melbourne)). (Daniel, Interview 2)

This excerpt indicates that Daniel became interested in *anime* through interaction with his peers and a sibling. Although Daniel stated that *anime* gradually 'stopped interesting me' (Interview 2), he still watched several episodes of Japanese *anime* and TV serials as a reward for finishing assessment tasks. Similarly, Joshua, Melissa and Thomas started watching *anime* when they were primary or high school students, having been influenced by peers or siblings. They started watching *anime* even though their school did not provide Japanese as a subject, or they had not chosen Japanese as a foreign language subject. They claimed that *anime* stimulated their interest in Japanese as a foreign language and became a catalyst for learning it in formal education settings. These students' interests in Japanese pop culture continually triggered enjoyment activities, such as watching Japanese *anime* and reading *manga*.

A key insight from the sociocultural approach relevant to this issue is that students' interests, which were socially constructed through past interactions with community members at their schools or family, were crucial in shaping their participation in their current activities. In her well-known study on language learning strategies from the viewpoint of Activity Theory, Gillette (1994) suggested that an individual's history, including his/her family's attitudes towards foreign languages and cultures, affected the formation of his/her motives and goals for learning an L2, and thus resulted in individual differences emerging in learning strategies and attitudes towards language study. A study by Gao (2010) also found significant influences from family members and teachers in the formulation of learners' motives and beliefs about language learning strategies throughout their learning histories. The examples of students in the present study also support these claims that their current activities were affected by their history, including community members' influences.

These students also reported on the continuous influence that their peers and siblings had on their interest in Japanese popular culture since the time they started studying Japanese at university. For instance, Thomas' classmates provided him with information on interesting *anime* series which they had watched (Interview 2). Melissa's peers at the *Manga* library often talked about Japanese TV serials which they had watched, and this also stimulated her interest in TV serials (Interview 3). These students' longitudinal involvement with such types of media was thus supported by the recommendations by their peers and siblings of interesting series.

### Long-term interests in other specific topics

Other than Japanese popular culture, students also reported on their long-term interests in specific topics, such as specialised topics related to their majors at university. Eric, for example, read an article from a product design engineering magazine that he bought in Japan during his intensive in-country summer programme. He explained the reason why he bought this magazine:

> I'm doing like a type of engineering, computer based machine and lots of stuff. So I was really interested in this sort of stuff …and when I was in Japan, I thought I felt weird not reading about it, so we ((Eric and his classmate who was majoring science at university)) thought it would be fun to get to a bookshop and to get some magazines, so I got this one, that was about machine computers, computer hardware, something like that. (Eric, Interview 2)

As explained in this excerpt, Eric's interest in his other major, engineering, drove him to buy the magazine. Patrick, who majored in law at a Japanese university, also read various legal texts in Japanese, such as websites based on a Japanese court case and textbooks that he utilised at the Japanese university. Patrick's interests in Japanese law clearly affected his reading activities during the period of my research. This finding is similar to the Chinese students in the study by Ma (2017) regarding how they utilised mobile technology to improve their English skills. The participants in Ma's study also read news websites related to their majors. These examples illustrate that interests gleaned from other areas of their lives might also become contributing factors towards out-of-class literacy practices.

### Temporary interests in specific topics

Students' temporary interests also provoked their voluntary literacy activities in the target language. To be more specific, participants searched for information on the internet when they became interested in particular topics and engaged in reading and viewing activities as a result. This type of interest seems to receive less attention in the area of L2 motivation research as well as out-of-class language learning studies. The following examples reveal that students' interests were stimulated by external factors, such as Japanese classes and peers, and that eventually these became connected with literacy activity opportunities.

As presented in Chapter 3, Scott searched for information about what he learned in Japanese class and read articles on the Japanese version of Wikipedia and a website. In the second semester of the data collection, Scott also searched for a website on Japanese pop songs and checked the lyrics as well as the English translations of several Japanese pop songs played in Japanese video games and *anime*. This activity was again triggered by one of the topics discussed in the classes of Level 9, the content-based course on Japanese popular culture:

> The week before in the seminar, we discussed it, 日本語の歌手と歌 ((*nihongo no kashu to uta* – Japanese singers and songs)). So, I was listening to some Japanese songs and I wanted to know the meanings ((of the lyrics)). (Scott, Interview 4)

Scott already knew the songs from having played Japanese video games. However, as the above excerpt indicates, undertaking study on Japanese songs in the classroom ultimately prompted him to check the lyrics and try to understand the meanings. Although Scott stated that he rarely undertook literacy activities related to Japanese popular culture (Interview 6), the class activity topics successfully aroused Scott's interest and generated extra opportunities to use the target language outside of the classroom.

Similar to learners' long-term interests, participants' peers and Japanese friends were another influential factor which could provoke temporary interests. For instance, Chris checked the lyrics of Japanese pop songs on the internet because his Japanese friend, who was an exchange student in Melbourne, recommended these songs to him (Interview 5). Joshua also reported an example in which his friend who was learning Japanese triggered his interest and resulted in him undertaking reading activity. As the friend was Chinese and talked to Joshua about the mid-autumn festival in China, they were intrigued about what this festival was called in Japanese and the differences this presented between China and Japan. This interest motivated Joshua and his friend to read the article about the festival on the Japanese version of Wikipedia.

From an Activity Theory standpoint, as discussed in relation to the students' long-term interests, these examples indicate that students' temporary interests were socially constructed by means of the influence of Japanese-related communities (i.e. Japanese classes in Scott's case) and their peers (i.e. Joshua's Japanese learner friend and Chris' Japanese exchange student). However, a crucial difference is their continuity. On the one hand, literacy activities prompted by long-term interests, particularly interests in Japanese popular culture, seemed to become a part of the students' lives in the form of hobbies. Although the amount of time available to engage in these activities was influenced by their circumstances (e.g. course schedule at university), students who were particularly interested in this media continually undertook these activities over the years. On the other hand, in regard to temporary interests, each activity was completed if the interest or question was satisfied. In other words, transient interests did not usually provide sustained opportunities for using Japanese over an extended period of time.

It is, however, interesting to note that the variety of literacy activities conducted by Chris, Patrick and Joshua, who constantly undertook non-class-related activities, indicates their longitudinal as well as temporary interests in a broad range of topics (Table 5.1). As discussed in an earlier section of this chapter (see Learners' beliefs and positive experiences of voluntary literacy activities), these students also stated beliefs about the usefulness of literacy activities which utilised authentic materials in order to improve their Japanese. The combination of their beliefs and their interests in various topics seemed to result in constant and various types of literacy activities.

## Multiple Motives

The foregoing sections illustrated that the students in this study often stated two predominant motives for non-class-related literacy activities: learning Japanese and entertainment. As described in Chapter 2, Leont'ev (1978: 123) points out the possibility for multiple motives for one activity: that is, an activity 'responds simultaneously to two or more motives'. Whereas a more important motive provides an activity's main meaning, a less important motive provides additional meaning but does not alter the primary meaning of the activity. Leont'ev (1978: 123) refers to these as 'sense-forming motives' and 'motive-stimuli', respectively. The following examples demonstrate how learning and enjoyment motives were combined, one being the sense-forming motive, while the other provides the motive-stimuli.

Grace was a student who considered learning Japanese to be a sense-forming motive; furthermore, she enjoyed the content as motive-stimuli. In her second diary entry after she returned from an in-country programme, she reported that she read a book that she bought in Japan. The book comprised of short stories written by contemporary Japanese novelists and included explanations about grammar and expressions in English and vocabulary lists. Grace described the reason why she selected this book:

> It's just real, like it's real Japanese, which is what I was always trying to do with French ((her other major at university))... this is something that is going to let me do that. And, it isn't just a difficult book, because if I tried to read a novel, it would be like too hard for me, but it has everything, everything explained really well, and it's got vocab and CDs so... it's a collection of short stories, so I love it <@@>. (Grace, Interview 3)

Grace's comment above illustrates that she was interested in literature and enjoyed the book, though her main reason for selecting this material was to learn Japanese using authentic materials, which she also employed while learning French. Grace also bought the well-known *manga* ドラえもん (*Doraemon*) in Japan because she could learn Japanese and enjoyed the story (Interview 3). This example shows that her aim of learning Japanese was a sense-forming motive whereas her interest or enjoyment gained from reading the books appeared to be motive-stimuli.

Melissa's case is an example of where the enjoyment of authentic material content was in fact the sense-forming motive, while the expectation of learning Japanese was the motive-stimuli. As mentioned previously, Melissa was a student whose interest in Japanese popular culture influenced her to start learning Japanese in the first place. She occasionally watched Japanese TV serials and *anime* with English subtitles, and tried to read some Japanese *manga* comics throughout her learning history. She explained the reason for undertaking these activities as follows: 'I do them for fun and they double as study, which is good' (Interview 2). Given that Melissa described several examples in which she learned new vocabulary and expressions or found items which she had learned in Japanese classes while enjoying pop culture materials, it is assumed that these experiences influenced her expectation that reading or viewing popular culture materials would help her learn Japanese, and this ultimately provided the motive-stimuli for her activities. Grace and Melissa's cases were examples of where it was possible to distinguish sense-forming motives and motive-stimuli. However, in a number of cases such distinctions were not nearly as clear-cut.

## Ambiguity of distinction between learning Japanese and entertainment

Kaptelinin and Nardi (2006) critically discussed Leont'ev's distinction between motives and claimed that this distinction is often ambiguous. They instead propose to view a poly-motivated activity as being comprised of different activity aspects exercised towards an object which is 'jointly defined by the whole set of motives' (Kaptelinin & Nardi, 2006: 149). Nancy's comments on her reading activity actually indicate this ambivalence. In her first diary study, Nancy reported reading a picture book based on a famous Japanese *anime* movie, もののけ姫 (*Mononoke hime – Princess Mononoke*). Although Nancy was unable to clearly articulate why she read this book, she suggested that the reason was to learn *kanji* (Interview 2). In fact, Nancy made a word list when she read this picture book. This concrete action also highlights her aim to learn vocabulary. In addition to this purpose, Nancy had another motive related to understanding the story:

> I didn't finish that ((reading the picture book)), I have to return it, but I'm planning to get it out again and keep reading it because I've seen もののけ姫 ((*Mononoke hime – Princess Mononoke*)), but it was in Japanese, and I didn't understand it at all. (Nancy, Interview 2)

Nancy watched this movie in Japanese because she watched it in Japan when she was a high school exchange student. Nancy's comment above implies that her desire to understand the story was another motive that triggered and regulated this reading activity (i.e. it encouraged her to continue reading the book), rather than merely adding extra meaning to the primary language learning activity.

Thomas' case also presents an example where two motives appeared to jointly promote his literacy activities related to Japanese popular culture. As already discussed, Thomas had watched Japanese *anime* or had read *manga* throughout his Japanese learning history because he was interested in this particular media format. It appears that his interests in *anime* and *manga* originally triggered these activities. However, he also obviously recognised the value of learning or practicing Japanese through entertainment activities:

> So when I can, I try to talk to a few Japanese friends, but when I can't, what I do generally is to watch some *anime* in Japanese or read some *manga*. And that can help me to keep like, you know, get used to speaking and listening to it. (Thomas, Interview 1)

For Thomas, enjoying *anime* as well as *manga* and practicing Japanese were two complementary motives for his reading and viewing activities. Chris, Joshua and Patrick, who regularly engaged in reading and writing, also highlighted both their interest in certain topics and their expectations for improving their Japanese language skills. These intertwined motives often jointly encouraged the students' engagement with the target language, although one of these motives may become dominant in a particular phase of undertaking literacy activities (see Spence-Brown, 2004). As stated in Chapter 2, the previous studies on out-of-class L2 learning have tended to view voluntary activities as one type of language learning strategies to improve L2 skills. However, it can be said that this exclusive view does not necessarily reflect the true nature of these activities.

## Learners' Interests and Expansion of Literacy Activities

It is evident that students in the current study often stated multiple motives that collaboratively prompted and encouraged their non-class-related literacy practices. However, analysis of the interview data suggests that students' interests in particular topics often play a more significant role than their Japanese learning motives in terms of expanding and transforming their literacy activities. Here, I will discuss how students' interests in particular topics and media sources may increase opportunities for L2 literacy practices and generally lead to them fulfilling their individual goals.

### Snowballing effects of interests

Students in the current study reported that their interests in a particular topic or media form prompted several associated literacy activities.

This is what Yap (1998: 26) termed the 'snowballing effect' of interests. In her study, Yap argued that an English as a second language (ESL) student's activity development was triggered by her interest in English pop songs, in the forms of listening activities and reading activities. As Lantolf (2000) points out, what begins as one activity can reshape itself into another during the course of its unfolding. For instance, participants who were fans of Japanese popular culture maintained interest in a given media format and continually watched Japanese *anime* and TV serials or read *manga* (see also Williams, 2006). These activities, which were triggered by students' long-term interests in Japanese popular culture, could be viewed as the snowballing effect of their interests. In addition, several examples in the current study show that the shift in students' interests eventually led to other types of activities that were linked to each other.

Melissa's case exemplifies the fact that her interests in a Japanese boy band, 嵐 (*Arashi*), prompted multiple and longitudinal activities in the target language, including viewing, listening and reading skills. In the interview, Melissa reported that she first undertook viewing activities after they were introduced to her by her sister's friend. The manner in which she became a fan of the boy band through her viewing activities is described below:

> …because 嵐 ((*Arashi* – her favourite idol group)) was the first one that I listened to. I think, I was already watching *anime* and drama as well, I like drama. And I saw the drama of ごくせん ((*Gokusen* – the title of the TV serial)), and I think that it had 松本潤 ((*Matsumoto Jun* – a member of the boy band)) in it. And my friends said he is in a band and gave me some of the band's music. I think that's how I started it, and I like the music, and music is easy for me to listen to because I drive. And so, I really got into it that way. (Melissa, Interview 1)

Melissa also reported that she bought boy band CDs and DVDs in Japan during an in-country programme at a sister university. These resources were mostly related to listening and watching. However, just as French learners of English in the study by Toffoli and Sockett (2010) utilised written forms of the lyrics of English pop songs, Melissa's activities occasionally included reading activities because she checked the lyrics on the internet when she wanted to understand the content of songs.

Joshua's activities related to Japanese pop songs also demonstrate the snowballing effects of learners' interests. Joshua became interested in Japanese pop songs through playing Japanese video games which utilised them. He then started listening to pop songs and occasionally checked the lyrics on the internet in order to understand their meanings. Likewise, Patrick reported a reading activity as an example of the cascade effect. He had watched DVDs of a Japanese TV serial on *rakugo* (Japanese sit-down comedy), which his brother borrowed from his Japanese friend, and became interested in the topic. He eventually borrowed several books on *rakugo* from the university's library and read one of them during the data collection period.

All of the above examples indicate that students' new interests emerged through an engagement with existing activities and prompted relevant activities involving different material types and language skills. It is also important to state that viewing or listening activities might lead to reading activities. In the case of Melissa and Joshua, they utilised text information in order to support their listening skills. Patrick also read books in order to gain deeper knowledge about the topic. Accordingly, it can be assumed that students tended to employ textual information for the purposes of promoting their understanding about particular topics.

### Learners' interests and continuation/discontinuation of activities

In addition to the aforementioned snowballing effects, learners' interests with regard to specific topics also influenced whether students continued or discontinued an activity. Here, I will firstly present Eric's unsuccessful experience of reading *manga* and then compare it with his successful experience.

Eric purchased several *manga* books and tried to read them as spontaneous reading activities throughout his learning history. However, Eric often discontinued reading *manga*. In his first diary entry, Eric reported a concrete example of an unsuccessful experience. Although he tried to read *manga* that was based on his favourite Japanese video game, he only read several pages over two days and eventually ceased reading it. The following excerpt illustrates why he abandoned this reading:

> …there were many words I didn't understand. I translated them, and I found them, but it was just too much. Like it was, every single word I didn't understand. So, I didn't get any word, you translate one word and then next straight away, 'What? I don't know that one either'. So, just word after word after word, I didn't understand it. So, I just gave up. Difficult. (Eric, Interview 2)

In the *manga* that Eric showed me at the time of the interview, he had written down the pronunciations and meanings for almost every single *kanji* character using his electronic dictionary. However, he had stopped writing down the pronunciations and meanings only after half a page because it was 'too clunky and messy' (diary entry on 2 September 2008). Eric's comments also imply that *manga* included a large amount of unfamiliar *kanji* and vocabulary for him, thereby making it too difficult to read. From an Activity Theory perspective, the above comment indicates that there was a crucial tension between Eric's vocabulary knowledge, which included *kanji*, and the language utilised in the *manga*.

As discussed in Chapter 4, Frank and Daniel tried to overcome this type of contradiction which was evident in class-related literacy practices in order to gain good academic results. In contrast, in Eric's case, this contradiction appeared to result in the discontinuation of his spontaneous reading activity. A possible reason for the discontinuation is that reading *manga* was a voluntary task, which implies that Eric did not have to actually complete it. Indeed, a study by Yap (1998) also found that several participants simply stopped undertaking activities when they perceived the activities to be too difficult for them.

Additionally, Eric did not recognise the positive outcomes of his spontaneous activities in terms of his academic results, despite his expectations as discussed in the earlier section of this chapter (see, Influence of Japanese classes: exchange value type of motive). In the interview, Eric also claimed:

> I always kind of felt that it wasn't doing anything. I would watch *anime*, and I would read *manga*, and I do it, thinking like I have to do this to get ((my Japanese)) better. But the vocabulary like in the *anime* and that sort of stuff, to be honest, I probably wouldn't even use it in class... it will make my better Japanese, but I'm not sure how much it actually helped my Japanese. (Eric, Interview 3)

The last sentence of the above excerpt indicates that Eric believed his voluntary activities would improve his Japanese language skills, but doubted the direct effect of such activities on his marks. Eric's self-doubt about the effectiveness of literacy activities for improving his performance in class may be another reason why he quickly ceased reading *manga*. Thus, students tended not to sustain literacy activities outside of class-time if these were too difficult and if they felt that the activities did not help their language learning.

In contrast to these unsuccessful attempts, Eric completed reading a whole *manga* book when he became interested in the story. Eric compared his successful and unsuccessful reading activities:

> (E refers to Eric and M refers to the author, Miho)
>
> **E:** That was the one *manga* that I read completely because really really like, it was just good.
>
> **M:** Ah okay, using like this dictionary?
>
> **E:** Yeah yeah, one by one, every word. Most of the other *manga*, it's good, but it's not, it's not enough for me to read, because I get bored very quickly, but this one, I wanted to know what happened, yeah it was pretty good. (Eric, Interview 2)

As previous studies on extensive L2 reading (e.g. Mori, 2004; Nishino, 2007) and the study by Pickard (1995) on motivation for out-of-class language learning demonstrate, Eric's comments here indicate that being interested in the story was a crucial factor in his efforts to read it to completion. Considering the fact that he looked up many words in the dictionary, there seemed to be a discrepancy between the Japanese in the *manga* and Eric's Japanese language skills. However, once Eric became interested in the *manga* story, he read it even though he had to rely heavily on his dictionary.

In relation to the concept of motive in Activity Theory, I would like to draw on Eric's successful reading activity. Although he did not clearly describe his motive related to this particular reading activity, it can be assumed that he initially aimed to improve his Japanese because he previously said in the interview: 'If I can read *manga*, I can say to myself, "even though this is really tiring, at least maybe I'll get a distinction", because this is going directly into my marks, like this is directly useful' (Interview 3). However, Eric also became interested in the story, which could be regarded as another emerging motive essential to his reading activity. This motive of pursuing his interest in the story energised Eric to continue reading the *manga*. This was in spite of the fact that his concrete strategies for reading this text remained the same.

Gillette (1994) demonstrated that even though students relied on similar strategies, strategy outcomes differed depending on their motives for L2 learning and goals related to tasks or to a particular language course. Although Gillette's study compared effective students with ineffective students, Eric's case implies that strategy outcomes varied even when a student changed his/her motive. It is also important to note that *manga* was recommended by Eric's ex-classmate as well as a good friend, Michelle (pseudonym). In the interview, Eric described how he gained information about *manga* from Michelle and subsequently purchased the book:

> (E refers to Eric and M refers to the author, Miho)
>
> M: Where did you get this *manga*?
> E: I got it in Japan. Do you remember Michelle? She told me about it. As she said I probably like it. And I was in Japan, I was just looking through ((at a book shop)), and I thought 'Oh my God, that's the one Michelle was talking about', but I wasn't sure because it looked like for girls, I didn't know if I liked it, but I got it. It was really good, yeah. (Eric, Interview 2)

According to Eric's third interview, Michelle worked as a volunteer at the *Manga* library and became interested in Japanese popular culture. This fact may imply that Michelle had more knowledge about Japanese *manga* than Eric. In addition, over the years she became a good friend to Eric, even outside of the Japanese classes. It can reasonably be assumed that she was familiar with Eric's preferences and could suggest *manga* that suited his interests. As a member of Eric's Japanese-related community, Michelle thus played an important role in assisting his reading activity by means of providing him with suitable information. Considering the fact that this was Eric's only example of successfully reading *manga*, his classmate's appropriate suggestion was an essential factor which led to the activity's completion.

Eric's case was the only clear example in the current study to demonstrate how learners' interests might emerge during activities and influence the success or failure of these activities. However, his case underscores what autonomous language learning researchers claim (e.g. Little *et al.*, 2002; Ushioda, 2000, 2011; van Lier, 1996; Williams & Burden, 1997): stimulating language learners' interests by choosing content appropriate to each student facilitates their positive attitudes towards language learning tasks.

## Roles of the Internet in Expanding Opportunities for Non-Class-Related Literacy Practices

As mentioned previously, participants engaged in various online literacy activities. Viewing activities were particularly related to the internet. In the activity system model that Engeström (1999) advocated, the internet could be understood as a mediating artefact (tool). However, information technology's functions are broad and 'can support and penetrate activities at all levels' (Kuutti, 1996: 34). In this vein, the internet seems to fundamentally differ from other tools that support learners' literacy activities, for instance, dictionaries that only address students' insufficient vocabulary knowledge. Here, I will discuss the affordances that the internet provides and whether or not they develop the participants' non-class-related literacy practices.

### Providing resources and connecting learners' interests to resources: Reading and viewing activities

It goes without saying that advances in computer technology have enabled language learners to easily gain foreign language resources even in home country settings (Ryan, 1997). A number of previous studies already revealed that L2 learners could access various material types and information via the internet (e.g. Inozu *et al.*, 2010; Lai *et al.*, 2015; Lin & Siyanova-Chanturia, 2015; Ma, 2017; Spratt *et al.*, 2002; Sylvén & Sundqvist, 2012; Toffoli & Sockett, 2010; Yi, 2005, 2007). My participants' diary entries also confirmed what the previous studies claimed. As Tables 5.1 and 5.2 show, participants read articles on the Japanese Wikipedia site, online discussion boards, online news and various websites. With regard to viewing activities, approximately half of the participants reported that they watched *anime*, video clips of Japanese pop songs and other types of TV shows on video-sharing sites. Several other students also borrowed DVDs from friends or siblings which contained material downloaded via the internet. The internet thus provided students with a broad range of materials relevant to the target language.

More importantly, the internet allowed students to easily connect to resources relevant to their interests. For instance, Alice, Joshua and Scott utilised Google in order to search for websites based on Japanese pop songs and *anime* songs when they wanted to know the lyrics. When participants wanted to gain information about a particular topic (i.e. person, event or item), they directly searched key words in Wikipedia and read relevant articles. These examples indicate that the internet allowed students to find information on various topics or information pertaining to these interests.

This ability of the internet to connect learners to resources that reflect their interests is essential in expanding students' opportunities for spontaneous activities outside of the classroom. According to Leont'ev (1978), a need becomes a motive when it meets an object. This implies that students' needs, which are to gain information or resources to satisfy their interests, may not become a motive for an activity if they are impossible or difficult to gain. This is because the need is not objectified; that is, the need does not become a motive for an activity. It is the internet's capability to provide information so readily which encourages students to turn a generalised interest into a specific research undertaking, and this is thus an opportunity to further promote reading and viewing activities.

Furthermore, this function of the internet produced opportunities for voluntary reading activities, even when students only had vague interests but wanted to read something in the target language. For instance, during his first diary entry, Joshua searched for Japanese words on Google and read question and answer sessions that were posted on a Japanese online discussion board. Joshua stated the reason as: 'あんまり理由がないけど、何か読みたかったから ((*Anmari riyū ga nai kedo, nani ka yomitakatta kara* – I did not have any particular reason, but I wanted to read something))' (Interview 2). Chris also reported that he sometimes undertook similar types of reading activities (typed some words in Japanese on a discussion forum and read questions and answers) in order to kill time. This type of activity is possible because the internet makes resources ready at hand and might be a salient feature of digital literacies in expanding the possibilities of autonomous language learning (Benson, 2013).

Another characteristic of internet resources which was significant to the current study was the multiplicity of languages available. This finding is similar to that of previous studies (e.g. Lam, 2000, 2004, 2009a, 2009b; Yi, 2005, 2007) as well as claims made by proponents of Multiliteracies. Daniel, Melissa and Thomas reported that they watched *anime* and Japanese TV serials with English subtitles. Kate, who is a Singaporean international student, reported that she usually watched Japanese TV serials with Chinese subtitles. In addition, websites based on the *anime* songs that Alice and Scott checked included Romanised versions of lyrics (i.e. the Japanese lyrics written in Roman alphabets) and English translations. It is assumed that these multilingual resources encourage learners to undertake literacy activities. This issue will be further discussed in Chapter 6 in terms of students' strategy usage.

### Connecting learners with peers: Online written communication

Previous studies based on out-of-class L2 learning and its use in FL contexts show that L2 learners had opportunities to engage in online written communication with native speakers or users of their target languages outside of the classroom (e.g. Hyland, 2004; Kurata, 2011; Pasfield-Neofitou, 2012; Sockett & Toffoli, 2012; Yap, 1998). In my study, however, students rarely reported online communication opportunities with Japanese speakers because of infrequent communications and the use of L1. Only Joshua reported his frequent online written communications, by means of social networking sites, in particular, Facebook and Twitter. According to his diary entries, Joshua utilised these sites almost every day during the data collection period. Hence, here I will focus on Joshua's experiences in order to discuss how social networking sites possibly expand or limit opportunities for target language use.

Joshua's online written communication on social networking sites considerably differed from those of the other students, not only in terms of frequency but also the utilisation of Japanese as the language of communication. In the beginning, Joshua only communicated on Facebook with his Australian friends whom he had recently met at the university (Interview 4). However, he became friends with Japanese international students and began to utilise Facebook to communicate with them. It can be said that Joshua's Facebook activities shifted from English-dominant communication to activities undertaken in Japanese when the community's dynamics changed due to the introduction of his Japanese-speaking friends.

Another feature of Joshua's case is that he extended his social network with Japanese speakers on Facebook or Twitter. The following is an example that Joshua reported in the interview:

> There is a person in Cambodia. So, just we met on Facebook somehow, but anyway, she has been learning Japanese for long time, I think. She doesn't speak English, so it's again, at one of the situations, she doesn't speak English, we can speak Japanese. (Joshua, Interview 4)

This Japanese learner from Cambodia first added Joshua as a friend on Facebook and then sent him messages. On Facebook and Twitter, Joshua also actively searched for Japanese speakers and tried to contact them if he was interested in what they wrote on these sites. Joshua's social relationships and opportunities for written communication were developed on such social networking sites in spite of the fact that he had not been to Japan. In her often-cited studies on L2 online communication, Lam (2000, 2004) discusses the case of a Chinese immigrant adolescent in the United States who met other ESL peers with the same interests (Japanese pop culture) on the internet and developed his English language skills through communicating with them. Joshua's experience also suggests that social networking sites have the potential to enable language learners to establish a new social network with target language users and eventually produce opportunities whereby the language can be used for communicating with peers.

In contrast to Joshua's case, the majority of participants utilised English as the language of communication on Facebook with their Japanese friends, although the reasons why they did this differed depending on each participant. For instance, Alice, Brenda and Nancy claimed that it was easier to communicate this way because their Japanese friends possessed a sound command of English. Melissa remarked that her Japanese friends' desire to practise English with her was the reason that she utilised English on Facebook. These comments highlight the fact that online communication between students and their Japanese friends is of a shared and reciprocal nature, although the communication partners may possess different motives. On the one hand, learners of Japanese appear to have two different motives – learning Japanese and keeping in touch with their peers. On the other hand, their Japanese friends might aim to practise English in addition to enjoying communication with English speaker friends. In other words, there might be a conflict between their mutual motives for practising their target languages. It is highly probable that participants chose English as a communication language because they prioritised socialising with their Japanese friends over practising Japanese. In her study on communication between Japanese learners and their peers, Kurata (2011) demonstrates that various factors influence learners' language choice, such as learners' self-image of being language learners, differences evident between asynchronous and synchronous communication and the norms of the communities to which Japanese learners and their peers belonged. Thus, the linking of students with their Japanese friends, exercised mainly in English-speaking contexts, does not necessarily produce opportunities for written communication in the target language.

Unlike Joshua, moreover, the other students tended to utilise social networking sites only for the purpose of maintaining contact with their Japanese friends or classmates. For instance, Melissa reported that she often asked Japanese exchange students if they had Facebook accounts when she became acquainted with them at the university. In the interview, she claimed:

> I like to connect with my friends that I know, that I met in person. I'm a bit scared about a sort of being friends with someone I don't actually know who they are <@@>. (Melissa, Interview 2)

Several other students expressed opinions similar to Melissa's comment about making friends on social networking sites. This implies that these students regarded social networking services as possibly being unsafe spaces in which to communicate with unacquainted individuals, although meeting new people is one of the features of these services. In other words, these participants used social networking services in order to enhance their existing social networks rather than to expand them, in agreement with what Mitchell (2012) points out as being one of the roles of Facebook.

Grace also explained her view on a communication feature evident in this type of online community in relation to her non-Japanese friends whom she met during an intensive programme in Japan:

> I mean Facebook is good, it connects you to the world, and I might occasionally write a message to them... but I don't know like, I won't have been able to have conversation with them, and generally, it won't be a very significant communication relationship. (Grace, Interview 3)

Grace's comment indicates that Facebook only provided loose connections with her friends. Scott also claimed that he usually utilised online chat services, such as MSN or Skype, for personal communication with Japanese speaker friends. In contrast to Joshua, Grace and Scott rarely used personal communication on Facebook. This is what van Lier (2000, 2004) described as affordance. On the one hand, social networking services have the potential to expand opportunities for online literacy activities. On the other hand, this potential differs depending on the shared objective, the individuals' perceptions about these services and how to utilise them (Menezes, 2011).

### Participating in online communities based on interests

In addition to social networking services, Joshua also participated in other online communities. These communities included an open source software group organised by Japanese programmers as well as a project aimed at English–Japanese machine translations. In the first interview about his Japanese learning background, Joshua described himself as an IT person, and this was one of the reasons why his interest in Japan and the Japanese language study commenced. Because of his interests in computer programming and machine translation, Joshua signed up to the mailing lists of these projects and he received emails from these groups. As a mediating artefact, the internet thus linked Joshua, his interests and the relevant online communities.

Individuals in these online groups discussed issues via email. For example, emails from the open source software group were written in Japanese and the sample email that Joshua submitted to me included computer programming jargon. As Joshua already knew the technical words, he reported that: 'こういうものは、まあOKですが、なんか

programming の言葉なんですから ((*Kōyū mono wa, mā* OK *nan desu ga, nanka programming no kotoba nan desu kara* – These words are okay for me because they are words for programming))' (Interview 2). According to his diary entry, Joshua skimmed this email for a few minutes with the help of an online dictionary. Emails relating to the machine translation project were written in English. In this form, community members discussed topics related to Japanese language, such as grammar, verb conjugations and word meanings. Although these emails were not actual Japanese reading opportunities, Joshua might assume new knowledge or reflect on what he had learned about the target language by reading them.

Here, it is important to concede that Joshua only read the emails and never wrote his opinions in response to the discussions. In other words, Joshua's participation in the communities was unidirectional in that he passively participated in the communities. Pasfield-Neofitou (2012) also identified a similar case of peripheral participation in an online community, with the student highlighting his/her lack of confidence in using L2 as one of the reasons for engaging in such peripheral participation. It appears that Joshua also did not have enough confidence to write emails in Japanese. Alternatively, he might not have any particular opinions about the topics. In addition, this way of participating might be influenced by a feature of the online communities: that is, the loose connections between members via emails. In this communication, members do not necessarily express their opinions about issues and Joshua seemed to have limited opportunities to use authentic language. However, it can also be argued that this feature allowed Joshua to participate in communities even if he did not have enough confidence to write in the target language or did not have any opinions.

It is also important to note that Joshua's participation in online communities was a distinctive occurrence with regards to the current study. This type of involvement in online communities might be difficult or beyond the expectations of many participants for several reasons, for instance, low self-evaluation about his/her Japanese proficiency level and unfamiliarity with or lack of knowledge about such online communities.

## Summary and Discussion

This chapter has explored factors that trigger students' non-class-related literacy activities. The detailed analysis of participants' task-specific motives has revealed that students' positive beliefs related to authentic language usage and their interests in specific topics prompt their voluntary L2 literacy activities. In particular, the significant role that learners' interests play in expanding opportunities for out-of-class Japanese literacy activities has become apparent. A number of examples demonstrated the snowballing effects of interests which triggered different types of activities. Furthermore, Eric's example of reading *manga* comics indicates that learners' interests in topics provide a driving force in accomplishing activities, even if the learners face difficulties. These findings support claims made by scholars in the field of learner autonomy in relation to selecting materials based on learners' interests being essential to promote their motivations and autonomous language learning (e.g. Little *et al.*, 2002; Ushioda, 2000; Williams & Burden, 1997).

Regardless of these assertions, the importance of learners' interests, in particular, temporary interests in topics, has been somewhat overlooked in many empirical studies based on out-of-class L2 learning of adult learners (e.g. Freeman, 1999; Hyland, 2004; Kalaja *et al.*, 2011; Palfreyman, 2006), though the research on ESL/EFL adolescents found that they undertook online literacy activities led by their interests (e.g. Black, 2008; Chandler-Olcott & Mahar, 2003a, 2003b; Lam, 2009b). This might be because these studies tended to view out-of-class L2 use activities as language learning strategies intended to improve target language skills. However, the examples in this chapter illustrated that students' L2 literacy activities were undertaken not only for learning Japanese but also for enjoyment. It can be argued that the narrow focus on language learning aspects might exclude a crucial factor to facilitate L2 out-of-class literacy activities, that is, learners' interests.

Focusing on the students' activity systems has assisted me in exploring several major factors that contributed to formulating learners' positive beliefs and their interests in topics. With regard to learners' beliefs, Japanese classes appear to affect students' understanding of the usefulness of non-class-related literacy practices in order to improve their Japanese language skills. With regard to learners' interests, I argued that students' community members, such as classmates, friends in Japanese-related communities and siblings, played significant roles in triggering their interests in Japanese popular culture. This was achieved by providing information and resources related to the media. Although previous research on L2 learning and social networks discussed linguistic or motivational support from peers and family members (e.g. Hamada *et al.*, 2006; Palfreyman, 2006, 2011), the findings in the current study shed light on the importance of peer networks as information providers who share similar interests with learners. Similarly, with the exception of a study by Lai (2015), existing research into out-of-class language learning has not paid much attention to the influence of language classes on students' voluntary L2 studies. Yet, as Scott's case demonstrates, it is worth noting that language classes have the potential to expand L2 literacy activities by triggering students' interests in topics.

Drawing on Activity Theory standpoints, this chapter also revealed the ways in which the internet expanded L2 practice opportunities: connecting students to resources related to their interests, connecting students with peers and enabling students to participate in online communities. Firstly, the internet enabled students' interests in topics meet objects (i.e. materials related to the topics); in other words, their interests become motives to trigger activities. Furthermore, Joshua's case exemplified that the internet can allows for more instances of online written communication with Japanese speakers by facilitating students to become acquainted with other Japanese speakers and accessing online communities. The internet is thus an important mediating artefact which expands L2 literacy practice opportunities and enables students to organise their personalised language learning environments based on their interests and preferences, as Ma (2017) and Sockett and Toffoli (2012) claim.

Benson (2013) explained that providing learners with target language materials was crucial in facilitating autonomous language learning, and self-access centres have flourished based on this idea. The internet has thus made such language resources easily attainable. In this digital age, triggering learners' interests might be more essential than preparing resources to promote voluntary L2 activities outside of the classroom because, as discussed above, learners' interests played an important role in both expanding and deepening literacy activities in a target language.

In this vein, it is also important to note the influence of Japanese pop culture on students' literacy activities. For the majority of the students in the current study, their interests in Japanese pop culture became a driving motivation to commence their Japanese study in formal education settings, and this also promoted opportunities for authentic language use over the course of their Japanese learning histories. In addition to this, the popularity of viewing activities indicates that Japanese pop culture and related materials were easily accessible to students via the internet and became common literacy activities. These examples in the present study have thus proved that a number of pop culture materials are available in a language other than English, and possibly contribute to learners' continuous engagements in this type of activity in the target language.

# 6 Language-Related Mediation in L2 Literacy Practices

Chapter 4 focused on students' class-related literacy practices in out-of-class contexts, while Chapter 5 examined their non-class-related literacy practices and demonstrated how their interest in particular topics – which were often influenced by members of their social networks – triggered various reading and viewing activities. The analysis in Chapter 5 also suggested that the internet has the potential to expand the opportunities for activities involving written language. In order to address the third research question of how the participants undertake their literacy activities outside of the classroom and what tools they use to support these activities, this chapter will focus on individual learners' techniques and, in particular, the manner in which students compensated for gaps in their language competence.

In order to accomplish the objects for each literacy activity, language learners employed various tools and signs, such as computers and their first or second language (L1 or L2). They also received support from their classmates, Japanese friends or teachers. In other words, participants' literacy activities are mediated by physical as well as symbolic tools and through means of social interaction. As learners of Japanese, the participants' language skills are not advanced enough for them to be able to undertake the range of activities that they need or wish to undertake in the target language. Accordingly, students have to compensate for this strategically by utilising other mediational means or alternatively by gaining assistance from community members.

This chapter will examine students' mediation for different activity types (reading, writing and viewing) in class-related and non-class-related literacy practices separately. Although Chapters 3 and 5 revealed that the distinction between the two types of literacy practices was not always clear-cut, different characteristics are evident between these practices. It is presumed that such differences influence how students read, write and watch in the target language. For each literacy activity type, I will examine how students selected and utilised tools as well as peer assistance which was available to them in their activity systems. I also identify problems that students experienced while engaging in their literacy activities.

## Mediation in Class-Related Literacy Practices

Drawing upon the concept of activity, I would like to suggest a number of factors in the students' activity system that affect their approaches towards literacy activities related to their Japanese classes: namely, objects (motives), community norms and rules, and the relationship between classmates. As discussed in Chapter 4, learners' concerns regarding academic results often became dominant motives for assessment tasks or learning Japanese at university. Hence, students often directed their efforts towards undertaking these tasks rather than engaging in non-class-related literacy practices. Furthermore, as mentioned in Chapter 4, a characteristic of this type of literacy practice is teachers' regulation over the tasks, which could be understood as being related to rules/norms and the division of labour. In other words, these factors evident in students' activity systems shaped the ways in which they read and wrote when preparing for classes and assessment tasks. Because of these factors, students utilised various mediational means, which will be discussed below.

## Reading activities

As discussed in Chapter 3, students' class-related literacy practices included various reading activities, such as reading textbooks to prepare for classes, quizzes and examinations, and reading paper-based or online materials to undertake research for essays, oral presentations and oral tests. The mediation for these reading activities was characterised by students' multiple use of dictionaries and utilisation of search engines, Google and Wikipedia.

### Multiple use of dictionaries

Participants' comments indicated that dictionaries were their first choice, and often their only tool, when they faced linguistic problems in their reading. As Table 6.1 shows, the most significant feature of students' dictionary use is that all participants, except Eric, utilised multiple dictionaries for class-related reading activities, in particular, handheld electronic dictionaries (hereafter, electronic dictionaries) developed for native speakers of Japanese and web-based online dictionaries (hereafter, online dictionaries) intended for either learners of Japanese or Japanese learners of English.

However, this data was collected in 2008 and 2009, and the most recent research shows that there has been a rapid change in learners' dictionary choice, with a shift from electronic dictionaries to dictionary applications on mobile phones and computers triggered by the growing prevalence of smartphones around 2010 (Suzuki, 2016). Indeed, as a teacher of Japanese, I have observed that my students have relied heavily on dictionary applications and Google Translate (which can be accessed through mobile phones) during classes since the early 2010s.

**Table 6.1** Students' dictionary use patterns for class-related reading practices

| Students | Japanese course | Paper dictionary (for learners) | | Electronic dictionary (for Japanese native speakers) | | Online dictionary (for learners or native speakers) | |
|---|---|---|---|---|---|---|---|
| | | B | M | B | M | B | M |
| Brenda | Level 7 | | | √ | | | |
| Grace | Level 7 | | | √ | | √√ | |
| Kate | Level 7 | | | √ | | √ | |
| Nancy | Level 7 | √ | | | | √ | |
| Melissa | Level 7 | | | √ | | √√ | |
| Joshua | Level 8 | | | √ | | √ | |
| Scott | Level 8 and 9 | | | √ | | √ | |
| Frank | Level 9 | | | √ | | √√ | |
| Alice | Level 10 | | | √ | | √ | |
| Eric | Level 10 | | | √ | | | |
| Lisa | Level 10 | | | √ | | √ | |
| Daniel | Level 11 | √ | | | | √ | |
| Thomas | Level 11 | | | √ | | √√ | |
| Patrick | Level 11 | | | √ | √ | | |
| Chris | Level 12 | | | √ | √ | | |

*Note*: √ = number of dictionaries that the students utilised; √√ = students utilised two different dictionaries; B = bilingual dictionaries; M = monolingual dictionaries.

The participants' use of multiple dictionaries was affected by a number of factors. Firstly, the advantages and limitations of each dictionary type in terms of *kanji* word search methods were closely connected with students' use of two forms of digital dictionaries. Electronic dictionaries with a stylus pen and online dictionaries offer learners simple *kanji* word search techniques. Figure 6.1 shows an example of an electronic dictionary that allows learners to write a *kanji* character on screen with a stylus pen and search *kanji* compounds in Japanese–English or Japanese monolingual dictionaries. Seven out of 15 students utilised this type of dictionary and all of them positively evaluated the dictionary because of the ease of looking up *kanji* compounds.

An online dictionary provides students with a similar technique, utilising the handwriting function provided by the input method editor (IME) pad for Windows. As Figure 6.2 shows, users can write a *kanji* character by using a mouse to choose a target *kanji* character from a list of alternatives provided on the screen. A number of dictionary applications on smartphones and tablets also allow learners to use the same word search technique by using their finger to write *kanji* characters on the screen. This handwriting function in digital dictionaries significantly reduces the burden of searching for *kanji* compounds when reading both digitised and hard copy materials (Yamane, 2007).

**Figure 6.1** Melissa's electronic dictionary with a stylus (used with permission from Sharp Cooperation)

In addition to handwriting functions, online dictionaries have another advantage in that they allow learners to cut and paste words and expressions when reading digitised texts (Pasfield-Neofitou, 2009). Furthermore, Frank and Thomas read websites by utilising *Rikaichan* (a web browser plug-in on Firefox), which automatically glosses individual words or *kanji* characters evident on websites.

However, the effectiveness of these word search techniques varies depending on the material type in question, as shown in Table 6.2. Due to the features of each dictionary type, students needed to use multiple dictionaries. For instance, Scott, who did not possess an electronic dictionary with a stylus, reported that he often needed to consult an online dictionary with the assistance of the IME pad handwriting function in order to read hard copy materials, such as textbooks and handouts.

In addition, students often found that their electronic dictionaries did not cover particular words, and this compelled them to consult online

**Figure 6.2** IME pad for Windows 10 (used with permission from Microsoft) and an online dictionary (Jim Breen's WWWJDIC http://nihongo.monash.edu/cgi-bin/wwwjdic?1C – used with permission from Mr Breen)

**Table 6.2** Available word search techniques and material types

| Dictionary resources | Word search methods | Hard copy | Digitised |
|---|---|---|---|
| Electronic | With a stylus (handwriting) | √ | √ |
|  | Without a stylus | ? | ? |
| Dictionary apps on mobile phones and tablets | With a handwriting function | √ | √ |
|  | Without a handwriting function | ? | ? |
| Online | With IME pad (handwriting) | √ | √ |
|  | Copy and paste | X | √ |

dictionaries. In relation to this point, Pasfield-Neofitou (2009) postulates that online dictionaries tend to cover newer lexica and phrases than offline tools because online resources are regularly updated and are not restricted in terms of capacity to store data.

Secondly, learners' Japanese proficiency level prompted their use of online dictionaries after an initial search in electronic dictionaries. Kate, Lisa and Scott reported that online bilingual resources developed for learners of Japanese were superior to the bilingual dictionaries for Japanese learners of English in terms of the explanation of word definitions. For example, in preparation for a vocabulary quiz, Kate first utilised her electronic dictionary to search for unknown words, and then consulted an online dictionary for learners of Japanese to identify the most appropriate translation words. She explained the reason as follows:

> I think it ((an online dictionary))'s better than ((electronic dictionaries)), coz they have explanations in English. Most of the electronic dictionaries are all Japanese, but this one has like in English and you have like example sentences in English ((English translations for Japanese example sentences)). (Kate, Interview 2)

In the same interview, Kate also explained that online dictionaries for learners of Japanese include grammatical information in English about target words, such as verb conjugations and adjective types. Given that Kate was enrolled in Level 7, which is equivalent to intermediate level, these advantages of learners' dictionaries were beneficial for her to read Japanese texts. It is also worth noting that Patrick and Chris, who had long-term stays in Japan, only utilised electronic dictionaries developed for native speakers of Japanese. Although they consulted both Japanese–English and English–Japanese dictionaries, their high level of Japanese literacy skills enabled them to utilise dictionaries for native speakers.

Finally, students' insufficient knowledge about the useful functions of online dictionaries affected their use of different dictionaries. Several students were not familiar with the handwriting function of the IME pad, though this function was particularly beneficial for those with desktop and laptop computers who needed to read paper-based materials. In the interview, for instance, Daniel asserted that online dictionaries were only useful for digitised texts. His comment implies that he did not recognise the handwriting function of the IME pad. In fact, Daniel recounted his reliance on his paper dictionary rather than online dictionaries for class-related reading activities because these reading materials were usually hard copy documents.

In relation to students' insufficient knowledge of dictionary functions, Grace's usage of multiple online dictionaries is an interesting example. Grace utilised an online dictionary for Japanese learners of English, *Eijiro* (http://eow.alc.co.jp), because it contained more expressions with English translations, which were useful for her to identify the most appropriate meaning from alternative translation words. However, the online dictionary did not automatically display pronunciations of *kanji*. She did not know that she could change the settings, and eventually employed another online dictionary for the sole purpose of checking the pronunciations of *kanji*. On the one hand, Grace's report could be interpreted as a creative use of multiple dictionaries. On the other hand, this example illustrates that students did not necessarily recognise the effective functions offered by various dictionaries.

From the viewpoint of Activity Theory, it can be claimed that a larger societal factor, the advancement in digital dictionary functions, considerably reduces the burden of searching for unfamiliar *kanji*, and therefore mediates students' reading activities more effectively than traditional paper dictionaries. In addition, the availability of various dictionaries provides students with choices to facilitate their reading activities. It is also useful to recall that the participants commented on their dictionary usage for class-related reading activities. As discussed in Chapter 4, students' concerns about academic results were a crucial motive for class-related tasks. This motive might encourage students to understand reading materials more fully because their vocabulary knowledge was assessed in various ways, such as through quizzes and examinations. Also, it is reasonable to assume that students were conscious of learning Japanese for class-related literacy practices because of their motives to acquire language skills. These may be supplementary reasons why the majority of students made a lot of effort to look up unfamiliar words by employing multiple dictionaries. However, as previous studies on dictionary use by language learners have established (e.g. Boonmoh, 2012; Loucky, 2010; Pasfield-Neofitou, 2009; Yamane, 2007), the examples of Daniel and Grace show that students did not fully understand the useful functions of such tools. In other words, providing information about electronic and online dictionaries in classes did not necessarily result in students utilising these tools effectively and efficiently. For instance, Grace believed that the online dictionary (*Eijiro*) was appropriate for her because her teacher recommended it to the class. However, given her method of utilising it, it seems that she needed the support of teachers, that is, more detailed instructions on or training in how to use its available functions.

### Google and Wikipedia as reading aids

As mentioned in Chapter 3, students in the current study also utilised Google and Wikipedia to search for unfamiliar words and expressions. The usage of Google and Wikipedia as dictionaries or corpora is slightly different from their original functions as a search engine and online encyclopaedia, respectively. This is what Wertsch (1998: 59) described as the 'spin-off' function of tools, which can be understood as a consequence of reshaping existing artefacts to meet an individual's needs. Scott reported that he utilised Wikipedia when preparing for class as follows:

> Translating a textbook passage (page 139, lines 20–36) in preparation for a seminar. I understood nearly everything (with the aid of a vocab list), which is perhaps unusual! … I looked at Wikipedia (in Japanese and English) for a list of the 'Tokyo Big 6 Universities' (http://ja.wikipedia.org/wiki/東京六大学). (Scott's diary entry on 3 September 2008)

Scott could not find a particular term in his language dictionary, and therefore searched for it on Wikipedia. In the interview based on this diary entry, Scott explained that he checked the entry in the Japanese version of Wikipedia after reading the English version because this version only included a small amount of information on that topic.

Frank also reported that he often utilised Google and Wikipedia to search for proper nouns, compound words and set phrases. The following excerpt illustrates an example of how Frank checked a phrase utilising Google:

> Homework – reading comprehension. Used an internet dictionary/IME pad for reading comprehension. Used Google to look up some expressions that were not in the dictionary, such as 敷居が低い ((*shikii ga hikui* - literally means that threshold is low, and in turn, implies having mass appeal )), and found a blog post about the term, although it didn't really help too much. (Frank's diary entry on 21 March 2009)

The reason why the blog post, which Frank found online, was not useful for his comprehension of the expression was because it only mentioned whether this expression (*shikii ga hikui*) was commonly used or not. As the excerpt above indicates, Google only enables language learners to access websites that contain unfamiliar words and expressions. In doing so, however, Google allows learners to access authentic language resources on the world wide web, and to guess the meanings of target words and phrases based on concrete examples and the context provided there. Frank also reported that he sometimes even utilised Google images in order to understand particular words because 'if I see a lot of pictures of that, I don't realise, but guess what must be right' (Interview 1). Unfortunately, Frank did not report any concrete example of this usage of Google in his diary entries. Nevertheless, it can be reasonably assumed that visual images provide students with hints on proper nouns (e.g. famous people, food and places) or cultural information, such as festivals and Japanese popular culture.

When considering students' use of Google and Wikipedia as reading aids, it is also useful to recall that the students were enrolled in intermediate and advanced level classes and needed to read various authentic Japanese texts, such as articles from Japanese newspapers, books and websites, as well as the course materials assigned for their assessment tasks. In particular, Levels 9–12 were content-based courses focusing on specific topics (shown in Table 3.1). Taking these circumstances into account, it is highly probable that students often encountered unfamiliar words and phrases that are not covered by language dictionaries. In addition, I speculate that this spin-off use of Google and Wikipedia has been significantly affected by out-of-class contexts, where it is often difficult to gain assistance from teachers and other classmates.

As a final comment, many of the articles on Wikipedia are available in both English and Japanese. In other words, it can be claimed that their L1 support on the internet might also be a crucial factor affecting why students utilise Google and Wikipedia to support their reading activities.

## Writing activities

All participants reported various writing activities associated with their Japanese classes, including writing to memorise vocabulary and example sentences, undertaking written homework (e.g. filling in worksheets) and writing essays. In addition, as pointed out in Chapter 3, oral assessment tasks also included writing, such as drafting scripts for their oral presentation and for the oral test, as well as preparing PowerPoint slides. In this section, I will examine how students employed tools and peer assistance when undertaking these writing activities for homework and assessment task purposes.

### Dictionary choice and example sentences

Similar to their dictionary selection for reading activities, the majority of the participants relied heavily on digital dictionaries when engaging in writing. Although 8 of the 15 students employed both electronic and online dictionaries, six students utilised electronic or online dictionaries alone. Only Brenda utilised a paper dictionary alongside an electronic dictionary for her writing activities. Although no quantitative difference was apparent in students' selection of electronic and online dictionaries, during the interviews, a number of students offered more positive comments about online dictionaries because of the ample example sentences available compared to dictionaries accessible via other media forms (see Pasfield-Neofitou, 2009).

Scott utilised Jim Breen's WWWJDIC (http://nihongo.monash.edu/cgi-bin/wwwjdic?1C), a dictionary for learners of Japanese, because it contains numerous example sentences for each lexicon entry. According to Scott, several example sentences were useful for him to compare alternatives and choose the most suitable words and expressions. Grace also mentioned that 'it's got a lot more examples' (Interview 2) than her electronic dictionary as the reason for utilising *Eijiro*, which is the online dictionary for Japanese learners of English. As is the case with reading activities, examples are important for writing activities because students need to choose appropriate Japanese words and expressions from a range of alternatives which these dictionaries suggest in order to express their opinions in essays or oral presentation tasks.

In addition, Lisa emphasised this advantage of online dictionaries in terms of checking grammatical items. Because of the ample example sentences provided by *Eijiro*, she utilised it not only to identify appropriate Japanese lexicon, but also to check grammatical points:

> So, when I looked it up, where they were used, and had copied the sentences, especially with the particles, because I'm not very good ((at particles)). (Lisa, Interview 2)

Particles in Japanese have a similar function to prepositions in English. As Lisa commented on in the above excerpt, it is often difficult for learners to choose an appropriate particle. In order to complete her sentence in a translation task for Level 10, Lisa checked which particle should be used before a particular word, 開発した (*kaihatsu shita* – the past form of the verb 'develop'). Although translation tasks may not be typical writing activities, this purpose of consulting dictionaries is crucial to writing activities for assessment tasks that demand grammatical accuracy. However, as has been noted above, *Eijiro* can be disadvantageous in the sense that this dictionary does not automatically display the pronunciations of *kanji*, and therefore students are required to utilise other online dictionaries for learners of Japanese. Regardless of these extra processes, Grace and Lisa relied heavily on this dictionary because it provides a number of examples from various authentic texts. Interestingly, Brenda's reason for consulting her paper dictionary was also related to issues of example sentences. Generally speaking, paper dictionaries only contain a few example sentences for each word. However, Brenda claimed that these example sentences are easier to understand than those available in her electronic dictionaries because her paper dictionary targets learners of Japanese and thus provides simple example sentences.

In relation to the students' concerns about example sentences in dictionaries, it is necessary to consider several crucial differences in the roles that dictionaries play in reading and writing activities. With regard to reading activities, students consulted Japanese–English or Japanese–Japanese dictionaries to gain information about the pronunciation of *kanji* compounds and to understand the meanings of target words or expressions. In other words, they used these dictionaries to deal with lexical problems rather than with syntax. This might be a crucial reason why students chose digital dictionaries, which offer simple word search methods. In contrast, for writing activities, students usually relied on English–Japanese dictionaries when attempting not only to identify appropriate Japanese words and phrases, but also for the purposes of solving grammatical problems in order to produce accurate sentences. Accordingly, students positively evaluated online dictionaries that provided ample example sentences. Such differences in preferences in dictionary choices indicate that students selected different tools for different types of activities. Situational factors, for example, being in front of a computer or engaging in a writing task in the class, might be one factor in students' dictionary choice, though no participants in this study reported such an influence.

As might be expected, the advanced students appeared to rely less on dictionaries compared to other students. In an interview on how he wrote an essay for Level 11, Thomas reported that 'I think I only used it ((his electronic dictionary)) for one or two words' (Interview 3). Chris and Patrick also reported that they only utilised their electronic dictionaries for their writing activities. It is thus reasonable to assume that their advanced Japanese language skills were sufficient for them to undertake writing activities with less reliance on other tools than lower level students.

### Google as a writing aid

Similar to the findings in the recent qualitative research on English as a second language (ESL) postgraduate student' essay writing (Park & De Costa, 2015) and writing strategies of advanced learners of Korean (Kang & Pyun, 2013), 3 out of the 15 students in the current study (Alice, Frank and Scott) utilised Google for their writing tasks. The use of Google as a writing aid is another example of the spin-off function of mediational means (Wertsch, 1998: 59), as examined previously for reading activities. Scott explained how he and his classmate utilised Google when they prepared a script for their oral test in Level 8:

> Also, we used Google… if we want to check whether a sentence sounds natural, then we search for it in Google and see if other Japanese people frequently use the same things. (Scott, Interview 3)

Frank also reported a similar example of using Google for writing answers in his reading comprehension homework:

> Sometimes, I would just put my answer into Google to see if it made sense (i.e. if there were lots of hits, then I assumed it must). (Frank's diary entry on 21 March 2009)

This use of Google search is similar to that of a corpus in that it allows students to check the appropriateness of phrases that they produced. Sha (2010) asserts that used as a corpus, Google can support students' L2 writing skills by evaluating the quantity of the language utilised in conjunction with an analysis of the context within the language. My study also observed that Scott and Frank applied these Google search features in order to increase the accuracy and appropriateness of grammar and phrases in their written texts. Furthermore, as Robb (2003) has claimed, free access and the sheer extent of its database, which includes colloquial language not usually included in existing corpora, are just two of Google's many advantages. Considering that free online Japanese corpora are rarely available, Google may be the only tool accessible by students.

More importantly, the comments above by Scott and Frank illustrate that Google appears to support students' self-revision as opposed to merely supporting their composition of texts. This point becomes more salient after comparing Google to the function of dictionaries. Language dictionaries provide users with lexical information about each entry, such as definitions of words, common idioms, example sentences and grammatical information (e.g. part of speech, verb conjugations). This information is useful to students when choosing appropriate words and composing sentences. However, as a Japanese language teacher, I often observe that the phrases and sentences that students produce sound unnatural, even though these texts are grammatically and semantically correct. As it is difficult for students to recognise appropriateness in terms of collocations and lexicogrammar (Halliday, 1994), the lack of naturalness of the texts that these language learners produce can be expected. Language dictionaries can rarely support these aspects of L2 writing. In contrast, as Frank claimed in the above excerpt, Google can support students in checking the appropriateness of their texts by providing a quantitative parameter (Sha, 2010). In cases where students cannot find any relevant examples that use the exact same expressions, as indicated in Scott's comment, they can revise their expressions based on similar examples which a Google search provides. It can be argued that Google complements the shortcomings of dictionaries, thereby also supporting students' self-editing processes.

From an Activity Theory perspective, this spin-off use of Google as a writing aid can be understood as the interaction of components in the students' activity systems. Since these writing activities were undertaken for assessment of their Japanese courses, students needed to improve their writing in terms of linguistic accuracy and appropriateness (e.g. grammar and appropriate word choices) in order to achieve their objectives. In fact, as mentioned in Chapter 4, Scott and Frank were conscious about gaining good marks and tended to prioritise class-related literacy practices. Moreover, given that both remarked upon their interests in Japanese as a language (see Chapter 4), it is highly probable that Scott and Frank hoped to enhance their Japanese language skills and thus devoted their attention to the grammatical accuracy and naturalness of their texts. The similar motives of Scott and Frank, the rules as well as norms related to the assessment tasks and the contextual feature as out-of-classroom activities (e.g. no help from teachers) may thus affect their creative use of Google as a tool to support their writing activities.

However, Alice, another student who utilised Google as a writing aid, claims that Google was not always useful for revising her translation tasks for Level 10. Elaborating on this point, Alice explained that the appropriateness of grammar varies depending on the context, namely, the appropriateness of texts from the perspective of lexicogrammar (Halliday, 1994). In a study on ESL students' corpus use for writing activities, Yoon (2008) found that a participant experienced difficulties in using corpora because of her English language skills and lack of training in using the technology. Although it is difficult to identify Alice's exact problem with using Google from the limited data provided, it can be assumed that she also experienced similar problems to the participant in Yoon's study. In addition, despite Google's potential as a writing aid, only three students in this study utilised this tool for their writing activities. This fact implies the necessity of the assistance of teachers or peers to recognise and learn the application of tools.

*L2 materials as language resources*

As touched upon in Chapter 3, writing activities undertaken for assessment tasks (i.e. writing essay drafts and scripts for oral presentations and speaking tests) were inextricably linked to reading activities. Previous studies on L2 writing also revealed that ESL/English as a foreign language (EFL) learners utilised literary books and journal articles as models for their writing (e.g. Lei, 2008; Yang *et al.*, 2004). Participants in this study also reported that they utilised written Japanese materials for assessment tasks, such as essays, oral presentations and oral examinations. These materials were not only drawn upon as information sources but also as helpful linguistic resources which could mediate their writing activities. Brenda, Kate and Scott actively utilised Japanese websites and articles on the Japanese version of Wikipedia for their assessment tasks. For instance, Brenda claims that 'the grammar and things ((in the

Japanese website)) helped me a lot' (Interview 2) when she prepared the script for her oral test.

Kate also referred to the usefulness of L2 materials in that she could directly utilise vocabulary and phrases from textual materials, such as essay drafts and scripts for oral tests. In an interview on preparing a script for her oral examination, Kate explained why she and her classmate read an article on the Japanese version of Wikipedia rather than the English version:

> So, it's easier than to check it in English and then translate coz... if it's about environment, all the vocabulary, it's very scientific, so it's very difficult for us to find one by one, so we just used this. (Kate, Interview 2)

Kate was an international student who could understand Chinese. We can assume that her knowledge of Chinese characters was advantageous in helping her utilise Japanese resources, though she reported in the interview that she still needed to look up pronunciations in her electronic dictionary as preparation for the oral examination.

As Grabe (2001: 29) asserts, it is generally acknowledged that insufficient L2 linguistic resources complicate L2 writing, particularly with regard to the expression of 'complex ideas with careful nuance'. The comments by Brenda and Kate above support Grabe's claim and demonstrate that Japanese materials help students employ contextually appropriate lexica and phrases in their writing. As indicated previously, linguistic accuracy and appropriateness are usually important assessment task criteria. It is likely that such emphasis on the linguistic accuracy and appropriateness required by assessment tasks presented an extra incentive for students to use Japanese source materials, even though these took more time to read. It is also assumed that the students chose Japanese materials in order to improve their language skills, although none of the students clearly reported this during the interviews.

At the same time, however, I acknowledge that such textual borrowing techniques, which are easily employed by utilising electronic source texts and copy and paste functions provided by computer technology, increase the risk of plagiarism (Barks & Watts, 2001; Bloch, 2001; Hirvela, 2005). This indicates that a conflict may exist between rules/norms and tool dimensions. Even though the textual borrowing technique is an effective and appropriate tool in terms of linguistic production and developing learners' L2 skills, it can nevertheless cause problems when it clashes with academic notions of originality, which is a reason why plagiarism is strictly forbidden in the rules of the assessment tasks.

Regardless of the usefulness of authentic materials to improve grammatical accuracy and find appropriate phrases and vocabulary, not all the participants utilised L2 written materials to gather information for their assessment tasks. There are several reasons why students read L1 resources and these emerged during the interviews. For instance, Daniel only read English resources for his oral presentation because 'that's the way that I can get as much information as possible in a short amount of time' (Interview 3). As explained in Chapter 4, Daniel recognised his low Japanese reading proficiency as a student in Level 11 and decided to read articles in his L1, English. Furthermore, although Scott preferred to utilise Japanese sources, he could not find Japanese websites related to the topic of his oral presentation, so due to time limitations, he utilised English resources. The students thus decided to employ L1 or L2 resources in relation to other individual and contextual factors, such as their L2 language skills, time limitations and the actual availability of the learning resources. Interestingly, both students who used English resources sought assistance from other students or Japanese friends in order to solve linguistic problems when composing work in their L2.

### Assistance from other students and native speakers

In addition to the tool mediations discussed above, Daniel, Nancy and Scott reported that they employed social mediation, which refers to support from their classmates or Japanese native speakers. Among these students, only Daniel relied heavily on assistance from his classmates and friends from other subjects when undertaking his assessment tasks, as discussed in Chapter 4. One possible interpretation of this result relates to students' concerns about the rules of the assessment tasks, which restrict help from Japanese native speakers, in order to assess each student's individual language skills. Because of this rule, students appeared not to seek assistance frequently, nor did they report this type of mediated action in the interviews. In addition, infrequent communication with Japanese native speakers, which was discussed in Chapter 5, may be another reason why there was little reliance on native speaker assistance.

More importantly, there was a notable difference between Nancy, Scott and Daniel in terms of the ways in which they obtained support with their assessment tasks from other people. On the one hand, Nancy and Scott only asked their Japanese friends to check their drafts, and asked questions about particular words and phrases. In other words, they relied on peer assistance in the revision process. On the other hand, Daniel asked his classmate and friends from other subjects to help him compose Japanese texts. As explained in Chapter 4, for instance, Thomas assisted Daniel in translating the script of his oral presentation. In the interview on preparing the oral presentation, Daniel described how Thomas assisted him in composing his presentation script:

> We had two computers, and I had one computer and typed the script, and how I would say it in English, and I emailed to him ((Thomas)) and then he would work on the translation. (Daniel, Interview 2)

The reason that Daniel depended almost entirely on Thomas' assistance in the production process can be explained in relation to other factors present in his activity system. Firstly, Daniel recognised the extent of his poor reading skills and therefore only read English resources in order to gather information for his oral presentation. However, as explored in the previous section, utilising English resources possibly triggered additional problems in terms of achieving linguistic accuracy, including the appropriateness of word selections. Daniel also admitted the extent of the deficiency of his Japanese formal speech style which was an important criterion of the oral presentation. Judging from his comments, he seemed to perceive that a crucial tension existed between his Japanese language skills and the task demands. In addition, Daniel only relied on his Japanese learners' paper dictionary and a relatively simple online dictionary. It is highly probable that Daniel could not utilise dictionaries effectively in order to fill the gap mentioned above. He thus had to rely on Thomas' assistance in executing the task and achieving his object (i.e. gaining a good mark, as mentioned in Chapter 4), despite the risk of violating the assessment rules.

In relation to agency in Activity Theory, Lantolf and Thorne (2006: 238) claim that the variability of possible mediated actions employed by subjects can be defined as 'constraints and affordances' in activity systems. In Daniel's case, his relatively poor Japanese language skills, his lack of ability to utilise dictionaries and the assessment criteria could be understood as constraints for selecting mediational means. In contrast, assistance from classmates and Japanese speaker friends might be interpreted as an affordance. In his diary entry concerning the preparation of the oral presentation, Daniel explained how Thomas' assistance was beneficial:

> It's amazing the amount of formal Japanese that Thomas knows and it was a bonus to have him beside me to study and prepare for the presentation. (Daniel's diary entry on 17 April 2009)

As this excerpt illustrates, Thomas was a capable peer who was well versed in formal Japanese which was an important aspect of the assessment. In addition, the relationship of Daniel and Thomas as classmates, as well as being close friends outside of the classroom, enabled the former to ask the latter for support. It can be argued that Daniel strategically employed this peer assistance under the constraints and affordances of social and contextual factors.

Participants as agents (subjects) of activities thus employed various mediational means in order to achieve their objects, such as preparing good work for assessments and developing their Japanese language skills, as discussed in Chapter 4. I also suggest that rules and norms related to the mediational means (e.g. restriction of native speaker's help in checking work) appeared to affect the ways in which students utilised available mediating artefacts and resources. Furthermore, it is important to acknowledge that the advanced students (Chris, Patrick and Thomas) rarely reported creatively using the physical tools and L2 resources such as those discussed above. They also used their dictionaries less often than other participants. It is reasonable to assume that their Japanese language skills were sufficiently internalised in order to complete assessment tasks without the need for such tools.

## Mediation in Non-Class-Related Literacy Practices

In contrast to class-related literacy practices, the teachers' control did not exist outside of the classroom, nor did the pressure or time constraints of assessments apply to non-class-related literacy practices. In addition, as discussed in Chapter 5, although students often expected to learn Japanese by means of their voluntary literacy activities, they had other motives, such as enjoying content, fulfilling their interests in certain topics and maintaining friendships with Japanese-speaking friends. These features of non-class-related literacy practices affected the ways in which students undertook each literacy activity and the mediational means they utilised. In the following sections, I will examine how students selected and employed various tools and resources in relation to other factors within their activity systems.

## Reading activities

As presented in Chapter 5, 11 out of 15 students undertook at least one paper-based or online reading activity during the data collection period. Among these activities, I presented examples of 4 students (Chris, Eric, Joshua and Patrick) who reported the details of their reading activities in their diary entries and interviews. Here, I will focus on students' dictionary use, which was often their only mediating artefact.

Before presenting a detailed analysis, it can be stated that the advantages of digital dictionaries discussed in relation to class-related tasks are common to all types of reading activities, and therefore, these 4 students employed electronic dictionaries or online dictionaries. However, one striking difference between their dictionary use in reference to class-related and non-class-related reading activities was the degree of their reliance on dictionaries. This appeared to be affected by their goals, the difficulty of materials and their Japanese language skills. I will particularly examine the dictionary use of these 4 students in relation to these factors.

### Dictionary use and objects/motives of the activity

Chris, Joshua and Patrick, who regularly undertook spontaneous reading activities, rarely utilised a dictionary during their reading activities. An obvious factor affecting students' non-use or limited use of dictionaries is a high reading proficiency in the target language, as mentioned in the previous chapters. Although Joshua was enrolled in intermediate level, his voluntary engagement in a variety of literacy activities indicates a good level of reading skill. In the interviews, Chris mentioned that he guessed the meanings of new expressions and set phrases in the novel he was reading based on the lexicon that he had learned in his previous Japanese classes. Patrick, who studied law at a Japanese university, read websites about a Japanese court case without a dictionary. Even though there were many legal terms, Patrick did not experience any difficulties because 'I've seen these before, they come up in family law' (Interview 2). These comments indicate that the advanced reading skill level of Chris, Joshua and Patrick was sufficient to enable them to read authentic texts without dictionaries.

Furthermore, the students' interview data suggests that their objectives for reading also influence their dictionary use. With regard to his reading of a Japanese novel, Chris explained why he rarely searched for unfamiliar words in a dictionary:

> If I don't understand one word or something like, ((it)) doesn't matter as far as I understand... as far as I understand, what I mean, the whole thing. (Chris, Interview 2)

This excerpt indicates that Chris did not consider looking up unfamiliar words and expressions in dictionaries necessary, as long as he could achieve his goal, that is, to understand the gist of the story. This supports previous studies which were seen in the findings of experimental settings, namely, that advanced students did not tend to rely on dictionaries or annotation for understanding the main idea of a text (e.g. Hulstijn, 1993; Hulstijn et al., 1996; Knight, 1994; Yamane, 2007).

I suggest, in addition, that Chris' goal was inextricably related to a feature of non-class-related reading activities, which crucially differs from class-related tasks in terms of the presence or absence of teacher assessment. In her study of a complex assessment and pedagogic task, Spence-Brown (2007) identifies the relationship between language learners' task engagements and their motives, and claims that students' concerns about assessments often dominated how they framed their task engagements. As discussed in Chapter 4, the majority of the students in the current study explained their concerns about receiving good marks. This implies that at least part of their motive in trying to understand the content of what they read comprehensively, and their consequent dictionary use, was to perform well in assessments, as well as to increase their knowledge for their own purposes. Although Chris did not clearly state his concerns about academic results, he utilised his electronic dictionary to help him understand reading resources for his essay task. In contrast, in the case of reading activities that were not related to Japanese classes, there was no pressure to perform well or to learn the target language. Given such a difference between assessment tasks and non-class-related literacy practices, it can be assumed that Chris was rather focused on entertainment or fulfilling his interests. Therefore, understanding the content was sufficient to achieving this goal, and dictionary use might have interfered with that purpose.

Despite his non-use of dictionaries, however, it is interesting to note that Chris wrote down unfamiliar words from the book in his diary entries and asked me to explain these words at the interviews. In particular, during his second diary entry, Chris mainly picked up onomatopoeia used in the novel but never searched for them in a dictionary 'because too lazy' (Chris's diary entry on 3 February 2009). His comment implies that he hoped to read the story without the distraction of consulting a dictionary. Moreover, in the interview on his diary entries, Chris described his reason for writing down these words:

> Like these words, I don't fully understand what they mean, but I think particular I like… these sorts of vocab which we never use, we don't have like any sort of common in English, I want to learn them. (Chris, Interview 3)

This statement illustrates that Chris' desire to learn new vocabulary also influenced his engagement with his reading materials. As discussed in Chapter 5, Chris highlighted his beliefs about the benefits of self-directed language use for improving his Japanese competence and appeared to have the motive of learning Japanese for his reading activities. Although he did not actively look up new words, he noticed them and at least sometimes wrote them down. In addition, Chris' example exhibits what Schmidt (1990: 132) calls *noticing*. Schmidt (1990) asserts that noticing is an essential factor in acquiring new knowledge based on input. The above excerpt and Chris' diary entries clearly indicate that noticing occurred during his reading activity regardless of his lack of dictionary use, and this might ultimately prompt his further acquisition of new vocabulary.

### Dictionary use and the difficulty of reading materials

As discussed above, students who regularly undertook reading activities (Chris, Joshua and Patrick) rarely used dictionaries, but when they did, it was related to the overall level of difficulty of the materials in relation to their language competence. In such cases, they employed dictionaries in the same way that the lower level students did (e.g. Nancy's reading of a picture book as mentioned in Chapter 5). This practice was similar to students who usually experienced a large gap between their language proficiency and the materials they were attempting to read.

Frawley and Lantolf (1985: 22) describe this reversion to earlier patterns as 'the principle of continuous access' to earlier developmental stages. Frawley and Lantolf claim that individual learners might seek assistance from other people or from physical tools when confronted with more difficult tasks than those for which they have successfully achieved self-regulation (see Lantolf, 2000; Lantolf & Aljaafreh, 1995; Lantolf & Thorne, 2006).

For instance, Patrick read a book on Japanese sit-down comedy and a number of legal texts either without or with minimum dictionary use. However, he reported extensive use of his electronic dictionary when reading a novel written in an old style of Japanese because the book included 'so many words that I don't understand' (Interview 2). In order to read the book, moreover, Patrick made his own word list. Interestingly, this approach is similar to the technique that intermediate students, who gained lower scores than other participants, employed in a study by Yamane (2007) on reading strategies by learners of Japanese. In other words, it can be interpreted that Patrick might need to access techniques acquired at an earlier stage of his language development because of the gap between his Japanese language proficiency level and that of the novel.

Joshua also reported a similar experience to that of Patrick. On the one hand, when reading posts on an online bulletin board, Joshua only skimmed them to understand their gist and rarely checked unfamiliar words in a dictionary. On the other hand, to read a Japanese novel written by a famous contemporary writer, he relied heavily on his electronic dictionary to check the meaning of *kanji* compounds. Based on Joshua's Japanese language skills as a student at intermediate level, it can be reasonably assumed that there was a critical gap between his reading skills and the level of Japanese needed to read the novel, which caused him to rely on the dictionary.

Another interesting fact to emerge from Joshua's example was his attempt to vary his habitual approach of skimming by instead retyping the book. In the interview, Joshua reported that he started retyping the book to pay particular attention to the multitude of unfamiliar words and described the difference between skimming and retyping the book:

> It's interesting because if I read it like this, I can skip over the words, and the meanings too. Whereas, I type everything up, then I have to really pay attention, so even if there are some words that I don't understand, like I kind of get the image better. (Joshua, Interview 5)

As Joshua mentioned in this excerpt, typing the text directed his attention to each word, and often forced him to consult his electronic dictionary because typing in Japanese requires learners to be aware of each *kanji* character's pronunciation. Hence, I speculate that typing the text was beneficial for Joshua, allowing him to control his cognitive processes and seek an external tool to support his reading activity. In addition, given that Joshua regarded these reading activities as opportunities for improving his Japanese competence (see also Chapter 5), this retyping technique might have been affected by his desire to improve his vocabulary by means of reading.

As indicated above, the dictionary use by these students was similar to that of advanced students in previous research studies undertaken on L2 reading and dictionary use. However, it is not necessarily the case that proficient L2 learners always undertake reading activities without external assistance. Rather, students' dictionary use seems to be jointly defined by the relationship between objects for activities, learners' Japanese language skills and the level of difficulty of the reading materials. In addition, I must note that it is impossible to simply compare students' dictionary use to that of class-related reading activities because the data I could collect varied. Although students who prioritised Japanese class tasks tended to give detailed information on their reading activities for the Japanese classes, they read less material outside of the classroom. Yet, the above examples still provide interesting differences in students' dictionary use in out-of-class settings.

### Inherent problems of dictionary use while reading manga

Eric's example of reading *manga* suggests that dictionaries are not always useful tools for reading certain type of materials. Pasfield-Neofitou (2009) points out that an emphasis on formal language registers is a problem inherent in electronic dictionaries. Eric reported similar disadvantages when comparing reading *manga* and an article in a specialised magazine.

In his diary entry about his reading of an article in a computer magazine, Eric explained how it differed from reading *manga*:

> This was probably one of the easier Japanese articles I read (much easier than *manga*!). I used the same strategy as I usually do – I just used my NDS ((Nintendo DS)) *kanji* dictionary every time I came across an unknown word. There were no expressions that couldn't be translated by my dictionary, unlike in *manga*. (Eric's diary entry on 7 September 2008)

In the interview, Eric further recounted the lexical problems that he experienced when reading *manga* in comparison to the article:

> They ((*manga*)) use different letters, or not like different ones, but like where I wouldn't expect them put in ひらがな ((*hiragana* – Japanese syllabary)) or, you know, カタカナ ((*katakana* – Japanese syllabary mainly utilised for loanwords)) maybe... and probably more importantly, so much colloquial Japanese, so, I just don't understand. This ((the article from a computer magazine)) was completely like, there was no colloquial stuff. (Eric, Interview 2)

These statements exemplify the problems characterising electronic dictionaries highlighted by Pasfield-Neofitou (2009). Online dictionaries contain a more comprehensive amount of vocabulary than any other type of dictionary and could potentially cover the type of colloquial language that is utilised in *manga*. However, Eric only utilised his Nintendo DS dictionary, which is the same type of dictionary as electronic dictionaries for native speakers of Japanese. Although he did not state any concrete reason for this, *manga* constituted hard copy material and his Nintendo DS dictionary might have been more useful than online dictionaries for looking up unfamiliar words because of the option of inputting words by handwriting with a stylus.

Eric's comment above also illustrates that unusual writing conventions, which are often employed in *manga* (e.g. using *hiragana* or *katakana* instead of *kanji*), might cause learners difficulty in identifying a target word in a dictionary. Given that Japanese classes rarely introduce this type of material as the main focus in the classroom, it is probable that Eric had not acquired knowledge concerning the distinctive conventions utilised in *manga*. From an Activity Theory perspective, Eric's experience highlights the conflicts (contradictions) which resonate between the activity of learning Japanese by attending a university course and the activity of self-directed Japanese usage in authentic contexts. Thus, Eric's lack of knowledge about the writing styles used in *manga* might have prevented him from utilising his dictionary effectively. Once again, Eric's comments exemplify that the effectiveness of tools vary in relation to learners' L2 skills and materials. Moreover, since these types of reading activities are often undertaken individually outside of the classroom, it is difficult to seek assistance from more capable peers or teachers. In light of this contextual feature of non-class-related reading activities, Eric might not have access to alternatives apart from his dictionary, even though it was not a very effective tool.

Schodt (1996: 29–30), who is a Japanese translator and interpreter, identifies Japanese *manga* as a useful language learning resource, particularly for colloquial Japanese, and recommends that learners read it. Indeed, as presented in Chapter 5, Eric was motivated to read *manga* in order to improve his Japanese. However, reading *manga* does not appear to be an easy task for learners as an individual activity outside of the classroom.

### Online reading and viewing activities related to Japanese popular culture

As indicated in Chapter 5, all participants, except Brenda, undertook at least one online reading or viewing activity related to Japanese popular culture. A significant mediation feature apparent in these types of activities is the reliance on students' L1s, which were either English or Chinese. In viewing activities, L2 written information also supported students' understanding of the content. In this section, I will explore the types of available support in L1 and L2, and the social and contextual factors which enabled the students to employ this support.

## L1 subtitles and translations

Students in the current study reported several L1 means of support for their viewing and online reading activities, such as L1 subtitles used in visual resources (i.e. Japanese serials, *anime*, movies and variety shows) and English translations of Japanese pop songs on the internet. For instance, Daniel, Melissa and Thomas watched Japanese serials and *anime* with English subtitles on video-sharing sites or DVDs borrowed from friends. Kate, who is a Singaporean international student, reported that she usually watched Japanese TV series with Chinese subtitles on the internet. Alice and Scott also utilised websites based on Japanese *anime* songs to check lyrics and meanings. Both types of websites not only provide Japanese versions, but also Romanised versions of the lyrics (utilising the English alphabet to write Japanese based on the pronunciations), as well as English translations for non-Japanese speakers.

A prime feature of L1 support is that it enables students to undertake activities in which they are interested regardless of their Japanese proficiency levels. In addition, this type of L1 support allowed students to focus on the content without distractions that might occur in utilising dictionaries or by not being able to understand the meaning. Given that the participants highlighted entertainment purposes for these activities together with the expectation of learning Japanese, it is highly probable that students chose to rely on their L1 when confronted with comprehension difficulties. Based on the advantages of L1 support afforded by subtitles, I suggest that the availability of support in their L1 was another factor that determined the dominance of viewing and other related activities (i.e. checking Japanese *anime* songs) in addition to their interests in Japanese pop culture as discussed in Chapter 5.

The majority of videos that the students utilised had been voluntarily translated by fans of Japanese popular culture. Fan translation started in the 1980s and has been termed 'fansubs' (Leonard, 2005: 282). According to Japanese popular culture researchers (e.g. Hatcher, 2005; Leonard, 2005), the subtitles of Japanese TV serials or *anime* and relevant websites have emerged in close association with the popularity of Japanese subcultures and its worldwide fandom. Hatcher (2005) further points out that the advent of computer technology has allowed fans to create and distribute fansubs more easily, as well as at a lower cost, though these materials are of dubious legal standing. It has also enabled fans to form communities on the internet and create websites (fansites) in order to provide relevant information (Hatcher, 2005). Students in the current study also accessed several video-sharing sites and relevant websites (e.g.

a website on Japanese *anime* songs) in order to gain access to materials with the assistance of their L1. The larger societal factors, that is, the popularity of Japanese subculture and the advancement of computer technology, have thus enabled students to access viewing materials mediated by L1 support. Although a number of the participants mentioned that fansubs significantly vary in their quality and accuracy, such L1 subtitles expanded opportunities for learners' viewing activities.

With regard to viewing activities with L1 subtitles, it seems that students still paid attention to audio information in the target language. For instance, Kate explained that she noticed that movie characters talked in a polite style of Japanese (Interview 2 on watching Japanese movies) similar to a French learner of English in a study by Sockett and Toffoli (2012) who noticed the way that people talk in English. An advanced level student, Patrick, also reported that he watched Japanese movies and TV series with English subtitles in order to compare his understanding with what the subtitles presented because it was a good exercise to improve his Japanese competence, in particular, his translation skills (Interview 3). Although the degree of attention paid to Japanese may differ among students, these examples imply that watching videos with L1 subtitles allowed for greater opportunities to be exposed to the target language by means of audio recordings outside of the classroom.

I admit that reading activities related to visual materials were limited. However, Melissa's experiences of watching Japanese *anime* discussed in Chapter 3 indicated the possibility of learning Japanese by drawing on written information presented in viewing activities with English subtitles. The examples of Melissa and Thomas in Chapter 5 also indicated that watching Japanese *anime* might help students learn the pronunciations of the words that they encounter in written forms in reading materials and textbooks. Given the positive effect of viewing activities on vocabulary acquisition (Rodgers & Webb, 2011; Webb, 2015), listening to newly learned words through viewing activities might contribute to the development of students' vocabulary. On the basis of these examples, it can be argued that viewing activities accompanied by L1 subtitles have the potential to enhance students' language skills in a target language, including its written forms.

*L2 text information*

Only 2 students watched videos of Japanese variety shows with Japanese subtitles, rather than English. According to Suto (2008), subtitles were originally utilised for displaying lyrics of songs or translations of foreign languages in Japanese TV programmes. Recently, subtitles have also frequently been employed especially in Japanese variety shows to clarify the main points made by cast members, for example, by showing what they say or placing an emphasis on particular parts of their talk

(Suto, 2008). This usage of subtitles in Japanese TV programmes thus fundamentally differs from the subtitle service aimed at people with hearing impairments.

Figure 6.3 is an example of Japanese subtitles in a Japanese news programme. The sentences in the lower part of the screenshot are subtitles of the main points of the news. As mentioned in Chapter 3, Lisa relied on Japanese subtitles in order to understand her favourite Japanese variety shows. The following diary entry illustrates how she understood the dialogue in the video by reading the Japanese subtitles:

> I sometimes take notes, pause and rewind the video to better understand the main points, especially the 'subtitles'. So watching a ten minute video is a very long process! I usually watch them twice to get a better understanding on second viewing. (Lisa's diary entry on 12 September 2008)

In the interview based on this diary entry, Lisa also claimed that it was often difficult to follow the content without Japanese subtitles, though she did not clearly identify the reason for this difficulty. However, considering the fact that Lisa had never visited Japan, she might not have acquired sufficient listening skills or colloquial vocabulary to understand authentic Japanese conversations. Furthermore, Lisa's knowledge of basic Chinese characters due to her linguistic heritage might become an additional advantage for understanding the subtitles. Frank, who also watched videos with Japanese subtitles, claimed that following natural conversations on Japanese variety shows was often difficult for him because the cast spoke very quickly. In his research on the effectiveness of watching videos with L2 subtitles, Vanderplank (1988) suggested that L2 subtitles would be beneficial for learners with weaker L2 listening skills and stronger reading skills. Drawing on the comments by Lisa and Frank, Japanese subtitles appear to support these students' listening skills and help them to understand the videos' content.

In the interview, however, Lisa reported that she often found unfamiliar words in Japanese subtitles and looked them up in her electronic

**Figure 6.3** An example of Japanese subtitles in a Japanese news programme (used with permission from NHK International, Inc.)

dictionary, an online dictionary or Google when she did not understand the content of the videos. It is easy to assume that a number of unfamiliar words appear in Japanese variety shows because of the cast's casually spoken manner. For example, Lisa explained that she searched for a Japanese word 'タメグチ (*tameguchi* – talking like friends)' which appeared in the subtitles:

> タメグチ was written in katakana ((one of the Japanese syllabaries that are basically utilised to write loan words)) and wasn't in my electronic dictionary, but online searches of it (google) clarified its meaning and significance. ALC ((the website provided with an online dictionary, *Eijiro*))'s explanation of ため口 was a start. (Lisa's diary entry on 12 September 2008)

Interestingly, Lisa utilised the same tools in the same way as she did for class-related reading activities, even though she claimed in the interview that she watched these videos purely for entertainment purposes and did not have to understand them perfectly. From an Activity Theory perspective, this may be due to the gap in Lisa's Japanese language skills as a tool compared with the language used on Japanese variety shows as the object of this particular activity being so significant. This subsequently forced her to utilise these tools in order to follow the content details so as to increase her enjoyment of the variety show. However, it can also be argued that as a Japanese language student, Lisa took up the affordances provided by the programme to increase her vocabulary, even though this was not her major motive for viewing.

I also suggest that Japanese subtitles appear to allow Lisa to easily grasp the *kanji* for unfamiliar words and thus enable her to consult dictionaries. Given that Lisa's listening skills might not be sufficient to understand the variety show, identifying unfamiliar words from the conversation would be an extremely difficult task for her. In addition, there are a number of homophones in Japanese that might prove problematic when selecting appropriate words from dictionary entries. Japanese subtitles can reduce these problems and help students undertake this type of activity.

### Peer assistance in an online community

With regard to viewing activities on YouTube, Lisa also reported that she often referred to other users' comments on the videos in order to understand the content of Japanese variety shows. This is another example of social mediation which was previously discussed in relation to peers' assistance for assessment tasks. The following excerpt illustrates how comments posted by viewers could assist Lisa and help her to understand a video:

(L refers to Lisa and M refers to the author, Miho)

L: Sometimes, people don't understand either, and say 'oh, what is he saying there', and another person, another user could reply 'oh, he is saying, you know, it's very rude', or something like that. That explains it.
M: That means non-native speakers ((of Japanese))?
L: Yep usually, and maybe native speakers of Japanese also… (Lisa, Interview 2)

Lisa also reported that she could understand some variety show punchlines because of clues provided in other viewers' comments on YouTube. According to Lisa's diary entry, these comments were written not only in English, but also in Japanese, although the latter were often difficult for her to understand. These examples suggest that Lisa could gain support from both her L1 and L2 for understanding the videos.

Interestingly, the ways in which this peer assistance occurred instantiates several characteristics of what Gee (2004: 83, 2007) calls an 'affinity space'. An affinity space is a 'supportive social structure' (Lam, 2009b: 305) which is often created on the internet by people sharing a common interest, such as video games or a particular genre of popular culture. An affinity space is in some ways similar to the community in which an activity resides. However, it is not a static community, but a fluid one, brought together temporarily through a common interest. Typical affinity spaces include online fan communities related to popular culture, for example, forums of digital games and Japanese *anime*. Although YouTube is not a specific fan community, it can still be viewed as an affinity space in that it is a video-sharing site, which allows anyone to freely access the site, post videos and enjoy the videos posted by other users (see Gee, 2004: 77–79). In an affinity space, people are encouraged and able to access other people's knowledge and they are also able to participate in the space in different ways and at different levels. For instance, referring to other users' comments to understand a video's content could be understood as utilising other people's knowledge in order to achieve goals. As Lisa implies in the excerpt above, English speakers who understand Japanese or Japanese speakers who understand English access YouTube via the internet, regardless of their physical separation, and can help each other. In addition, YouTube allows users to select how they utilise the service. Whereas some of the other viewers posted comments, Lisa did not join in the conversation and only passively observed the comments. These features of YouTube as an affinity space thus enabled Lisa to employ useful information provided by other users in order to understand the content without having to rely on English subtitles.

## Writing activities

As indicated in Chapters 3 and 5, students in the current study rarely had opportunities to participate in non-class-related writing activities, or even online communication with their Japanese speaker friends. Only Joshua constantly engaged in writing activities in an online or offline setting on his computer. These included writing short messages on Twitter, communicating with Japanese-speaking friends on Facebook and writing a personal diary in Japanese. Joshua also wrote blogs during his leave of absence from university. In this section, I will discuss Joshua's case because he supplied detailed data.

For his non-class-related writing activities, the only tool that Joshua utilised was an online dictionary. Joshua did not give any particular reason for his dictionary selection. However, when considering that his writing activities were undertaken on a computer, it is reasonable to assume that the ease of access to an online dictionary is one of the possible reasons for his dictionary selection. In addition, Joshua utilised not only an English–Japanese but also a Japanese–English dictionary for confirming words which he already knew.

It is also notable that Joshua actively utilised the grammar patterns and expressions which he learned in his Japanese classes. For instance, in his personal diary, Joshua utilised a set phrase '判で押したように (*han de oshita yoo ni* – without exceptions)' and a grammar pattern '～にちがいない (*~ni chigainai* – must)', both of which Joshua had recently learned in his Japanese class. With regard to the reason for utilising these expressions, Joshua explained the following:

> I sometimes, like I would try to be more expressive, so I think of that, a certain expression something like that. (…) I was trying to be, as you said literary, so I was thinking about the expressions that I used, which is just probably why I ended up using '判で押したように ((*han de oshita yoo ni*))' just because it's a kind of, sounds of like something great. (Joshua, Interview 3)

This statement indicates that Joshua drew on the knowledge that he learned in his Japanese classes to polish his writing. With regard to his usage of a casual speech style in his personal diary, as well as on Twitter and Facebook, Joshua claimed that he utilised the knowledge that he had gained in his previous upper-beginner Japanese classes rather than by initiating communication with Japanese native speakers on social networking services. These comments thus demonstrate that his Japanese classes served as what Engeström (1987) calls an instrument-producing activity by fostering his linguistic tools for his non-class-related writing activities.

Needless to say, there were several other examples of Japanese classes being able to provide instrument-producing activities for students' non-class-related literacy activities: Chris' reading activity of a Japanese novel in this chapter and the viewing activities of Melissa and Thomas discussed in Chapter 5. It is reasonable to say that at least these students identified distinct connections between their formal learning and their non-class-related literacy practices.

## Summary and Discussion

This chapter has analysed how learners engaged with literacy activities by utilising a number of physical and symbolic tools, and peer assistance. The analysis revealed the significant impact that computer technology, including digital dictionaries, Google and Wikipedia, exercised on students' Japanese literacy practices. In particular, for class-related literacy practices, less proficient students (e.g. intermediate students, such as Frank and Scott) creatively employed digital tools to supplement their insufficient knowledge of the target language and culture. However, it was also found that students did not necessarily recognise the most effective ways of utilising these digital tools and needed to be provided with opportunities to master how to utilise tools by means of expert support, such as teachers or more capable and informed classmates. With regard to non-class-related literacy practices, the internet and Japanese pop culture provided various materials with L1 subtitles, which allow students to undertake literacy activities related to this media, regardless of their L2 proficiency.

Another significant finding is that participants' selection of mediational means and the manner in which they utilised these resources were shaped by a combination of multiple factors. These factors included not only students' objectives for each literacy activity, but also the rules or norms, the availability of support from community members, their Japanese language skills and societal factors, such as the popularity of Japanese popular culture. This finding exemplified learners' agency from an Activity Theory perspective. Lantolf and Pavlenko (2001) as well as Lantolf and Thorne (2006) claim that learners' agency is co-constructed with particular sociocultural environments and various contextual factors that surround learners. Gao (2010) and Gao and Zhang (2011), moreover, assert that such a sociocultural perspective of agency does not underestimate learners' agency, but rather enables researchers to understand how they exercise their agency in their learning process. Indeed, participants in the present study actively selected or often devised means of accessing mediating artefacts (e.g. dictionaries, Google, Wikipedia) and support from classmates and Japanese friends, but at the same time their decisions were constrained or supported by various social and contextual factors, as stated above. In relation to class-related literacy practices, I suspect that learners' motives/objects for performing assessment tasks, combined with the rules or norms of the assessment tasks, triggered students' creative use of online tools. In contrast, in their pursuit of voluntary literacy activities, while the learners expected to improve their Japanese competence, they undertook such activities mainly for enjoyment purposes or to pursue their interests. Additionally, their voluntary literacy activities were not restricted by rules or norms in terms of task approaches. These factors shaped the ways in which learners tended to employ relatively effortless means, for example, relying on their L1 in viewing activities or skimming the material, insofar that they could understand the contents, which was their main goal for non-class-related literacy practices. Moreover, Patrick's example of reading a novel written in an old style of Japanese was indicative of how the same person chose different strategies in relation to his motives/goals, the materials and his Japanese language skills.

The influence of social and contextual factors on language learners' approaches to tasks has been overlooked in the experimental or quantitative research on reading and writing strategies to date, despite the fact that prominent researchers have advocated its importance (e.g. Atkinson, 2002; Gao, 2010; Grenfell & Macaro, 2007; Oxford & Schramm, 2007). Traditionally, as already described in Chapter 1, previous studies in this area have focused mainly on cognitive aspects, and have often compared reading and writing processes between proficient and less proficient learners. This tendency stems from the primary aim of learning strategy research, which is to identify effective strategies in order to support language learners (Grenfell & Macaro, 2007). However, considering the fact that learners' mediated actions are defined in association with various other factors, it is questionable whether effective strategies undertaken in experimental settings are also useful in real target language learning and usage situations.

That said, it is beneficial, as well as necessary, to provide language learners with opportunities to gain information about useful tools and approaches that other students employ. For instance, Japanese Level 10, which was a content-based course specialising in interpreting and translation, provided students with opportunities to introduce and discuss the techniques which they and their classmates employed when undertaking assessment tasks. Students enrolled in this course positively evaluated these opportunities. For instance, Alice reported that she became familiar with Google's function as a writing aid upon hearing about it in a Level 10 classroom discussion. Following this, she commenced employing the technique, though she had 'never even thought to use that before' (Alice, Interview 2). This example demonstrates that the provision of these opportunities in Japanese classes extends the range of available mediational means that students may employ. Unfortunately, however, other students reported that they rarely had opportunities to share their L2 literacy practice techniques in the classroom.

Finally, the potential of non-class-related literacy practices as learning activities was also noteworthy. As I described by drawing on Chris's example, it is highly probable that language learners might notice new linguistic items (e.g. lexica and set phrases) while engaging in reading or even viewing activities with L1 subtitles. As argued by Schmidt (1990), this noticing might eventually develop into the acquisition of new knowledge of the target language. Joshua's writing activities also clearly show that literacy activities which are unrelated to Japanese classes evolved into opportunities to use knowledge acquired in Japanese classes and other related activities (e.g. assessment tasks). Also, Lisa's experience of using YouTube indicates the potential for L2 acquisition based on peer assistance provided by online communities. At the same time, however, Eric's experience of reading *manga* indicates the gap between the language that learners study in class and the language used for non-class-related literacy activities. Although this issue was not examined in detail in this study due to unavoidable data collection limitations, it is necessary to further investigate language learning affordances provided by voluntary L2 literacy practices, including the role of classes as an instrument-producing activity.

# 7 L2 Literacy Practices and Language Learning in Out-of-Class Contexts

The study presented in this volume examines the second language (L2) literacy practices of 15 students of Japanese outside the classroom. In contrast to previous studies which examined either class-related tasks or voluntary L2 learning and use activities, the current study explores both types of literacy practices holistically. The previous chapters have presented a detailed examination on L2 out-of-class literacy practices, focusing on the types of literacy activities undertaken by the participants, the factors influencing opportunities for these activities and the ways in which learners undertook such activities in naturalistic contexts. Such a detailed examination has made a contribution to identifying the possibilities for learning and using a target language in foreign language (FL) contexts.

The present chapter will first summarise the major findings which broaden the understanding of related topics in second language acquisition (SLA), such as out-of-class autonomous language learning, motivation and reading and writing strategies. I will further discuss the implications for pedagogy with an emphasis on the roles of language classes to promote L2 literacy activities outside of the classroom, followed by suggestions for future research emerging from the major findings.

## Out-of-Class L2 Literacy Practices and Language Learning: Major Findings

This study has explored three main questions, as set out in Chapter 1. Chapter 3 explored the literacy activities that participants actually undertook in Japanese outside of the classroom and the features of these activities, including the similarities and differences between class-related and non-class-related literacy practices. Chapters 4 through 6 detailed the major findings of this current study, drawing on Activity Theory (Engeström, 1999, 2001; Leont'ev, 1978). Chapters 4 and 5 focused on class-related and non-class-related literacy practices, respectively, in order to analyse individual and contextual factors which influenced

L2 literacy activity opportunities. Chapter 6 then described the ways in which learners read, wrote and watched programmes in their L2 by exploring the use of various external resources, such as online tools and peer assistance.

## Types of literacy activities

Drawing on the four factors (arrangement, assessment, content and pedagogy) developed from Benson's (2011) framework for out-of-class language learning, Chapter 3 revealed the various types of reading and writing activities which students undertook, as well as the differences and similarities between class-related and non-class-related literacy practices. Predictably, for the majority of the participants in the current study, preparation for assessment tasks as well as in-class activities (e.g. reading activities) represented the main opportunities drawn upon to utilise reading and writing skills. Assessment tasks in particular, even tasks which assessed students' oral skills, involved a number of reading and writing activities, such as reading websites and book chapters, writing essays and preparing scripts for oral presentations and speaking tests. Reading and writing skills were also utilised as a means to memorise the vocabulary and grammar items required for quizzes and examinations. In other words, literacy skills were crucial elements needed to successfully complete Japanese courses, at least at the university where the participants studied.

Regarding non-class-related literacy practices, this study has identified that writing activities, including online written communication with Japanese speakers, rarely took place for most of the students. Among this study's participants, viewing activities, such as watching Japanese TV shows, *anime* and movies, were found to be the most popular and common activities. A closer examination of each student's literacy activities also revealed a variety of materials and topics utilised for the students' voluntary reading, although activity amounts differed considerably between individuals. These materials included not only online resources (e.g. websites listing the lyrics of Japanese pop songs, online discussion boards, friends' blog posts) but also print media (e.g. novels, picture books, *manga*, local Japanese newspapers), which were often not dealt with in the classroom.

In contrast, it was found that reading materials for assessment and in-class tasks were relatively limited to formal or academic styles of Japanese. Although some of the assessment tasks (e.g. essays and oral presentations) allowed students to choose their own topics and reading materials, students were required to read resources written in relatively formal Japanese because of the assessment criteria, such as Japanese newspaper websites, books and articles on Wikipedia. This is a clear reflection of teachers' intentions. These findings indicated that the language used in materials for class-related tasks and non-class-related literacy practices appeared to differ. This is evident in Eric's experience of reading *manga* which was illustrated in Chapter 6. Conversely, learners' voluntary reading materials appeared to provide learners with learning opportunities for new vocabulary and expressions that were not introduced in the classroom, as Chris' comments indicated in Chapter 6.

However, similarities between class-related and non-class-related literacy practices were also identified in terms of materials, pedagogical factors and content. With regard to materials, articles on Wikipedia were utilised for assessment tasks, preparation for in-class reading activities and voluntary reading. Similar to non-class-related literacy practices, no direct teacher instructions or structured materials were available in reading and writing activities for a number of assessment tasks. In relation to the content, Scott's reading activities discussed in Chapters 3 and 5 were triggered by the topics in his Japanese classes, similar to a finding reported in a study by Lai (2015) about the influence of activities in language classes on out-of-class learning activities. Such similarities indicate that the boundary between class-related and non-class-related literacy practices is not always clear-cut, and a number of links between these two types of practices may exist.

## Motives/objects as driving force for literacy activities

Drawing upon Activity Theory, the present study has provided an insight into the nature of learners' motives (and objects) as a driving force for both class-related and non-class-related literacy practices. With regard to class-related literacy practices, students' concerns about receiving a good mark were found to be closely related to their focus on assessment tasks and preparation for in-class reading activities. More importantly, the analysis of the experiences of Frank and Daniel in Chapter 4 demonstrated that their concerns about academic results triggered a change in their learning routines in order to fill the gap evident between their Japanese language skills and task demands. Daniel's case further demonstrated that his motive/object for gaining a good mark prompted the transition of his activity system: selecting friends for improving his Japanese learning environment. However, Daniel's experience of writing an essay also indicated that he abandoned his other purpose of learning Japanese at university, which was to improve his Japanese language skills, in order to concentrate on achieving good academic results.

In addition, it was found that students appeared to lose their incentive to undertake class-related tasks when they could not identify the connections between these tasks and their purposes for learning Japanese, for example, improving their Japanese language skills for their future careers. Conversely, identifying the possible usefulness of task contents in relation to students' own motives might encourage them to undertake challenging and demanding tasks, as summed up in Eric's experiences at different levels of courses reported in Chapter 4. This finding supports the observation of Russell and Yañez (2003) that the important link between the goals of students and the aim of first language (L1) academic writing tasks is also applicable within L2 settings.

Regarding students' non-class-related literacy practices, two main motives were identified, namely learning Japanese and entertaining themselves, including pursuing their interests. The motive of entertainment was closely related to students' interests in Japanese popular culture or certain other topics. In most of the cases, learners stated these two motives as reasons, and they appeared to jointly promote students' literacy activities. However, a number of examples in this study indicated that participants' interest in particular media or topics, including temporary interests, played a more important role than did their motive for learning Japanese in terms of expanding their literacy activity opportunities. In order to pursue their interests, students often undertook a number of activities, which required different types of language skills. The example of Melissa in Chapter 5 illustrated that her interest in a Japanese pop group led to opportunities for her to engage in viewing and listening activities, and occasionally triggered reading activities (e.g. checking pop song lyrics). Moreover, motives related to Japanese pop culture were different from the other task-specific motives in that they constantly produced opportunities for L2 use activities, usually over a long period of time.

In the field of SLA, learners' interest in a target language or language learning itself has attracted attention from the perspectives of intrinsic motivation of self-determination theory (Noels *et al.*, 1999, 2000). However, Sundqvist and Sylvén (2016) suggest the significance of entertainment/leisure activities in the efforts of young Swedish learners to improve their English language skills. The findings of the present study support this assertion by Sundqvist and Sylvén and have further contributed to our knowledge of how important learners' interest in a particular media and topics is in expanding and deepening the opportunities for L2 literacy activities in out-of-classroom contexts. It has, moreover, empirically confirmed the claim by scholars in the field of learner autonomy that triggering learners' interests is essential in promoting motivation and autonomous language learning (e.g. Little *et al.*, 2002; Ushioda, 2000, 2011; Williams & Burden, 1997).

## Learners' beliefs and the role of language classes

In relation to motives, the participants' beliefs were also found to play an important role in encouraging students to undertake literacy activities outside of the classroom. On the one hand, the analysis of class-related literacy practices in Chapter 4 found that students who focused more on assessment tasks and class preparations had positive beliefs about classroom-based learning. On the other hand, the students who had positive beliefs about the effectiveness of voluntary L2 use activities in improving their language skills tended to engage in reading or viewing activities regularly, or undertook a variety of voluntary activities.

Interestingly, the participants' language classes appeared to have a significant impact on developing both their beliefs about learning in formal education settings and also beliefs about non-class-related literacy practices. For the former, successful experiences as well as enjoyment in relation to the class-related tasks were key factors in learners having positive beliefs about class-related literacy practices, as Frank's comments in Chapter 4 indicated. Grace's case in the same chapter illustrated the change in her preferred out-of-class activities reflecting the change in her beliefs which were influenced by teaching styles in the in-country programme. These examples explained the direct influence of the language classes (or language teachers) on developing students' beliefs.

This study also found that recognising the links between Japanese classes, class-related tasks and non-class-related literacy practices contributed to fostering students' positive beliefs about the usefulness of non-class-related literacy practices on L2 acquisition. The comments by Melissa and Thomas in Chapter 5 indicated that they clearly noticed such links, which resulted in their positive beliefs and became a motivator for their listening, reading and viewing activities outside the classroom, along with the purpose of entertaining themselves. Language classes thus can be viewed as an important community with the potential to facilitate out-of-class L2 learning and use activities through fostering beliefs.

However, it was also found that not all of the participants realised the positive effects of their voluntary literacy activities on their L2 learning in the classroom, and vice versa. Eric's case in Chapter 5 indicates that learners' doubts about the effectiveness of literacy activities for improving Japanese language skills valued in the classroom may demotivate them to undertake L2 use activities outside the classroom. This finding indicates that teachers' help is necessary for learners to recognise the usefulness of their voluntary L2 learning and use activities in improving their language skills.

### Community members as information providers

In terms of expanding opportunities for non-class-related literacy practices, the participants' friends, classmates and siblings were found to play an important role as information providers related to learners' interests, in particular, about Japanese pop culture. This role was somewhat different from those focused on in previous studies, such as communication partners in a target language (Kurata, 2011; Pasfield-Neofitou, 2012) and teaching the language (Palfreyman, 2006, 2011). As Daniel's comment in Chapter 5 exemplified, siblings and friends often introduced Japanese pop culture to learners, and learners' interest in this media was a motivator to commence or continue to study Japanese. The information about *anime*, Japanese TV shows and pop songs provided by siblings, friends and classmates also triggered a number of voluntary L2 viewing and reading activities. Although participants often individually undertook these activities, their interests in this media were developed and supported by members of their social networks. It is also important to note that wider societal factors, such as advancements in information and communication technology (ICT) and the popularity of Japanese pop culture overseas, allowed learners to pursue their interests in this media on the internet, as discussed in Chapters 5 and 6.

More importantly, Eric's successful experience of reading *manga* in Chapter 5 demonstrated the importance of recommendations by peers who know learners' interests and preferences. Such appropriate suggestions about materials and resources possibly prompt learners' strong interests in topics which can drive them to accomplish activities even if they face linguistic difficulties. Learners' peers and siblings thus played a significant role in expanding the opportunities of L2 literacy activities as well as promoting their experience in their voluntary activities in a target language.

The examples of Scott's extra reading activities were again noteworthy in that his language classes triggered his interest. In Chapter 4, it was found that students often experienced a discrepancy between what they needed to do for the classes and what they would have liked to do in the target language. However, Scott's reading activities exemplified that language classes possibly overcome this discrepancy by creating a link between language classes and voluntary L2 activities at the content level.

## The role of the internet in expanding literacy activity opportunities

As predicted in Chapter 1, the internet has been shown to be a significant tool in expanding L2 literacy activity opportunities outside of the classroom. Most of the participants utilised the internet for both class-related and non-class-related literacy practices. This finding is of particular importance when considering possible opportunities for L2 learning and use in home country settings.

Chapter 5 discussed the function of the internet in expanding the opportunities of L2 literacy practices from an Activity Theory perspective. Among them, the most notable was to connect learners' interests to materials and resources. Students utilised the internet in order to find information and read websites when they became interested in certain topics, or even when they did not have any particular purpose in mind, as illustrated in Joshua's and Chris's examples of passing their time by reading in Chapter 5. The internet thus enabled students to access a variety of authentic materials based on their interests in a relatively minor FL compared to English, and to organise a more personalised language learning environment even though the participants were physically outside of the country (Ma, 2017; Sockett & Toffoli, 2012).

In addition, as a number of previous studies already found (e.g. Lam, 2000, 2009b; Ma, 2017; Palfreyman, 2011; Pasfield-Neofitou, 2012; Sockett & Toffoli, 2012), the analysis of Joshua's case in Chapter 5 illustrated that the internet connects language learners to their peers or to online communities based on their interests, producing rich opportunities for literacy activities in their L2. Social networking sites (SNSs) were found to allow Joshua to expand his peer network to include Japanese speakers and to gain numerous opportunities for natural interactions in the target language. Participating in online communities also provided Joshua with reading activities, such as emails from these communities' mailing lists. However, the use of SNSs and participation in online communities related to the target language was only observed in Joshua's case. Lai and Gu's (2011) study also found a similar tendency of a lower use of technology to develop social networks for language learning. Although there might be a number of reasons behind this finding, as discussed in Chapter 5, it implies that interventions by teachers are necessary to enable learners to utilise such significant features of the internet to enhance language learning opportunities outside of the classroom (Levy, 2009; Ushioda, 2011).

### Selection and use of resources

Chapter 6 discussed the ways in which students undertook literacy activities as a mediational means from an Activity Theory perspective, with particular emphasis on the resources utilised in order to support activities in their target language. The analysis revealed that a number of language-related resources, including dictionaries, online tools (Google and Wikipedia), peer assistance and L1 as well as L2 information (e.g. English and Japanese subtitles in videos), were utilised in order to facilitate students' literacy activities. L2 materials were also employed as linguistic resources, however, only for class-related tasks.

Among these resources, digital dictionaries (online and handheld electronic dictionaries) were the most commonly used for both class-related and non-class-related literacy practices because of the ease of searching for *kanji* words. However, the effectiveness of each type of dictionary varied depending on the types of materials in question. Furthermore, online dictionaries surpassed other types of dictionaries in terms of the number of example sentences available, with some of the students stating this as a reason for using them for writing activities and translation tasks. These differences for each type of dictionary appeared to be one of the factors triggering students' strategic use of multiple dictionaries depending on the targets of the tasks.

In addition to language dictionaries, Google and Wikipedia were found to support students' literacy activities as a dictionary or corpus. A number of students utilised these online tools to assist their reading activities by searching for vocabulary and set phrases which were not covered by language dictionaries. Google also served as a corpus for writing activities by allowing students to check the appropriateness or grammatical accuracy of their writing. These online resources have great potential to facilitate the use of authentic materials and to support individual writing activities. At the same time, however, the present study identified that not every student fully recognised the features and advantages of these online resources as well as the dictionaries, and often only relied on information provided by their teachers in the classroom. This finding suggested that they required more information and training in order to use these tools effectively.

One other resource utilised as a mediational means was peer assistance. With regard to class-related tasks, examples of peer assistance were identified only in the area of writing activities. These included corrections by Japanese native speakers or help received from classmates or Japanese speaker friends in drafting essays and scripts for speeches. In this study, however, only a few students reported such peer assistance. As mentioned earlier, assessment task rules restricted students as they avoided seeking peer help because this may have been viewed as unfair practice.

Similarly, only one example of peer assistance for non-class-related literacy practices was observed in Lisa's viewing activities on YouTube; this was examined in Chapter 6. This peer assistance occurred in the form of other users' comments in English or Japanese, which Lisa utilised for understanding the contents of the videos. This is indicative of the peer assistance characteristically observed in online communities, which enables target language speakers who do not know each other but share common interests to support each other. In this respect, moreover, literacy practices involving online communities significantly differ from other literacy activities usually undertaken by students independently.

Drawing on Activity Theory, the analysis also revealed that the students' selection and usage of resources was the result of the interaction of several factors in their activity systems. The students' multiple as well as creative use of digital dictionaries and online resources for their assessment tasks was indicative of the mutual influence of their motives for gaining a good mark, the rules related to assessment tasks and the features as well as limitations of linguistic resources. Reliance on L1 subtitles in viewing activities appeared to reflect learners' motives for enjoying the content and availability of such materials. Patrick's reading activity in Chapter 6 also illustrated how his motives, Japanese proficiency level, and the style of Japanese used in a novel defined his way of reading it. Both opportunities for out-of-class literacy practices and also actual processes of literacy activities are thus co-constructed by various subjective, contextual and societal factors, as claimed by several researchers who have examined language learning activities from sociocultural perspectives (Gao, 2010; Lantolf & Pavlenko, 2001; Lantolf & Thorne, 2006). Conversely, these findings challenge whether strategies that were found to be effective as the result of experimental research are also useful in real situations of target language learning and use.

### Links between Japanese classes, class-related tasks and non-class-related literacy practices

Based on the major findings mentioned so far, how students' non-class-related literacy practices and their Japanese classes as well as class-related tasks influenced each other will be clarified.

As illustrated in Figure 7.1, the current study identified a number of links or influences between language classes, including class-related tasks, and voluntary L2 literacy activities. One of the examples of such links was the influence of language classes on non-class-related literacy practices at the content level; an example of this is Scott's experiences, as illustrated in Chapters 3 and 5. The topics in his Japanese classes aroused his interest and eventually triggered extra reading activities outside of the classroom in order to pursue these interests. Eric's comments in Chapter 5 indicate that students might undertake voluntary L2 literacy activities with a strong desire to improve their target language skills to gain a good mark. This example can also be regarded as one of the influences of language classes on voluntary L2 learning and use activities.

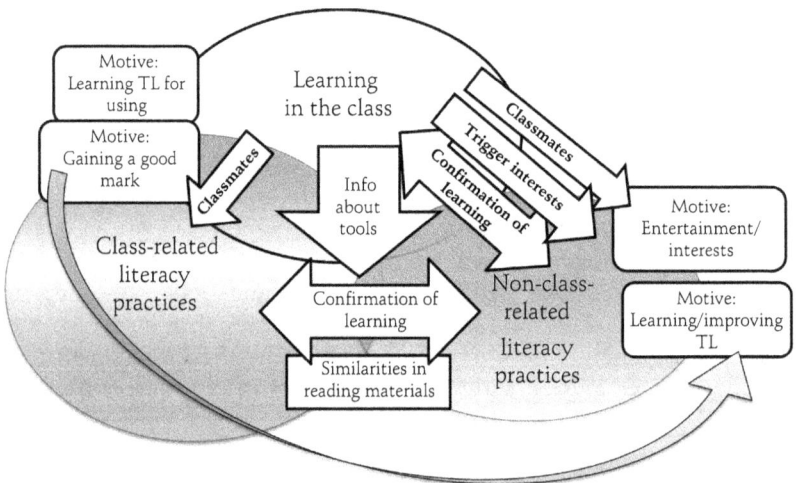

**Figure 7.1** Links between language classes/class-related tasks and non-class-related literacy practices

The Japanese classes were also found to impact on both class-related and non-class-related literacy practices in two more different ways: providing students with information about tools (e.g. dictionaries) and presenting a social space to find peers (classmates) who assist in class-related tasks as well as share similar interests in entertainment/leisure activities involving the L2. As the arrows in Figure 7.1 show, these links are more likely to be unidirectional influences from the language classes on out-of-class L2 literacy practices.

A closer examination of participants' experiences gained during their literacy activities also identified a link at the language level. On the one hand, vocabulary and expressions that students learned in their Japanese classes became resources for undertaking literacy activities other than class-related tasks. I found several examples of this, such as Melissa's viewing activities cited in Chapter 5 and Joshua's writing activities discussed in Chapter 6. On the other hand, students learned the lexicon that they noticed in their voluntary literacy activities, as new vocabulary in the classroom or class-related tasks. Thomas' comments in Chapter 5 also imply that this link was likely to result in opportunities for confirming what learners learned both in and outside of the classroom. As mentioned in the previous section, identifying the connections between Japanese classes, class-related tasks and non-class-related literacy practices was found to foster students' positive beliefs about the usefulness of their voluntary L2 use activities on their L2 acquisition. Such positive beliefs, in turn, appeared to motivate students to further engage in non-class-related literacy practices. Moreover, the similarities in material types for assessment preparation and voluntary reading activities (e.g. articles on Wikipedia) were also identified, as discussed in Chapter 3.

The current study thus revealed that language classes and out-of-class L2 learning and use activities were inseparable. Based on these findings, it could be said that the language classes formed the main communities in a variety of ways for L2 literacy practices outside of the classroom. In other words, language classes (and teachers who organise the classes) can facilitate autonomous language learning in out-of-class contexts by building or reinforcing these links.

## Recommendations for Language Teaching in Formal Settings

Based on the links between language classes and out-of-class L2 literacy practices identified above, this section will present recommendations for the ways in which language classes facilitate out-of-class autonomous language learning.

### Developing learners' beliefs

As we have seen in the cases of Melissa and Thomas, enabling learners to recognise the link between their literacy activities for entertainment purposes and learning in the class is one of the main means by which to foster the learners' positive beliefs/attitudes for the extra activities in L2 outside the classroom. Moreover, Grace's experience at the in-country programme exemplified how language classes/teachers can develop such beliefs in a relatively short period of time.

In order to achieve this, utilising authentic materials that learners (want to) read and watch in their daily lives for in-class activities may be effective in making learners take note of the concrete rewards of their voluntary literacy activities in their L2. In such cases, as I discussed elsewhere (Inaba, 2014), teachers' instructions are crucial in illustrating what students can learn through authentic materials. This way of employing authentic materials in the classroom may also heighten the connection between learners' motives related to the use value of learning and studying a target language in the classes. As discussed in Chapter 4, this connection will positively affect learners' attitudes towards class-related tasks.

### Triggering learners' interests

Triggering learners' interests is another important factor in expanding the opportunities for L2 literacy activities, with a focus on things other than language learning. As Scott's example indicates, the topics (contents) presented in language classes have the potential to stimulate learners' interests, which may prompt them to perform extra literacy activities outside the classroom. Allowing learners to select materials in language classes or for assessment tasks may be one way of stimulating learners' interests. Integrating learners' interests in in-class learning activities might also prompt students to 'talk as "people" rather than as simply "language learners"' (Ushioda, 2011: 206) in a target language and motivate them to engage in their learning processes. In order to achieve this, the internet should be utilised in the classroom as a tool that enables learners to gain/access on-the-spot materials in order to pursue their interests. In relation to the utilisation of authentic materials associated with the internet, Thorne and Reinhardt (2008) maintain the importance of integrating digital literacies into advanced language courses in order to bridge language learning and students' language use activities in their current and future lives. In other words, such in-class activity will also become a model for their non-class-related literacy practices and may help them develop the capacity for autonomous language learning outside the classroom.

At the same time, however, teachers are often required to utilise particular textbooks or course books and might not be allowed to arrange these activities in the classes. Having said that, as Sundqvist and Sylvén (2016) suggested, being acquainted with students' interests is crucial for teachers to arrange effective learning tasks in the classroom. Given that

Scott became interested in the topics of the textbook related to his nationality (topic about an Australian diplomat) and his hobby (songs used in video games), learning about students' interests, backgrounds and personal experiences will enable teachers to select more suitable textbooks and topics for assessment tasks.

Another suggestion is to organise opportunities for the students to share their interests in various topics (e.g. favourite novelists, sport players and movies) with each other and to recommend resources and materials. Given that classmates and friends were key information providers of Japanese pop culture and actually prompted a number of voluntary viewing and reading activities, this type of activity is beneficial for triggering or developing students' interests further. Sundqvist and Sylvén (2016), for example, recommend that students keep a language diary to record their entertainment activities in their L2 as a starting point for sharing their interests with teachers. By sharing their language diary not only with teachers but also with classmates, students gain useful information about resources and materials which suit their interests and may lead to the successful experience of L2 use activities, as Eric's example of reading *manga* indicated.

## Supporting literacy skills required for out-of-class literacy practices

The current study also identified the discrepancy in the materials for class-related tasks and those for learners' non-class-related literacy practices. These differences seem to cause a number of difficulties in terms of the utilisation of authentic materials based on the learners' interests. In Eric's case, his inadequate knowledge of the writing conventions of *manga* created problems in searching for unfamiliar words in a dictionary. This increased the difficulty he experienced while reading *manga*. The materials related to Japanese popular culture (e.g. *manga*, videos of *anime* and variety shows) also included colloquial language, which language classes and textbooks do not fully deal with. Employing authentic materials in in-class activities that students actually use or would like to use for entertainment purposes may in fact be beneficial to teach and practice the literacy skills required for reading and watching such materials.

As mentioned previously, not all students fully recognised the advantages presented by each dictionary resource. In order to support literacy practices outside the classroom, it is recommended that teachers provide learners not only with information about dictionary resources, but also with opportunities for training in the ways in which to use them effectively. It may also be necessary for language teachers to update their information about the advantages and limitations of dictionaries and online resources, for example, the dictionary applications available on mobile phones. Furthermore, as mentioned in Chapter 6, many of the participants highlighted the fact that there were few opportunities for sharing information with their classmates about effective ways of utilising online tools, for instance, using Google in order to improve grammatical accuracy in writing. As Alice's comments in Chapter 6 indicated, the provision of opportunities to discuss the ways in which learners use tools is likely to be beneficial in developing their skills in using these resources for both class-related and non-class-related literacy practices.

### Arranging more writing tasks

Another insight gained from the current study is that class-related tasks may present key opportunities for writing activities outside the classroom. Even cases of online written communication in the target language were rarely reported by the participants in the current study, despite their contact with Japanese speaker friends via SNSs, online chat and emails. Given this tendency as well as the learners' efforts in the class-related tasks, it is recommended that language classes should provide for a greater number of writing tasks, not only essays for academic writing but also tasks using a colloquial style of language. As a growing number of reports indicates (e.g. Dizon, 2016; Sockett & Toffoli, 2012; Vurdien, 2013), writing activities or project work utilising online communication channels (e.g. Facebook, blogs) may benefit learners in terms of developing their literacy skills in a target language in a way that allows them to engage in online written communication outside of the classroom. Considering that students in this study were reluctant to become acquainted with unknown people on SNSs, creating an online learning community based on teacher's initiatives may be beneficial. In addition, this type of project work may contribute to creating a learning community which will possibly be maintained after the completion of the course.

### Bridging between learners' motives and language classes

I have discussed so far how language classes can facilitate out-of-class L2 literacy activities, in particular, non-class-related literacy practices. I now move on to recommendations on how to promote class-related literacy practices. Chapter 4 showed that there often exists a disparity between students' objectives of using a language outside the classroom and the contents or topics of language classes. As previously mentioned, employing materials that students actually use or want to use outside the classroom in in-class activities might be one way to overcome this contradiction. However, it is reasonable to assume that there is sometimes no room to change materials and topics dealt with in the class due to curriculum constraints. For such cases, asking students to set up their own learning objectives in relation to the use value type of motive (e.g. improving writing skills to communicate with friends on SNS) and classroom-based learning might be one solution to fill the gap between learners' motives and what they learn in the classes. These individual goals can serve as sub-goals attainable for one semester or an entire academic year, which is one of the effective ways to support the learning process (Dörnyei & Ushioda, 2011).

Furthermore, it might be possible to set up learners' objectives including their motives for gaining a good mark. For example, consider the goal of 'watching Japanese movies without English subtitles'. In order to achieve this goal, not only are good listening skills required, but also a broad range of vocabulary and sociolinguistic knowledge. These concrete skills can be connected to in-class or class-related activities as well as gaining a good mark in the following way: memorising vocabulary for examination and in-class tests (i.e. to achieve objectives of language classes) will contribute to gaining good academic results (i.e. exchange value type of motive) and developing learners' vocabulary required to understand Japanese movies (i.e. use value type of motive). Rewards for learning (e.g. gaining a good grade) as motivational strategies are controversial (Dörnyei & Ushioda, 2011). However, given the significance of students' enthusiasm to gain a good mark, as discussed in Chapter 4, integrating concrete goals in terms of academic results may be effective to maintain learners' engagement in class-related tasks.

## Directions for Future Research

This study demonstrated that L2 literacy practices outside of the classroom are an important area for exploring L2 learning and its use in naturalistic contexts. However, certain methodological limitations should be considered for future research. One of the limitations is the number of participants. The present study only investigated a sample of 15 intermediate and advanced participants over a one to two semester period. Although the analysis in the students' narrative data revealed a number of influential factors to facilitate out-of-class L2 learning and use activities, these findings cannot be generalised. Further research is needed to gather data relevant to larger groups. Moreover, greater amounts of data in different contexts are required, such as the cases of learning a target language in FL contexts, particularly in the areas where target languages are not particularly popular or not supported by education policies, and less accessible resources and communities related to the languages. Studies involving quantitative research methods should also be considered, in other words, mixed method approaches (see Dörnyei, 2007). For example, conducting a questionnaire based on the major findings from interviews might be useful to identify whether such findings are applicable to other students too.

Regarding the data collection method, the combination of a diary study with photos and interaction interviews was found to be beneficial in obtaining rich information about learners' L2 literacy practices outside of the classroom in less intrusive ways. However, as has previously been acknowledged in Chapter 2, self-reporting data utilising retrospective techniques such as this cannot be considered to be completely accurate. Another limitation which this report encountered was the actual time period of the diary entries. The one-week diary did not cover infrequent activities, for instance, online written communication with Japanese speakers. Although the interviews allowed me to obtain information regarding what the participants undertook between their diary entries, I acknowledge that information gleaned from such data could potentially be limited. It is necessary to explore the possibility of developing different types of data collection methods, for example, creating learning diary mobile apps which enable learners to access and keep a learning diary without much effort.

Theoretically, Activity Theory proved to be an effective framework for the study, as it provided me with a systematic and analytical lens with which to examine out-of-class L2 literacy practices holistically in connection with the motivational factors behind them and affordances as well as constraints of contextual and societal factors. This framework may be worth utilising in other research on L2 learning strategies or out-of-class language learning, particularly for cases in which learners interact in formal educational settings or actively participate in communities related to target languages. Moreover, the concept of motives in combination with the activity system model may offer a useful framework for examining the dynamic interrelation between motivation and actual L2 learning and use activities situated in a particular context.

A number of directions for future research can also be suggested based on the major findings of this study. The influence of learners' interests in Japanese popular culture for L2 literacy activities and materials selection was significant. In relation to this point, the role of learners' interests as motives for authentic language use activities should be explored further so as to understand how students' interests enhance their engagements in particular literacy activities, and eventually, facilitate language learning processes. Furthermore, given that a few students even started to watch Japanese *anime*, TV shows and variety shows with English subtitles before commencing their Japanese study, out-of-class L2 literacy activities undertaken by beginner students also represent an important area for future research. This research topic is also crucial to explore the possibility of utilising authentic materials at the early stage of learning.

The potential of L2 acquisition by means of viewing activities should be investigated further. There are already a number of studies that have discussed how to use visual materials (e.g. movies and videos) in language classes (e.g. Chapple & Curtis, 2000; Herron *et al.*, 1998; Weyers, 1999) as well as experimental research on the effectiveness of viewing activities in terms of vocabulary acquisition, listening skills and the effectiveness of using L1 or L2 subtitles (e.g. Huang & Eskey, 1999; Taylor, 2005; Yuksel & Tanriverdi, 2009). However, few studies to date have investigated L2 acquisition opportunities in naturally occurring viewing activities. As this study illustrates, however, the L2 text information that appears in TV shows and *anime* not only supports learners' content understanding but may also possibly influence the development of their L2 literacy skills. Even though the present study briefly touched upon this topic, further research will be necessary in order to determine the language learning opportunities provided by viewing activities. In relation to this issue, peer assistance on video-sharing sites is another interesting topic. As the role of online communities of game players and literacy or L2 learning have started to attract more attention (Chik, 2011, 2013, 2014; Gee, 2004, 2007), L1 support by peers in other types of online communities may deserve further scholarly attention in order to explore the potential for L2 learning.

I have highlighted the importance of class-related literacy practices for university student participants and identified that class-related tasks represented the main opportunities for reading and writing activities for the majority of the participants. This fact raises the question of how students keep or develop their literacy skills (or manage their L2 learning in general) after completing their language courses at university. I have briefly mentioned Chris' case as an example of self-study after the completion of his Japanese course. Obviously, there is a need for further research into the roles of L2 literacy practices as a means of self-study following the completion of formal education.

In conclusion, the current research has shed valuable light on L2 literacy practices outside of the classroom, particularly in FL contexts. It described the reasons for and how language learners undertake activities requiring L2 literacy skills under the influence of various social and contextual factors. The findings presented in this book will provide insights for L2 educators to understand L2 learning and usage activities in learners' out-of-class lives. Moreover, this study will therefore promote further research into this topic and support practitioners to enhance their teaching practices in order to assist language learners to master a target language.

# Appendix 1
# Background Interview

The following questions form a sample of the kind of background interview conducted with the student participants at the outset of the data collection period.

(1) What is your first language?
(2) What languages do you speak?
(When did you learn it? When do you use it?)
(3) When did you start to learn Japanese?
Which institution (primary school, high school)? How long?
(4) Why did you start to study Japanese?
(5) What textbook did you use at primary school/high school?
(6) When did you start to learn Japanese at university?
(7) Which level did you start to study?
(8) Why did you decide to study Japanese at university (or the focal university)?
(9) What textbook did you use at university?
(10) Why do you study Japanese now?
(11) What do you think of your Japanese proficiency level?
(12) What did (do) you do for learning Japanese? How do you learn Japanese so far?
(13) Do you want to use Japanese in future? Why?
(14) Have you ever been to Japan? Yes – Why? How long?
(15) Do you have any Japanese friends or acquaintances in Melbourne or in Japan?
(16) How did you get acquainted with them?

# Appendix 2
# Interaction Interview

The following questions form a sample of the kind of interaction interview conducted with the student participants after each diary study.

**Questions about each diary entry**

(1) Could you explain about this diary entry with more details? What did you do?
(In the case of class-related tasks, I also asked 'what else did you do for this assignment?')
(2) Why did you do this activity? (Why did you choose this topic and material?)
(3) How did you gain the information about this topic or material?
(4) Did you have any problem or difficulty while undertaking this activity?
If yes, could you explain about the problem?
(5) Did you notice any new vocabulary or expressions?
(6) Did you use any tools (e.g. dictionaries, websites and reference books) during this activity? What did you use?
(7) Why did you choose these tools?
(8) How did you use these tools? Could you show me how you used them?
(9) Did you have any problem using these tools?
(10) How did you gain information about the tools, and when did you start using them?
(11) Why did you ask your friend (or classmates) to help out with this activity?
(12) What did your friend actually do?

**Related questions**

(1) Did you often do the same or similar type of activity?
(2) If yes, what did you do? When did you do it? (or when did you start doing this type of activity?)

(3) Do you use any other dictionaries or particular books for reading and writing in Japanese? What do you use?
(4) How did you gain the information about these tools, and why did you start using them?

## Questions about literacy activities between diary studies

(1) Did you do any other assignments, homework and preparations for quizzes since the last interview?
(2) If yes, what did you do?
(3) Did you do any other activities using Japanese other than those for your Japanese classes?
(4) If yes, what did you do? When? Why?
(5) Do you have any other comments?

# Appendix 3
# Final Interview

The following questions form a sample of the kind of final interview conducted with the student participants.

### Regarding the participants' social network and communication with Japanese speakers

(1) Do you have any other Japanese speaker friends or acquaintances in Melbourne, or anywhere else in the world?
(2) How do you communicate with them?
(3) How often?
(4) What language do you use? English or Japanese (or both)?

### Regarding the participants' literacy activities over the data collection period

(1) Did you do other reading/writing activities outside the classroom other than the things that you already told me?
(2) If yes, what did you do? Why?
(3) Did you have anything that you really want to do in Japanese outside the classroom, but you couldn't do it?
(4) If yes, what couldn't you do? Why couldn't you do it?'?
(5) Do you think that your activities in Japanese outside the classroom have changed over this semester? For example, did you start new activities in Japanese?

### Regarding the participants' Japanese classes, including in-class literacy activities

(1) Could you tell me about typical activities or tasks in the classroom?
(2) What do you think was useful that you learned (or practiced) in the Japanese classes this semester?
(3) Was there anything that you wanted to do in the Japanese classes, but there was no chance to do it?
(4) If yes, what did you want to do?

(5) Do you have anything else that you hope to do in the Japanese classes?

### Regarding the participants' recognition of the relationship between class-related and non-class-related literacy practices

(1) How do you think the activities that you engaged in outside the classroom affect your learning in the Japanese classes?
(2) How about vice versa? Do you think what you learned in the Japanese classes affected (has affected) your activities outside the classroom?

### Regarding the participants' observations about the improvements in their literacy skills, and the change of learning styles and motivations/goals

(1) What do you think your current Japanese language proficiency level is, in particular, reading and writing ability?
(2) What approach do you like for learning Japanese?
(3) Do you think your learning style has changed over the data collection period?
(4) Do you think your purpose for learning Japanese has changed from the start of this data collection until now? What is your goal for learning Japanese now?

# Appendix 4
# Semi-Structured Interview with the Teachers

The following questions form a sample of the kind of semi-structured interview conducted with the teacher participants. These interviews were conducted in Japanese.

### Questions to the course coordinators

(1) What were the anticipated outcomes of this unit? – to unit coordinators
(2) What activities did you conduct in the lectures/tutorials/seminars?
(3) Why did you choose these activities?
(4) What did the students have to do in these activities?
(5) What did the students actually do?
(6) What assignments/quizzes/exams did the students have to do during this course?
(7) What are the purposes of these tasks?

### Questions to all the teachers

(1) What activities or tasks did you do in your classroom?
(2) Did your students ask you questions related to what they didn't understand in the classroom or what they did outside the classroom in Japanese during this semester?
(3) For example? What kind of questions did they ask?
(4) What impressions do you have about students' literacy abilities, needs and interests outside the classroom?
(5) Did your students tell you about these things? Did you have any chance to talk about these things with students?
(6) Is there anything else about the activities or other things occurring in the classroom that you may want to convey to me?

# Appendix 5
# Diary about Literacy Activities

The following diary entries are examples of the actual diary entries (Frank's diary entries)

### Date: 11 June

| | |
|---|---|
| What? | Doing the '歌心' reading and vocab |
| When? How long? | 8:30–9:30 |
| Where? | Home |
| With whom? | By myself |
| Comments | Just re-reading the article for revision, and revising any bits I had forgotten with my old vocab sheet that I had made during the semester. |

### Date: 12 June

| | |
|---|---|
| What? | 'Diplomacy' reading; starting essay for the exam |
| When? How long? | 10:00–11:30 |
| Where? | Home |
| With whom? | By myself |
| Comments | Again, just revised an article that we had studied during the semester in class. As it was an online version, I used a *Rikaichan* plugin for Firefox (internet browser) that helped me read *kanji*/vocab that I had forgotten since I studied it in class… The plugin allows you to hover your mouse cursor over a word, and it provides a translation/reading. |

Article can be found at http://www.glocom.ac.jp/j/publications/2005/08/post_30.html (although we were given a slightly shorter edited version).

Screenshot of the *Rikaichan* plugin:

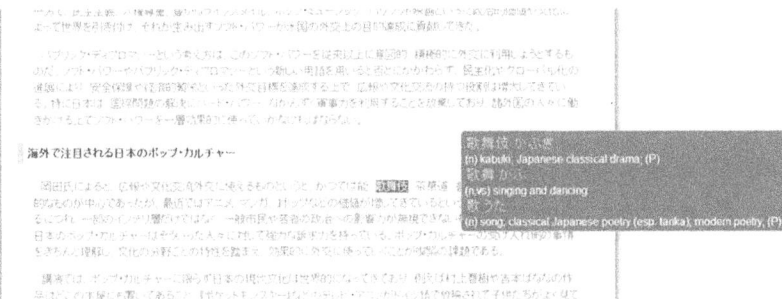

\* This is the screenshot of 'Pop Culture and Public Diplomacy' at the website of GLOCOM (Center for Global Communications)

# References

Ahearn, L. (2001) Language and agency. *Annual Review of Anthropology* 30, 109–137.
Akahori, K. (2002) Using multimedia in the network society. In K. Nakajima (ed.) *Learning Japanese in the Network Society* (pp. 1–24). Calgary: University of Calgary Press.
Akyel, A. and Erçetin, G. (2009) Hypermedia reading strategies employed by advanced learners of English. *System* 37 (1), 136–152.
Allen, J. and Labbo, L. (2001) Giving it a second thought: Making culturally engaged teaching culturally engaging. *Language Arts* 79 (1), 40–52.
Allen, J., Fabregas, V., Hankins, K.H., Hull, G., Labbo, L. and Lawson, H.S. (2002) PhOLKS Lore: Learning from photographs, families, and children. *Language Arts* 79 (4), 312–322.
Allen, L. (1996) The evolution of a learner's beliefs about language learning. *Carleton Papers in Applied Language Studies* 13, 67–80.
Anderson, N.J. (2005) L2 learning strategies. In E. Hinkel (ed.) *Handbook of Research in Second Language Teaching and Learning* (pp. 757–771). Mahwah, NJ: Lawrence Erlbaum Associates.
Ariew, R. and Ercetin, G. (2004) Exploring the potential of hypermedia annotations for second language reading. *Computer Assisted Language Learning* 17 (2), 237–259.
Atkinson, D. (2002) Toward a sociocognitive approach to second language acquisition. *The Modern Language Journal* 86 (4), 525–545.
Bailey, K.M. (1991) Diary studies of classroom language learning: The doubting game and the believing game. In E. Sadtono (ed.) *Language Acquisition and the Second/Foreign Language Classroom* (pp. 60–102). Singapore: SEAMEO Language Centre.
Barab, S., Barnett, M., Yamagata-Lynch, L., Squire, K. and Keating, T. (2002) Using activity theory to understand the systemic tensions characterizing a technology-rich introductory astronomy course. *Mind, Culture and Activity* 9 (2), 76–107.
Barcelos, A.M.F. (2003) Researching beliefs about SLA: A critical review. In P. Kalaja and A.M.F. Barcelos (eds) *Beliefs about SLA* (pp. 7–33). Dordrecht/Boston, MA: Kluwer Academic.
Barks, D. and Watts, P. (2001) Textual borrowing strategies for graduate-level ESL writers. In D. Belcher and A. Hirvela (eds) *Linking Literacies: Perspectives on L2 Reading–Writing Connections* (pp. 246–267). Ann Arbor, MI: The University of Michigan Press.
Barton, D. (1994) *Literacy: An Introduction to the Ecology of Written Language*. Oxford: Blackwell.
Benson, P. (2001) *Teaching and Researching Autonomy in Language Learning*. Harlow/New York: Longman.
Benson, P. (2007) Autonomy in language teaching and learning. *Language Teaching* 40 (1), 21–40.

Benson, P. (2011) Language learning and teaching beyond the classroom: An introduction to the field. In P. Benson and H. Reinders (eds) *Beyond the Language Classroom* (pp. 7–16). Basingstoke: Palgrave Macmillan.

Benson, P. (2013) Learner autonomy. *TESOL Quarterly* 47 (4), 839–843.

Benson, P. and Chik, A. (2011) Towards a more naturalistic CALL: Video-gaming and language learning. *International Journal of Computer-Assisted Language Learning and Teaching* 1 (3), 1–13.

Benson, P. and Cooker, L. (2013) The social and the individual in applied linguistics research. In P. Benson and L. Cooker (eds) *The Applied Linguistic Individual: Sociocultural Approaches to Identity, Agency and Autonomy* (pp. 1–16). Sheffield: Equniox.

Black, R.W. (2005) Access and affiliation: The literacy and composition practices of English-language learners in an online fanfiction community. *Journal of Adolescent and Adult Literacy* 49 (2), 118–128.

Black, R.W. (2008) *Adolescents and Online Fan Fiction*. New York: Peter Lang.

Bloch, J. (2001) Plagiarism and the ESL student: From printed to electronic texts. In D. Belcher and A. Hirvela (eds) *Linking Literacies: Perspectives on L2 Reading–Writing Connections* (pp. 209–228). Ann Arbor, MI: The University of Michigan Press.

Block, D. (1995) Social constraints on interviews. *Prospect* 10, 35–48.

Block, D. (2003) *The Social Turn in Second Language Acquisition*. Edinburgh: Edinburgh University Press.

Bolger, N., Davis, A. and Rafaeli, E. (2003) Diary methods: Capturing life as it is lived. *Annual Review of Psychology* 54, 579–616.

Boonmoh, A. (2012) E-dictionary use under the spotlight: Students' use of pocket electronic dictionaries for writing. *Lexikos* 22, 43–68.

Camitta, M. (1993) Vernacular writing: Varieties of literacy among Philadelphia high school students. In B. Street (ed.) *Cross-Cultural Approaches to Literacy* (pp. 228–246). Cambridge: Cambridge University Press.

Chandler-Olcott, K. and Mahar, D. (2003a) Adolescents' anime-inspired 'fanfictions': An exploration of Multiliteracies. *Journal of Adolescent and Adult Literacy* 46 (7), 556–566.

Chandler-Olcott, K. and Mahar, D. (2003b) 'Tech-savviness' meets Multiliteracies: Exploring adolescent girls' technology-mediated literacy practices. *Reading Research Quarterly* 38 (3), 356–385.

Chapple, L. and Curtis, A. (2000) Content-based instruction in Hong Kong: Student responses to film. *System* 28 (3), 419–433.

Chik, A. (2011) Learner autonomy development through digital gameplay. *Digital Culture and Education* 3 (1), 30–44.

Chik, A. (2013) Naturalistic CALL and digital gaming. *TESOL Quarterly* 47 (4), 834–839.

Chik, A. (2014) Digital gaming and language learning: Autonomy and community. *Language Learning and Technology* 18 (2), 85–100.

Chun, D.M. (2006) CALL technologies for L2 reading. In L. Ducate and N. Arnold (eds) *Calling on CALL: From Theory and Research to New Directions in Foreign Language Teaching. CALICO Monograph Series 5* (pp. 69–98). San Marcos, TX: CALICO.

Chun, D.M. and Plass, J.L. (1996) Effects of multimedia annotations on vocabulary acquisition. *The Modern Language Journal* 80 (2), 183–198.

Cope, B. and Kalantzis, M. (2000) Multiliteracies: The beginnings of an idea. In B. Cope and M. Kalantzis (eds) *Multiliteracies: Literacy Learning and the Design of Social Futures* (pp. 3–8). London: Routledge.

Crawford Camiciottoli, B. (2001) Extensive reading in English: Habits and attitudes of a group of Italian university EFL students. *Journal of Research in Reading* 24 (2), 135–153.

Cumming, A., Busch, M. and Zhou, A. (2002) Investigating learners' goals in the context of adult second-language writing. In S.E. Ransdell and M.L. Barbier (eds) *New Directions for Research in L2 Writing* (pp. 189–208). Dordrecht/London: Kluwer Academic.

Deci, E.L. and Ryan, R.M. (1995) Human autonomy: The basis for true self-esteem. In M. Kernis (ed.) *Efficacy, Agency, and Self-esteem* (pp. 31–49). New York, NY: Plenum.

de Bot, K. and Evers, R. (2007) Determinants of contact, proficiency, and attitudes. In M. Berns, K. de Bot and U. Hasebrink (eds) *In the Presence of English: Media and European Youth* (pp. 71–88). New York: Springer.

de Kretser, A. and Spence-Brown, R. (2010) *The Current State of Japanese Language Education in Australian Schools*. Carlton South, Australia: Education Services Australia.

de Morgado, N.F. (2009) Extensive reading: Students' performance and perception. *The Reading Matrix* 9 (1), 31–43.

Dickinson, L. (1987) *Self-Instruction in Language Learning*. Cambridge: Cambridge University Press.

Dippe, G. (2006) The missing teacher: Contradictions and conflicts in the experience of online learners. *Proceedings of the Fifth International Conference on Networked Learning 2006*. See http://www.networkedlearningconference.org.uk/past/nlc2006/abstracts/pdfs/P38%20Dippe.PDF (accessed 25 October 2017).

Dizon, G. (2016) A comparative study of Facebook vs. paper-and-pencil writing to improve L2 writing skills. *Computer Assisted Language Learning* 29 (8), 1249–1258.

Donato, R. and McCormick, D. (1994) A sociocultural perspective on language learning strategies: The role of mediation. *The Modern Language Journal* 78 (4), 453–464.

Dörnyei, Z. (2005) *The Psychology of the Language Learner: Individual Differences in Second Language Acquisition*. Mahwah, NJ/London: Lawrence Erlbaum Associates.

Dörnyei, Z. (2007) *Research Methods in Applied Linguistics*. Oxford: Oxford University Press.

Dörnyei, Z. (2009) The L2 motivational self system. In Z. Dörnyei and E. Ushioda (eds) *Motivation, Language Identity and the L2 Self* (pp. 9-42). Bristol: Multilingual Matters.

Dörnyei, Z. and Ushioda, E. (2011) *Teaching and Researching Motivation* (2nd edn). London: Routledge.

Du Bois, J.W. (1991) Transcription design principles for spoken discourse research. *Pragmatics* 1 (1), 71–106.

Duff, P. (2006) Beyond generalizability: Contextualization, complexity, and credibility in applied linguistics research. In M. Chalhoub-Deville, C.A. Chapelle and P. Duff (eds) *Inference and Generalizability in Applied Linguistics: Multiple Perspective* (pp. 65–95). Amsterdam: John Benjamins.

Duff, P. (2008) *Case Study Research in Applied Linguistics*. Mahwah, NJ: Lawrence Erlbaum Associates.

Ellis, R. (2008) *The Study of Second Language Acquisition* (2nd edn). Oxford: Oxford University Press.

Engeström, Y. (1987) *Learning by Expanding: An Activity-Theoretical Approach to Developmental Research*. See http://lchc.ucsd.edu/mca/Paper/Engestrom/expanding/toc.htm (accessed 25 October 2017).

Engeström, Y. (1999) Activity theory and individual and social transformation. In Y. Engeström, R. Miettinen and R.L. Punamaki (eds) *Perspectives on Activity Theory* (pp. 19–38). New York: Cambridge University Press.

Engeström, Y. (2001) Expansive learning at work: Toward an activity theoretical reconceptualization. *Journal of Education and Work* 14 (1), 133–156.

Engeström, Y. and Miettinen, R. (1999) Introduction. In Y. Engeström, R. Miettinen and R. Punamäki (eds) *Perspectives on Activity Theory* (pp. 1–16). New York: Cambridge University Press.

Engeström, Y., Engeström, R. and Sunito, A. (2002) Can a school community learn to master its own future? An activity-theoretical study of expansive learning among middle school teachers. In G. Wells and G. Claxton (eds) *Learning for Life in the 21st Century* (pp. 211–224). Oxford: Blackwell.

Eskey, D. (2005) Reading in a second language. In E. Hinkel (ed.) *Handbook of Research in Second Language Teaching and Learning* (pp. 563–580). Mahwah, NJ: Lawrence Erlbaum Associates.

Fatemeh, A., Ali, R. and Masood Rahimi, D. (2013) The effects of captioning texts and caption ordering on L2 listening comprehension and vocabulary learning. *Applied Research on English Language* 2 (2), 51–64.

Finders, M. (1996) Queens and teen zines: Early adolescent females reading their way toward adulthood. *Anthropology and Education Quarterly* 27 (1), 71–89.

Firth, A. and Wagner, J. (1997) On discourse, communication, and (some) fundamental concepts in SLA. *The Modern Language Journal* 81 (3), 285–300.

Frawley, W. and Lantolf, J.P. (1985) Second language discourse: A Vygotskyan perspective. *Applied Linguistics* 6 (1), 19–44.

Freeman, M. (1999) The language learning activities of students of EFL and French at two universities. *Language Learning Journal* 19 (1), 80–88.

Fukunaga, N. (2006) 'Those anime students': Foreign language literacy development through Japanese popular culture. *Journal of Adolescent and Adult Literacy* 50 (3), 206–222.

Gao, X.A. (2010) *Strategic Language Learning: The Roles of Agency and Context*. Bristol: Multilingual Matters.

Gao, X. and Zhang, L.J. (2011) Joining forces for synergy: Agency and metacognition as interrelated theoretical perspectives. In G. Murray, X. Gao and T. Lamb (eds) *Identity, Motivation and Autonomy in Language Learning* (pp. 25–41). Bristol: Multilingual Matters.

Gass, S. and Mackey, A. (2000) *Stimulated Recall Methodology in Second Language Research*. Mahwah, NJ/London: Lawrence Erlbaum Associates.

Gee, J.P. (1992) *The Social Mind: Language, Ideology, and Social Practice*. New York: Bergin and Garvey.

Gee, J.P. (2004) *Situated Language and Learning: A Critique of Traditional Schooling*. New York/London: Routledge.

Gee, J.P. (2007) *Good Video Games+Good Learning: Collected Essays on Video Games, Learning and Literacy*. New York: Peter Lang.

Gee, J.P. (2008) *Social Linguistics and Literacies: Ideology in Discourses* (3rd edn). New York: Routledge.

Gibson, V. (1995) An analysis of the use of diaries as a data collection method. *Nurse Researcher* 3 (1), 66–73.

Gillette, B. (1994) The role of learner goals in L2 success. In J.P. Lantolf and G. Appel (eds) *Vygotskian Approaches to Second Language Research* (pp. 196–213). Norwood, NJ: Ablex Pub. Corp.

Grabe, W. (2001) Reading–writing relations: Theoretical perspectives and instructional practices. In D. Belcher and A. Hirvela (eds) *Linking Literacies: Perspectives on L2 Reading–Writing Connections* (pp. 15–47). Ann Arbor, MI: The University of Michigan Press.

Graham, J. (2005) Video websites pop up, invite postings, *USA Today*, 21 November 2005. See https://usatoday30.usatoday.com/tech/news/techinnovations/2005-11-21-video-websites_x.htm (accessed 25 October 2017).

Grenfell, M. and Macaro, E. (2007) Claims and critiques. In A.D. Cohen and E. Macaro (eds) *Language Learner Strategies: Thirty Years of Research and Practice* (pp. 9–28). Oxford: Oxford University Press.

Hall, R. (2009) Towards a fusion of formal and informal learning environments: The impact of the read/write web. *Electronic Journal of E-Learning* 7 (1), 29–40.

Halliday, M.A.K. (1994) *An Introduction to Functional Grammar* (2nd edn). London: E. Arnold.

Hamada, M., Hayashi, S., Fukunaga, Y., Humino, M. and Miyazaki, T. (2006) Nihongo gakushūsha to gakushū kankyō no sōgo sayō o megutte [Interactions between Japanese language learners and learning environments]. In Kokuritsu kokugo kenkyūjyo (ed.) *Nihongo Kyōiku no Aratana Bunmyaku: Gakushū Kankyō, Sesshoku Bamen, Komyunikēshon no Tayōsei [The New Context of Japanese Language Education: Learning Environments, Contact Situations, and the Diversity of Communication]* (pp. 67–101). Tokyo: Aruku.

Haneda, M. (2005) Investing in foreign-language writing: A study of two multicultural learners. *Journal of Language, Identity, and Education* 4 (4), 269–290.

Haneda, M. (2007) Modes of engagement in foreign language writing: An activity theoretical perspective. *Canadian Modern Language Review* 64 (2), 297–327.

Hatcher, J.S. (2005) Of otakus and fansubs: A critical look at anime online in light of current issues in copyright law. *Script-ed* 2 (4), 514–542.

Heath, S.B. (1983) *Ways with Words: Language, Life and Work in Communities and Classrooms*. New York: Cambridge University Press.

Helft, J. (2007) Netflix to deliver movies to the PC, *The New York Times*, 16 January. See http://www.nytimes.com/2007/01/16/technology/16netflix.html (accessed 25 October 2017).

Herron, C., York, H., Cole, S.P. and Linden, P. (1998) A comparison study of student retention of foreign language video: Declarative versus interrogative advance organizer. *The Modern Language Journal* 82 (2), 237–247.

Hirvela, A. (2005) Computer-based reading and writing across the curriculum: Two case studies of L2 writers. *Computers and Composition* 22 (3), 337–356.

Huang, H.-C. and Eskey, D.E. (1999) The effects of closed-captioned television on the listening comprehension of intermediate English as a second language (ESL) students. *Journal of Educational Technology Systems* 28 (1), 75–96.

Huang, J. (2011) A dynamic account of autonomy, agency and identity in (T)EFL learning. In G. Murray, X. Gao and T. Lamb (eds) *Identity, Motivation and Autonomy in Language Learning* (pp. 229–246). Bristol: Multilingual Matters.

Huang, J. and Benson, P. (2013) Autonomy, agency and identity in foreign and second language education. *Chinese Journal of Applied Linguistics* 36 (1), 7–28.

Hulstijn, J.H. (1993) When do foreign-language readers look up the meaning of unfamiliar words? The influence of task and learner variables. *The Modern Language Journal* 77 (2), 139–147.

Hulstijn, J.H., Hollander, M. and Greidanus, T. (1996) Incidental vocabulary learning by advanced foreign language students: The influence of marginal glosses, dictionary use, and reoccurrence of unknown words. *The Modern Language Journal* 80 (3), 327–339.

Holec, H. (1981) *Autonomy in Foreign Language Learning*. Oxford: Pergamon. (First Published 1979, Strasbourg: Council of Europe.)

Hyland, F. (2004) Learning autonomously: Contextualising out-of-class English language learning. *Language Awareness* 13 (3), 180–202.

Inaba, M. (2013) What is the role of 'language classes' in autonomous learning?: The implications from Japanese language learners' L2 activities outside the classroom. In *The European Conference on Language Learning*. Proceedings of the European Conference on Language Learning, Brighton, UK, 18–21 July. See http://papers.iafor.org/conference-proceedings/ECLL/ECLL2013_proceedings.pdf (accessed 25 October 2017).

Inaba, M. (2014) Pop culture and second language learning: Utilising visual and audio materials in Japanese classes', *Högskolepedagogisk reflektion och praktik: proceedings från humanistiska och teologiska fakulteternas pedagogiska inspirationskonferens 2012* [Proceedings of the Fourth Pedagogical Conference 2012]. Lund, Sweden, 7 November.

Inaba, M. and Kurata, N. (2017) Nihongo gakushūsha no mochibēshon no henka to sono yōin: Ōsutoraria to suwēden no gakusē no jirē kara [Changes in motivation among Japanese language learners and their causes: Case studies of Australian and Swedish students]. *Nihongo Kyōiku Gakkai Shunki Taikai Yokōshū* [Proceedings of Japanese Language Education Spring Conference], 21–31. Tokyo, Japan, 20–21 May. See http://www.nkg.or.jp/pdf/yokou-17spring.pdf (accessed 25 October 2017).

Inozu, J., Sahinkarakas, S. and Yumru, H. (2010) The nature of language learning experiences beyond the classroom and its learning outcomes. *US-China Foreign Language* 8 (1), 14–21.

Japan Foundation (2011) *Survey Report on Japanese-Language Education Abroad 2009*. Tokyo: Japan Foundation. See https://www.jpf.go.jp/e/project/japanese/survey/result/dl/2009/2009_00.pdf (accessed 25 October 2017)

Japan Foundation (2017a) *Nihongo Kyōiku Kuni Chīki Betsu Jyōhō 2016: Ōstoraria* [Country and Regional Information about Japanese Language Education 2016: Australia]. Tokyo: Japan Foundation. See https://www.jpf.go.jp/j/project/japanese/survey/area/country/2016/australia.html (accessed 25 October 2017).

Japan Foundation (2017b) *Survey Report on Japanese-Language Education Abroad 2015*. Tokyo: Japan Foundation. See https://www.jpf.go.jp/j/project/japanese/survey/result/dl/survey_2015/Report_all_e.pdf (accessed 25 October 2017)

Jones, F.R. (1998) Self-instruction and success: A learner-profile study. *Applied Linguistics* 19 (3), 378–406.

Kalaja, P. and Barcelos, M.F. (2003) Introduction. In P. Kalaja and M.F. Barcelos (eds) *Beliefs about SLA* (pp. 1–4). New York: Springer.

Kalaja, P., Alanen, R., Palviainen, Å. and Dufva, H. (2011) From milk cartons to English roommates: Context and agency in L2 learning beyond the classroom. In P. Benson and H. Reinders (eds) *Beyond the Language Classroom* (pp. 47–58). Basingstoke: Palgrave Macmillan.

Kamada, O., Sugimoto, F., Tomiyama, Y., Miyatani, A. and Yamamoto, M. (1998) *Authentic Japanese: Progressing from Intermediate to Advanced*. Tokyo: The Japan Times.

Kang, Y.-S. and Pyun, D.O. (2013) Mediation strategies in L2 writing processes: A case study of two Korean language learners. *Language, Culture and Curriculum* 26 (1), 52–67.

Kaptelinin, V. and Nardi, B.A. (2006) *Acting with Technology: Activity Theory and Interaction Design*. Cambridge, MA/London: MIT Press.

Kawashima, K. and Kumano, N. (2011) Anime manga no nihongo jugyō eno katsuyō [Making use of anime and manga for Japanese language classes]. *2011nendo Nihongo Kyōiku Jissen Hōramu Hōkoku* [Report on the Forum of Japanese Language Teaching Practices, 2011]. See http://www.nkg.or.jp/pdf/jissenhokoku/2011_RT3_kawashima.pdf (accessed 25 October 2017).

Knight, S. (1994) Dictionary use while reading: The effects on comprehension and vocabulary acquisition for students of different verbal abilities. *The Modern Language Journal* 78 (3), 285–299.

Konishi, M. (2003) Strategies for reading hypertext by Japanese ESL learners. *The Reading Matrix* 3 (3), 97–119.

Kurata, N. (2011) *Foreign Language Learning and Use: Interaction in Informal Social Network*. London: Continuum.

Kuutti, K. (1996) Activity theory as a potential framework for human–computer interaction research. In B.A. Nardi (ed.) *Context and Consciousness: Activity Theory and Human-Computer Interaction* (pp. 18–44). Cambridge, MA: The MIT Press.

Lai, C. (2015) Perceiving and traversing in-class and out-of-class learning: Accounts from foreign language learners in Hong Kong. *Innovation in Language Learning and Teaching* 9 (3), 265–284.

Lai, C. and Gu, M. (2011) Self-regulated out-of-class language learning with technology. *Computer Assisted Language Learning: An International Journal* 24 (4), 317–335.

Lai, C., Zhu, W. and Gong, G. (2015) Understanding the quality of out-of-class English learning. *TESOL Quarterly* 49 (2), 278–308.

Lam, W.S.E. (2000) L2 literacy and the design of the self: A case study of a teenager writing on the Internet. *TESOL Quarterly* 34 (3), 457–482.

Lam, W.S.E. (2004) Second language socialization in a bilingual chat room: Global and local consideration. *Language Learning and Technology* 8 (3), 44–65.

Lam, W.S.E. (2006) Re-envisioning language, literacy, and the immigrant subject in new mediascapes. *Pedagogies: An International Journal* 1 (3), 171–195.

Lam, W.S.E. (2009a) Multiliteracies on instant messaging in negotiating local, translocal, and transnational affiliations: A case of an adolescent immigrant. *Reading Research Quarterly* 44 (4), 377–397.

Lam, W.S.E. (2009b) Literacy and learning across transnational online spaces. *E-learning and Digital Media* 6 (4), 303–324.

Lamb, M. (2004) 'It depends on the students themselves': Independent language learning at an Indonesian state school. *Language, Culture and Curriculum* 17 (3), 229–245.

Lamb, M. (2007) The impact of school on EFL learning motivation: An Indonesian case study. *TESOL Quarterly* 41 (4), 757–780.

Lantolf, J.P. (2000) Introducing sociocultural theory. In J.P. Lantolf (ed.) *Sociocultural Theory and Second Language Learning* (pp. 1–26). Oxford: Oxford University Press.

Lantolf, J.P. (2013) Sociocultural theory and the dialectics of learner autonomy/agency. In P. Benson and L. Cooker (eds) *The Applied Linguistics Individual: Sociocultural Approaches to Identity, Agency and Autonomy* (pp. 17–31). Bristol, CT: Equinox.

Lantolf, J.P. and Aljaafreh, A. (1995) Second language learning in the zone of proximal development: A revolutionary experience. *International Journal of Educational Research* 23 (7), 619–632.

Lantolf, J.P. and Pavlenko, A. (2001) (S)econd (L)anguage (A)ctivity: Understanding learners as people. In M.P. Breen (ed.) *Learner Contributions to Language Learning: New Directions in Research* (pp. 141–158). Harlow/New York: Longman.

Lantolf, J.P. and Genung, P.B. (2002) 'I'd rather switch than fight': An activity-theoretic study of power, success, and failure in a foreign language. In C. Kramsch (ed.) *Language Acquisition and Language Socialization: Ecological Perspectives* (pp. 175–196). London: Continuum.

Lantolf, J.P. and Thorne, S.L. (2006) *Sociocultural Theory and the Genesis of Second Language Development*. Oxford/New York: Oxford University Press.

Lantolf, J.P. and Johnson, K.E. (2007) Extending Firth and Wagner's (1997): Ontological perspective to L2 classroom praxis and teacher education. *The Modern Language Journal* 91 (Focus Issue), 877–892.

Laufer, B. and Hill, M. (2000) What lexical information do L2 learners select in a call dictionary and how does it affect word retention? *Language Learning and Technology* 3 (2), 58–76.

Lave, J. and Wenger, E. (1991) *Situated Learning: Legitimate Peripheral Participation*. Cambridge: Cambridge University Press.

Lei, X. (2008) Exploring a sociocultural approach to writing strategy research: Mediated actions in writing activities. *Journal of Second Language Writing* 17 (4), 217–236.

Leki, I. (1995) Coping strategies of ESL students in writing tasks across the curriculum. *TESOL Quarterly* 29 (2), 235–260.

Leki, I. (2002) Second language writing. In R.B. Kaplan (ed.) *Oxford Handbook of Applied Linguistics* (pp. 60–72). Oxford: Oxford University Press.

Leonard, S. (2005) Progress against the law: Anime and fandom, with the key to the globalization of culture. *International Journal of Cultural Studies* 8 (3), 281–305.
Leont'ev, A.N. (1978) *Activity, Consciousness and Personality.* Engelwood Cliffs, NJ: Prentice Hall.
Leont'ev, A.N. (1981) *Problems of the Development of the Mind.* Moscow [London]: Progress; Distributed by Central Books.
Leung, C.Y. (2002) Extensive reading and language learning: A diary study of a beginning learner of Japanese. *Reading in a Foreign Language* 14 (1), 66–81.
Levy, M. (2009) Technologies in use for second language learning. *Modern Language Journal* 93 (1), 769–782.
Lin, P.M.S. and Siyanova-Chanturia, A. (2015) Internet television for L2 vocabulary learning. In D. Nunan and J.C. Richards (eds) *Language Learning beyond the Classroom [eBook].* New York: Routledge.
Little, D., Ridley, J. and Ushioda, E. (2002) *Towards Greater Autonomy in the Foreign Language Classroom.* Dublin: Authentik.
Littlewood, W. (1999) Defining and developing autonomy in East Asian contexts. *Applied Linguistics* 20 (1), 71–94.
Loucky, J.P. (2010) Comparing electronic dictionary functions and use. *CALICO Journal* 28 (1), 156–174.
Lwo, L. and Lin, M.C.T. (2012) The effects of captions in teenagers and multimedia L2 learning. *ReCALL* 24 (2), 188–208.
Ma, Q. (2017) A multi-case study of university students' language-learning experience mediated by mobile technologies: A socio-cultural perspective. *Computer Assisted Language Learning* 30 (3–4), 183–203.
Mackey, A. and Gass, S.M. (2005) *Second Language Research: Methodology and Design.* Mahwah, NJ: Lawrence Erlbaum Associates.
Mahiri, J. and Sablo, S. (1996) Writing for their lives: The non-school literacy of California's urban African American youth. *The Journal of Negro Education* 65 (2), 164–180.
Makino, S. (2008) Nihongo, Nihon bunka kyōiku to anime: 'Sen to chihiro no kamikakushi' no baai [Japanese language, culture education and anime: Reasons and method: A case of 'Spirited Away']. In Y. Hatasa (ed.) *Gaikokugo to shite no Nihongo Kyōiku: Takabuteki Shiya ni Motozuku Kokoromi [Japanese as a Foreign Language Education: Multiple Perspectives]* (pp. 61–81). Tokyo: Kuroshio shuppan.
Manchón, R.M., Roca de Larios, J. and Murphy, L. (2007) A review of writing strategies: Focus on conceptualizations and impact of first language. In A.D. Cohen and E. Macaro (eds) *Language Learner Strategies: Thirty Years of Research and Practice* (pp. 229–250). Oxford: Oxford University Press.
Mason, B. and Krashen, S.D. (1997) Extensive reading in English as a foreign language. *System* 25 (1), 91–102.
Mayer, R.E. (2008) Multimedia literacy. In J. Corio, M. Knobel, C. Lankshear and D.J. Leu (eds) *Handbook of Research on New Literacies* (pp. 359–376). New York: Lawrence Erlbaum Associates.
McDonough, J. and McDonough, S.H. (1997) *Research Methods for English Language Teachers.* London/New York: Martin's Press.
Menezes, V. (2011) Affordances for language learning beyond the classroom. In P. Benson and H. Reinders (eds) *Beyond the Language Classroom* (pp. 59-71). Basingstoke: Palgrave Macmillan.
Merriam, S.B. (1998) *Qualitative Research and Case Study Applications.* San Francisco, CA: Jossey-Bass.
Ministry of Foreign Affairs of Japan (2017) *Kaigai Zairyū Hōjinsū Chōsatōkē: Hēsē 29 nen ban* [*Annual Report of Statistics on Japanese Nationals Overseas: Summary, 2017*]. See http://www.mofa.go.jp/mofaj/files/000293757.pdf (accessed 15 July 2018).
Mitchell, K. (2012) A social tool: Why and how ESOL students use facebook. *CALICO Journal* 29 (3), 471–493.

Miyazaki, S. (2006) Gengo shūtoku kenkyū no aratana tenkai [New directions in language acquisition research]. In S. Miyazaki (ed.) *Shinjidai no Nihongo Kyōiku o Mezashite: Waseda kara Sekai e Hasshin [Japanese Language Education in the New Age: Dissemination from Waseda to the World]* (pp. 8–25). Tokyo: Meiji Shoin.

Mori, S. (2004) Significant motivational predictors of the amount of reading by EFL learners in Japan. *RELC Journal* 35 (1), 63–81.

Muraoka, H. (2002) Shitsumon chōsa: Intabyū to ankēto [Surveys: Interviews and questionnaires]. In J.V. Neustupný and S. Miyzaki (eds) *Gengo Kenkyū no Hōhō: Gengogaku, Nihongogaku, Nihongo Kyōikugaku ni Tazusawaru Hito no tameni [Techniques for Language Research: For Researchers in the Field of Linguistics, Japanese Linguistics and Japanese Applied Linguistics]* (pp. 125–142). Tokyo: Kuroshio shuppan.

Murray, G. (2004) Two stories of self-directed foreign language learning. *Proceedings of the Independent Learning Association Conference*, Melbourne, Australia, 13–14 September 2003. See http://citeseerx.ist.psu.edu/viewdoc/download?doi=10.1.1.124.4139&rep=rep1&type=pdf (accessed 25 October 2017).

Murray, G. (2008) Pop culture and language learning: Learners' stories informing EFL. *Innovation in Language Learning and Teaching* 2(1), 2-17.

Murray, G. (2014) Exploring the social dimension of autonomy in language learning. In G. Murray (ed.) *Social Dimensions of Autonomy in Language Learning* (pp. 3–11). Basingstoke: Palgrave Macmillan.

Murray, G. and Kojima, M. (2007) Out-of-class language learning: One learners' story. In P. Benson (ed.) *Learner Autonomy 8: Insider Perspectives and Autonomy in Language Learning and Teaching* (pp. 25–40). Dublin: Authentik.

Nash, T. and Yuan, Y. (1992) Extensive reading for learning and enjoyment. *TESOL Journal* 2 (2), 27–31.

Neilsen, L. (1998) Playing for real: Performative texts and adolescent identities. In D. Alvermann, K.A. Hinchman, D.W. Moore, S.F. Phelps and D.R. Waff (eds) *Reconceptualizing the Literacies in Adolescents' Lives* (pp. 3–26). London: Lawrence Erlbaum Associates.

Nelson, C. and Kim, M. (2001) Contradictions, appropriation, and transformation: An activity theory approach to L2 writing and classroom practices. *Texas Papers for Foreign Language Education* 6 (1), 37–62.

Neustupný, J.V. (1991) *On Romanizing Japanese*. Melbourne: Melbourne Japanese Studies Centre.

Neustupný, J.V. (2002) Dēta o dō atsumeru ka [How to collect data]. In J.V. Neustupný and S. Miyzaki (eds) *Gengo Kenkyū no Hōhō: Gengogaku, Nihongogaku, Nihongokyōikugaku ni Tazusawaru Hito no tame ni [Techniques for Language Research: For Researchers in the Feld of Linguistics, Japanese Linguistics and Japanese Applied Linguistics]* (pp. 15–33). Tokyo: Kuroshio shuppan.

Nishino, T. (2007) Beginning to read extensively: A case study with Mako and Fumi. *Reading in a Foreign Language* 19 (2), 76–105.

Noels, K.A., Clément, R. and Pelletier, L.G. (1999) Perceptions of teachers' communicative styles and students' intrinsic and extrinsic motivation. *The Modern Language Journal* 83 (1), 23–34.

Noels, K.A., Pelletier, L.G., Clément, R. and Vallerand, R.J. (2000) Why are you learning a second language? Motivational orientations and self-determination theory. *Language Learning* 53 (S1), 33–64.

Norton, B. (2000) *Identity and Language Learning: Gender, Ethnicity and Educational Change*. London: Longman.

Nunan, D. (1992) *Research Methods in Language Learning*. Cambridge/New York: Cambridge University Press.

Nunan, D. and Richards, J.C. (2015) Preface. In D. Nunan and J.C. Richards (eds) *Language Learning beyond the Classroom [eBook]*. New York: Routledge.

Ohta, A.S. (2000) Rethinking interaction in SLA: Developmentally appropriate assistance in the zone of proximal development and the acquisition of L2 grammar. In J.P. Lantolf (ed.) *Sociocultural Theory and Second Language Learning* (pp. 51–78). Oxford: Oxford University Press.

Oxford, R.L. (2003) Towards a more systematic model of L2 learner autonomy. In D. Palfreyman and R.C. Smith (eds) *Learner Autonomy Across Cultures: Language Education Perspectives* (pp. 75–92). Basingstoke: Palgrave Macmillan.

Oxford, R.L. and Schramm, K. (2007) Bridging the gap between psychological and sociocultural perspectives on L2 learner strategies. In A.D. Cohen and E. Macaro (eds) *Language Learning Strategies: Thirty Years of Research and Practice* (pp. 47–68). Oxford: Oxford University Press.

Pailliotet, A.W. and Mosenthal, P.B. (2000) *Reconceptualizing Literacy in the Age of Media, Multimedia, and Hypermedia*. Norwood, NJ: JAI/Ablex.

Palfreyman, D.M. (2006) Social context and resources for language learning. *System* 34 (3), 352–370.

Palfreyman, D.M. (2011) Family, friends, and learning beyond the classroom: Social networks and social capital in language learning. In P. Benson and H. Reinders (eds) *Beyond the Language Classroom* (pp. 17–34). Basingstoke: Palgrave Macmillan.

Park, J.H. and De Costa, P. (2015) Reframing graduate student writing strategies from an Activity Theory perspective. *Language and Sociocultural Theory* 2 (1), 25–50.

Pasfield-Neofitou, S.E. (2009) Paper, electronic or online? Different dictionaries for different activities. *Babel* 43 (2), 12–18.

Pasfield-Neofitou, S.E. (2012) *Online Communication in a Second Language: Social Interaction, Language Use and Learning Japanese*. Bristol: Multilingual Matters.

Pearson, N. (2004) The idiosyncrasies of out-of-class language learning: A study of Mainland Chinese students studying English at tertiary level in New Zealand. *Proceedings of the Independent Learning Conference*, Melbourne, Australia, 13–14 September 2003, https://docplayer.net/22480303-The-idiosyncrasies-of-out-of-class-language-learning-a-study-of-mainland-chinese-students-studying-english-at-tertiary-level-in-new-zealand.html.

Pickard, N. (1995) Out-of-class language learning strategies: Three case studies. *Language Learning Journal* 12 (1), 35–37.

Pickard, N. (1996) Out-of-class learning strategies. *ELT Journal* 50 (2), 150–159.

Rama, P.S., Black, R.W., Van Es, E. and Warschauer, M. (2012) Affordances for second language learning in world of Warcraft. *ReCALL* 24 (3), 322–338.

Riazi, A. (1997) Acquiring disciplinary literacy: A social-cognitive analysis of text production and learning among Iranian graduate students of education. *Journal of Second Language Writing* 6 (2), 105–137.

Richards, K. (2003) *Qualitative Inquiry in TESOL*. New York: Palgrave Macmillan.

Robb, T. (2003) Google as a quick 'n dirty corpus tool. *The Electronic Journal for English as a Second Language* 7 (2). See http://tesl-ej.org/ej26/int.html (accessed 25 October 2017).

Rodgers, M.P.H. and Webb, S. (2011) Narrow viewing: The vocabulary in related television programs. *TESOL Quarterly* 45 (4), 689–717.

Rush, L.S. (2003) Taking a broad view of literacy: Lessons from the Appalachian Trail thru-hiking community. *Reading Online* 6 (7).

Russell, D.R. and Yañez, A. (2003) 'Big picture people rarely become historians': Genre systems and the contradictions of general education. In C. Bazerman and D.R. Russell (eds) *Writing Selves/Writing Societies: Research from Activity Perspectives [eBook]* (pp. 331–362). Fort Collins, CO: The WAC Clearinghouse and Mind, Culture, and Activity. See https://wac.colostate.edu/books/selves_societies/russell/russell.pdf (accessed 25 October 2017).

Ryan, R.M. and Deci, E.L. (2000) Self-determination theory and the facilitation of intrinsic motivation, social development, and well-being. *American Psychologist* 55 (1), 68–78.

Ryan, S.M. (1997) Preparing learners for independence: Resources beyond the classroom. In P. Benson and P. Voller (eds) *Autonomy and Independence in Language Learning* (pp. 215–224). New York: Longman.

Sakar, A. and Ercetin, G. (2005) Effectiveness of hypermedia annotations for foreign language reading. *Journal of Computer Assisted Learning* 21 (1), 28–38.

Sakuma, K. (2006) Kaigai ni manabu nihongo kyōiku: Nihongo gakushū no tayōsei [Learning from overseas institutions and teaching in Japanese language education: Diversity of Japanese learning]. In Kokuritsu Kokugo Kenkyūjyo (ed.) *Nihongo Kyōiku no Aratana Bunmyaku: Gakushū Kankyō, Sesshoku Bamen, Komyunikēshon no Tayōsei [The New Context of Japanese Language Education: Learning Environment, Contact Situation and Diversity of Communication]* (pp. 33–65). Tokyo: Aruku.

Sankó, G. (2006) The effects of hypertextual input modification on L2 vocabulary acquisition and retention. *UPRT 2006: Empirical Studies in English Applied Linguistics*. See http://vmek.niif.hu/04900/04902/04902.pdf#page=149 (accessed 25 October 2017).

Santos, T., Atkinson, D., Erickson, M., Matsuda, P.K. and Silva, T. (2000) On the future of second language writing: A colloquium. *Journal of Second Language Writing* 9 (1), 1–20.

Sasaki, M. (2006) Paradaimu shihuto saikō [Reconsideration of a paradigm shift]. In Kokuritsu Kokugo Kenkyūjyo (ed.) *Nihongo Kyōiku no Aratana Bunmyaku: Gakushū Kankyō, Sesshoku Bamen, Komyunikēshon no Tayōsei [The New Contexts of Japanese Language Education: Learning Environment, Contact Situation and Diversity of Communication]* (pp. 259–283). Tokyo: Aruku.

Schmidt, R.W. (1990) The role of consciousness in second language acquisition. *Applied Linguistics* 11 (2), 129–158.

Schodt, F.L. (1996) *Dreamland Japan: Writings on Modern Manga*. Berkeley, CA: Stone Bridge Press.

Schultz, K. (2002) Looking across space and time: Reconceptualizing literacy learning in and out of School. *Research in the Teaching of English* 36 (3), 356–390.

Schultz, K. and Hull, G. (2002) Locating literacy theory in out-of-school contexts. In G. Hull and K. Schultz (eds) *School's Out!: Bridging Out-of-School Literacies with Classroom Practice* (pp. 11–31). New York/London: Teachers College Press.

Scribner, S. and Cole, M. (1981) *The Psychology of Literacy*. Cambridge: Harvard University Press.

Sha, G. (2010) Using Google as a super corpus to drive written language learning: A comparison with the British National Corpus. *Computer Assisted Language Learning* 23 (5), 377–393.

Shibata, T. (2008) Anime o riyō shita nihongo kyōiku: Gakusei no hyōka to ōraru samarī no bunseki o chūshin to shite [Japanese Language Education using anime: Focusing on students' feedback and analysis of the oral summary]. In Y. Hatasa (ed.) *Gaikokugo toshite no Nihongo Kyōiku: Takakuteki Shiya ni Motozuku Kokoromi [Japanese as a Foreign Language Education: Multiple Perspectives]* (pp. 83–102). Tokyo: Kuroshio shuppan.

Silverman, D. (2005) *Doing Qualitative Research: A Practical Handbook* (2nd edn). London: Sage.

Sockett, G. (2014) *The Online Informal Learning of English*. Basingstoke: Palgrave Macmillan.

Sockett, G. and Toffoli, D. (2012) Beyond learner autonomy: A dynamic systems view of the informal learning of English in virtual online communities. *ReCALL* 24 (2), 138–151.

Spack, R. (1997) The acquisition of academic literacy in a second language: A longitudinal case study. *Written Communication* 14 (1), 3–62.

Spence-Brown, R. (2004) Authentic assessment? The implementation of an 'authentic' teaching and assessment task. Unpublished PhD thesis, University of Melbourne.

Spence-Brown, R. (2007) Learner motivation and engagement in a pedagogic and assessment task. In H. Marriott, T. Moore and R. Spence-Brown (eds) *Learning Discourses and Discourses of Learning* (pp. part three, 1–15). Melbourne: Monash University ePress.
Spratt, M., Humphreys, G. and Chan, V. (2002) Autonomy and motivation: Which comes first? *Language Teaching Research* 6 (3), 245–266.
Stake, R.E. (2005) Qualitative case studies. In N.K. Denzin and Y.S. Lincoln (eds) *The Sage Handbook of Qualitative Research* (pp. 443–466). Thousand Oaks, CA: Sage.
Street, B. (1984) *Literacy in Theory and Practice*. New York: Cambridge University Press.
Street, B. (1993) *Cross-Cultural Approaches to Literacy*. Cambridge: Cambridge University Press.
Street, B. (1995) *Social Literacies: Critical Approaches to Literacy in Development, Ethnography and Education*. London/New York: Longman.
Street, B. (2000) Literacy events and literacy practices: Theory and practice in the New Literacy Studies. In M.M. Jones and K. Jones (eds) *Multilingual Literacies: Reading and Writing Different Worlds* (pp. 17–30). Amsterdam: John Benjamins.
Street, B. (2003) What's 'new' in New Literacy Studies? Critical approaches to literacy in theory and practice. *Current Issues in Comparative Education* 5 (2), 77–91.
Sundqvist, P. (2011) A possible path to progress: Out-of-school English language learners in Sweden. In P. Benson and H. Reinders (eds) *Beyond the Language Classroom* (pp. 106–118). Basingstoke: Palgrave Macmillan.
Sundqvist, P. and Wikström, P. (2015) Out-of- school digital gameplay and in-school L2 English vocabulary outcomes. *System* 51, 65–76.
Sundqvist, P. and Sylvén, L.K. (2016) *Extramural English in Teaching and Learning: From Theory and Research to Practice*. London: Palgrave Macmillan.
Suto, H. (2008) Teroppu ga shichōsha ni ataeru eikyō [Influences of telops on the receivers' interpretation]. *Informatics* 1 (2), 13–20. See https://m-repo.lib.meiji.ac.jp/dspace/bitstream/10291/7908/1/informatics_1-2_13.pdf (accessed 25 October 2017).
Suzuki, T. (2016) Nihongo gakushūsha wa jisho kara donoyōni kotoba o sagasu noka: chūkyū jyōkyū nihongo gakushūsha nanamei no jisho shiyō ni tsuite no chōsa jirē hōkoku kara [How do Japanese language learners find words from a dictionary? Studies of dictionary use by seven mid to pre-advanced learners]. *Nihongo Nihon Kenkyuu* [*Journal for Japanese Studies*] 6, 1–24.
Sylvén, L.K. and Sundqvist, P. (2012) Gaming as extramural English L2 learning and L2 proficiency among young learners. *ReCALL* 24 (3), 302–321.
Tabata-Sandom, M. (2016) How do learners of Japanese read texts when they use online pop-up dictionaries? *Reading Matrix* 16 (2), 98–109.
Taylor, A. (2006) The effects of CALL versus traditional L1 glosses on L2 reading comprehension. *CALICO Journal* 23 (2), 309–318.
Taylor, G. (2005) Perceived processing strategies of students watching captioned video. *Foreign Language Annals* 38 (3), 422–427.
Thomson, C.K. (1997) Kaigaino nihongo kyōiku ni okeru risōsu no katsuyō [Japanese language learning resources for overseas learners and teachers]. *Sekaino Nihongo Kyōiku* [*Japanese Language Education around the Globe*] 7, 17–29.
Thorne, S.L. (2008) Transcultural communication in open internet environments and massively multiplayer online games. In S. Magnan (ed.) *Mediating Discourse Online* (pp. 305–307). Amsterdam: John Benjamins.
Thorne, S.L. and Reinhardt, J. (2008) 'Bridging activities', new media literacies and advanced foreign language proficiency. *CALICO Journal* 25 (3), 558–572.
Toffoli, D. and Sockett, G. (2010) How non-specialist students of English practice informal learning using web 2.0 tools. *Asp la revue du Geras* 58, 125–144.

Toohey, K. and Norton, B. (2003) Learner autonomy as agency in sociocultural settings. In D. Palfreyman and R.C. Smith (eds) *Learner Autonomy across Cultures: Language Education Perspectives* (pp. 58–74). Basingstoke: Palgrave Macmillan.
Ushioda, E. (2000) Tandem language learning via e-mail: From motivation to autonomy. *ReCALL* 12 (2), 121–128.
Ushioda, E. (2001) Language learning at university: Exploring the role of motivational thinking. In Z. Dörnyei and R. Schmidt (eds) *Motivation and Second Language Acquisition* (pp. 93–125). Honolulu, HI: Second Language Teaching and Curriculum Center, University of Hawaii.
Ushioda, E. (2009) A person-in-context relational view of emergent motivation, self and identity. In Z. Dörnyei and E. Ushioda (eds) *Motivation, Language Identity and the L2 Self* (pp. 215–228). Bristol: Multilingual Matters.
Ushioda, E. (2011) Language learning motivation, self and identity: Current theoretical perspectives. *Computer Assisted Language Learning* 24 (3), 199–210.
van Lier, L. (1996) *Interaction in the Language Curriculum: Awareness, Autonomy and Authenticity*. New York: Longman.
van Lier, L. (2000) From input to affordance: Social interactive learning from an ecological perspective. In J.P. Lantolf (ed.) *Sociocultural Theory and Second Language Learning* (pp. 245–259). Oxford: Oxford University Press.
van Lier, L. (2004) *The Ecology and Semiotics of Language Learning: A Sociocultural Perspective*. Dordrecht: Kluwer Academic.
van Lier, L. (2008) Agency in the classroom. In J.P. Lantolf and M.E. Poehner (eds) *Sociocultural Theory and the Teaching of Second Languages* (pp. 163–188). London: Equinox.
Vanderplank, R. (1988) The value of teletext sub-titles in language learning. *English Language Teaching Journal* 42 (4), 272–281.
Vurdien, R. (2013) Enhancing writing skills through blogging in an advanced English as a foreign language class in Spain. *Computer Assisted Language Learning* 26 (2), 126–143.
Vygotsky, L.S. (1978) *Mind in Society: The Development of Higher Psychological Processes*. Edited by M. Cole, V. John-Steiner, S. Scribner and E. Souberman. Cambridge: Harvard University Press.
Vygotsky, L.S. (1981) The genesis of higher mental functions. In J.V. Wertsch (ed.) *The Concept of Activity in Soviet Psychology* (pp. 144–188). Armonk, NY: M.E. Sharpe.
Webb, S. (2015) Extensive viewing: Language learning through watching television. In D. Nunan and J.C. Richards (eds) *Language Learning Beyond the Classroom[eBook]*. New York: Routledge.
Wells, G. (2002) The role of dialogue in activity theory. *Mind, Culture and Activity* 9 (1), 43–66.
Wenger, E. (1998) *Communities of Practice: Learning, Meaning, and Identity*. Cambridge: Cambridge University Press.
Wertsch, J.V. (1998) *Mind as Action*. New York: Oxford University Press.
Wertsch, J.V., Tulviste, P. and Hagstrom, F. (1993) A sociocultural approach to agency. In E.A. Forman, N. Minick and C.A. Stone (eds) *Contexts for Learning: Sociocultural Dynamics in Children's Development* (pp. 336–356). New York: Oxford University Press.
Weyers, J.R. (1999) The effect of authentic video on communicative competence. *The Modern Language Journal* 83 (3), 339–349.
Williams, K. (2006) The impact of popular culture fandom on perceptions of Japanese language and culture learning: The case of student anime fans. Unpublished PhD thesis, University of Texas. See https://repositories.lib.utexas.edu/bitstream/handle/2152/2657/williamsk52898.pdf?sequence=2&isAllowed=y (accessed 25 October 2017).

Williams, M. and Burden, R.L. (1997) *Psychology for Language Teachers: A Social Constructivist Approach*. Cambridge: Cambridge University Press.

Winke, P., Gass, S. and Sydorenko, T. (2010) The effects of captioning videos used for foreign language listening activities. *Language Learning and Technology* 14 (1), 65–86.

Yamada, Y. (2005) Chūgakusei e no nihongo shien: seito no riterashī to nihongo o musubu katsudō [Supporting Japanese for an international student at a junior high school: Activities to connect student's literacy and Japanese]. *Waseda Daigaku Nihongo Kyōiku Jissen Kenkyū* 3, 43–52.

Yamagata-Lynch, L.C. (2010) *Activity Systems Analysis Methods*. New York: Springer.

Yamane, N. (2007) The effects of dictionary aids on reading Japanese in computer and hardcopy environments. Unpublished MA thesis, Monash University.

Yamashita, J. (2004) Reading attitudes in L1 and L2, and their influence on L2 extensive reading. *Reading in a Foreign Language* 16 (1), 1–19.

Yang, N.D. (1999) The relationship between EFL learners' beliefs and learning strategy use. *System* 27 (4), 515–536.

Yang, L., Baba, K. and Cumming, A. (2004) Activity systems for ESL writing improvement: Case studies of three Chinese and three Japanese adult learners of English. *Angles on the English-Speaking World* 4, 13–33.

Yap, S.S. (1998) Out-of-class use of English by secondary school students in a Hong Kong Anglo-Chinese school. Unpublished MA thesis, The University of Hong Kong.

Yi, Y. (2005) Asian adolescents' out-of-school encounters with English and Korean literacy. *Journal of Asian Pacific Communication* 15 (1), 57–77.

Yi, Y. (2007) Engaging literacy: A biliterate student's composing practices beyond school. *Journal of Second Language Writing* 16 (1), 23–39.

Yoon, H. (2008) More than a linguistic reference: The influence of corpus technology on L2 academic writing. *Language Learning and Technology* 12 (2), 31–48.

Yuksel, D. and Tanriverdi, B. (2009) Effects of watching captioned movie clip on vocabulary development of EFL learners. *Turkish Online Journal of Educational Technology* 8 (2), 48–54.

Zimmerman, D.H. and Wieder, D.L. (1977) The diary: Diary-interview method. *Urban Life* 5 (4), 479–498.

# Index

Ahearn, L. 28
Activity Theory 4, 16–18, 20–22, 24–26, 28–30, 160 (*see also* activity system, agency, community, contradictions, motives, object, rules, and tools and resources)
   instrument-producing activity 142, 145
   subject-producing activity 71
activity system 21, 22, 24–26, 28, 30, 67–70, 160
   central activity system 21, 25, 67, 69
   collective activity system 22
   linked activity system 68, 69
   multiple activity system 69
   past activity system 69, 70, 97
affinity space 141
affordance 108, 112, 140, 145
   and constrain (*also* constrain and) 130, 160
agency 13, 17, 26–29, 86, 87, 130, 143
   mediated agency 28
autonomy (*also* learner autonomy) 9, 26–29, 44, 47, 114, 149
   self-access/teacher-led autonomy 46
   full autonomy 46, 64
   autonomous language learning (*also* autonomous learning) 2–4, 9, 10, 14, 27, 45, 47, 108, 109, 114, 115, 149, 155, 156
   reactive autonomy 27

Barab, S. 26, 65
Barcelos, A.M.F. (*also* Barcelos, M.F.) 71, 93
beliefs (*also* learners' beliefs) 12, 13, 16, 17, 70–73, 86, 93–95, 98, 101, 113, 114, 133, 149, 150, 155–156

Benson, P. 1, 2, 4, 9, 11, 12, 14, 27–29, 45–47, 109, 115, 147
Burden, R.L. 108, 114, 149

classification for out-of-class language learning 45
   settings and modes of practices 47–48
   arrangement, assessment, content and pedogamy 48, 56, 61, 63, 64, 147
Chik, A. 10, 47, 58, 59, 161
class-related literacy practices 5, 23, 29, 30
community 17, 24, 43, 68, 113, 114, 150, 160
   community members 22, 81, 98, 114, 150
   online communities 12, 58, 112, 113, 114, 145, 152, 153, 161, 112, 113, 140
   fan communities (*also* fandom) 12, 92, 137, 141
   learning community 12
contradictions (*also* conflicts, dilemma, discrepancy, gap and tension) 25, 26, 30, 77–79, 81–87, 105–107, 111, 116, 130, 136, 140, 148, 158

De Costa, P. 3, 17, 18, 125
diary study (with photos) 37, 39, 40, 44, 159
Dörnyei, Z. 159

Engeström, Y. 21, 22, 24, 25, 26, 30, 67, 70, 74, 81, 86, 94, 96, 108, 142, 146
exchange value and use value (*also* exchange and use value) 25, 26, 74, 76, 84, 86, 87

exchange value 26, 74, 75, 77, 79, 80–82, 85, 87, 96, 106, 159
use value 26, 75–77, 79, 81–84, 85, 87, 156, 158, 159

Fukunaga, N. 2, 39, 90

Gao, X. (*also* Gao, X.A.) 4, 13, 23, 25, 27, 29, 71, 73, 98, 143, 144, 154
Gee, J.P. 2, 141, 161
Genung, P.B. 73, 86
Gillette, B. 16, 23, 77, 87, 98, 107
goal 21, 23, 28, 30, 131–133, 141, 159
goal-directed action (*also* goal-oriented action) 21, 25
Gu, M. 15, 152

Haneda, M. 3, 16, 17, 71
Holec, H. 27
Huang, J. 27, 28
Hyland, F. 10, 11, 12, 14, 45, 92, 110, 114

Inozu, J. 10, 14, 45, 92, 108
interests 11, 12, 97–101, 103–105, 108, 109, 111–115, 156–157
interests in Japanese pop culture 98, 149, 150, 151, 160
long-term interests 97, 98, 100, 104
snowballing effect of interests 103, 104
temporary interests 99, 100

Jones, F.R. 29, 45, 46, 47, 61, 64

Kalaja, P. 4, 13, 27, 71, 114
Kaptelinin, V. 23, 102
Kim, M. 26, 81
Kurata, N. 6, 57, 92, 110, 111, 150
Kuutti, K. 25, 108

(L2/language) learning strategies 13, 22, 24, 25, 71, 72, 93, 98, 103, 114, 144, 160
strategy choice 71
strategy use 14, 15, 16, 18, 19, 20, 23, 25
Lai, C. 2, 10, 11, 14, 15, 108, 114, 148, 152

Lam, W.S.E. 3, 11, 109, 111, 114, 141, 152
Lantolf, J.P. 20, 21, 27, 28, 69, 70, 73, 86, 104, 130, 134, 143, 154
learning history (*also* history of learning Japanese, and learners' history) 67, 71, 73, 79, 102, 103, 105, 115
Lei, X. 3, 16, 17, 25, 127
Leont'ev, A.N. 21, 22, 23, 49, 74, 96, 101, 102, 109, 146
Lin, P.M.S. 10, 14, 92, 108
Little, D. 108, 114, 149
Littlewood, W. 27, 28

Ma, Q. 11, 12, 15, 99, 108, 115, 152
mediation 20, 24, 25, 44, 116, 136 (*see also* assistance, and tools and resources)
mediational means (*also* mediating artefacts) 21, 24, 30, 43, 108, 112, 116, 117, 130, 131, 143, 144, 152, 153
mediated action 129, 130, 144
social mediation 129
tool mediation 129
Menezes, V. 4, 27, 112
motivation 11, 13, 17, 18–20, 24, 30, 64, 97, 106, 114, 115, 146, 149
intrinsic motivation 97, 149
motives 22–24, 25, 43, 68, 74–78, 81–87, 92, 93, 96–98, 107, 111, 117, 131, 132, 143, 148, 149 (*see also* goals, motivation, interests and object)
motive-stimuli 23, 101, 102
multiple motives 18, 23, 24, 101, 103
sense-forming motives 23, 101, 102
Multiliteracies 90, 109
digital literacy 11, 34, 109, 156
multimodality 90
Murray, G. 11, 12, 28, 45

Nardi, B.A. 24, 102
Nelson, C. 26, 81
New Literacy Studies 2, 3, 5
literacy, literacy activity and literacy practices 4, 5
non-class-related literacy practices 5, 29, 30
emails 60, 158

(Japanese) pop songs (*also* anime songs) 58, 73, 99, 100, 104, 108–110, 137, 138
online communication (*also* online chat) 56, 60, 90, 92, 93, 110–112, 142, 158
reading activities 57, 58, 61–63, 99, 104–106, 109, 131–133, 135–138, 140
video games 47, 56, 59, 97, 99, 100, 104, 105, 141
viewing activities 59, 61, 62, 90, 92–96, 99, 103, 104, 108, 109, 136, 138, 140, 160–161
noticing 133, 144

object 20–21, 22–24, 25–27, 43, 68, 74, 77–85, 102, 109, 116, 131, 143, 148

Palfreyman, D.M. 11, 12, 13, 114, 150, 152
Park, J.H. 3, 17, 18, 125
Pasfield-Neofitou, S.E. 6, 110, 113, 119, 120, 121, 124, 135, 136, 150, 152
Pavlenko, A. 28, 143, 154
Pearson, N. 10, 11, 45, 92
Pickard, N. 10, 11, 92, 106

Riazi, A. 3, 16, 53
rules (*also* rules and/or norms) 21–22, 24–26, 28, 30, 68, 84, 85, 117, 127–130, 143, 153
Russell, D.R. 25, 26, 69, 83, 84, 149

Siyanova-Chanturia, A. 10, 14, 92, 108
social network 12, 13, 110–112, 114, 151
  peer assistance 15, 17, 30, 116, 123, 129, 130, 140, 141, 145, 152, 153
  peer network 114, 152
social networking sites (*also* social networking services and SNSs) 22, 90, 110, 111, 112, 142, 152, 158
sociocultural perspectives (*also* sociocultural approach) 2–4, 9, 13, 16, 17, 19, 25, 27, 28, 71, 73, 98, 143
  ontogenesis 73
  microgenesis 73

spin-off function of tools (*also* spin-off function of mediational means) 122–123, 125–126
Sockett, G. 10, 11, 12, 14, 15, 92, 104, 108, 110, 115, 138, 152, 158
Spack, R. 3, 16, 53, 71, 73
Spence-Brown, R. 7, 23, 24, 85, 87, 103, 132
Spratt, M. 10, 14, 45, 92, 108
Sundqvist, P. 10, 108, 149, 156, 157
Sylvén, L.K. 10, 108, 149, 156, 157

Thorne, S.L. 10, 20, 21, 28, 69, 70, 130, 134, 143, 154
Toffoli, D. 10, 11, 12, 14, 15, 92, 104, 108, 110, 115, 138, 152, 158
tools and resources 8, 15, 131 (*see also* social network)
  dictionary choice (*also* dictionary use) 117–122, 123–125, 131–136
  ICT (*also* internet) 14–15, 61, 108–113, 156
  Japanese captions (*also* subtitles) 59, 90, 138–140
  linguistic resources (*also* foreign language resources) 108, 122, 127–129, 152–154
  L1 subtitles and translation (*also* fansub) 137–138
  online resources (*also* online tools) 19–20, 120, 152, 153, 157, 158

Ushioda, E. 24, 108, 114, 149, 152, 156, 159

van Lier, L. 3, 28, 108, 112
Vygotsky, L.S. 20, 21

Wertsch, J.V. 122, 125
Williams, K. 2, 90, 104
Williams, M. 108, 114, 149

Yamane, N. 19, 20, 118, 121, 132, 134
Yang, L. 3, 16, 17, 53, 127
Yañez, A. 25, 26, 69, 83, 84, 149
Yap, S.S. 10, 11, 45, 92, 93, 96, 104, 106, 110

Zhang, L.J. 29, 143

For Product Safety Concerns and Information please contact our EU Authorised Representative:

Easy Access System Europe

Mustamäe tee 50

10621 Tallinn

Estonia

gpsr.requests@easproject.com

www.ingramcontent.com/pod-product-compliance
Lightning Source LLC
Chambersburg PA
CBHW070612300426
44113CB00010B/1504